Baggage

CONFESSIONS OF
A GLOBE-TROTTING
HYPOCHONDRIAC

Jeremy Leon Hance

Health Communications, Inc.
Boca Raton, Florida
www.hcibooks.com

Library of Congress Cataloging-in-Publication Data
is available through the Library of Congress

© 2020 Jeremy Leon Hance

ISBN-13: 978-07573-2206-8 (Paperback)
ISBN-10: 07573-2206-9 (Paperback)
ISBN-13: 978-07573-2207-5 (ePub)
ISBN-10: 07573-2207-7 (ePub)

Publisher: Health Communications, Inc.
         1700 NW 2nd Avenue
         Boca Raton, FL 33432-1653

Cover design by Larissa Hise Henoch
Interior design and formatting by Lawna Patterson Oldfield
Photos are copyright of Jeremy Hance and Tiffany Roufs, unless otherwise specified.

For Tiffany
Believe me, you'll see why

Know thyself.

Inscribed on the forecourt of the
Temple of Apollo at Delphi.

Contents

Acknowledgments

While writing is largely a solitary occupation, a book requires a community. In this case, a global one.

Let's start with Rhett Butler, without whom this book would not exist, nor would many of these adventures. Rhett, the founder of Mongabay, the best online news source for the environment, has been my mentor since the very beginning of my career. Thank you, Rhett, for over a decade of opportunities and tutelage. A special thank you as well to everyone at Mongabay.

For my indefatigable, clear-eyed, and ever-supportive agent, Alice Speilburg, who took a chance on an environmental journalist writing a very personal memoir. Few first-time authors are ever so lucky.

For Allison Janse with HCI Books, who saw something special in an undeniably unusual book, and for Camilla Michael for adopting this somewhat misshapen baby and much improving its contours, thank you.

Incredible gratitude to Artsmith for funding a week of writing on Orcas Island and to Jill McCabe Johnson for her outstanding hospitality. Gratitude as well goes to the Writer's Colony at Dairy Hollow for a fortnight of writing in Eureka Springs, with special thanks to Sharon Spurlin. Both programs gave me not only precious writing time but also time in nature, a chance to read my work to an audience, and peerless communities of like-minded artists—y'all know who you are.

A thank you to novelist Diane Hammond for advice on writing, publishing, and living. A thank you to Linda Carbone for making my proposal shine. Thanks to excellent beta readers Benjamin Klas, Kris Klas, Erin Cary, Brittany

Lynk, and, of course, Tiffany Roufs. Thanks, as well, to dear friends Thomas Christie, Emily Christy, Morgan Erickson-Davis, and Frank Janick for unwavering support and always inquiring, "How's the book?" The answer is now, thank God, "It's done."

This book takes place in eight countries, each of which required a crowd of guides, scientists, and locals to get me from one end to the other. To each of them—some mentioned in this book, many not—I give a special thanks. For those who work in nature tourism, *thank you*. Your work is vital. A special shout out to the staff, administrators, and guides at Pantiacolla in Peru, Warana Lodge in Suriname, Iwokrama River Lodge in Guyana, Tabin Wildlife Resort in Malaysia, Napo Wildlife Lodge in Ecuador, and Explora Ecotour in the Dominican Republic.

Many of the places I visited, however, were not tourist lodges but science stations or conservation groups. To that end, a multitude of thanks to STINASU in Suriname, the Iwokrama International Center for Rain Forest Conservation and Development, Hutan in Malaysia, the Yasuni Research Station and Tiputini Biodiversity Station in Ecuador, Yabi in Indonesia, the Sumatran Rhino Sanctuary in Sumatra, the Little Fireface Project in Java, and the Last Survivors Project in the Dominican Republic, a program by Durrell Wildlife Conservation Trust and the EDGE program.

I've spent over a decade interviewing thousands of scientists and conservationists. Many of my views are now distillations of their sweat-filled, years-long, passion-fueled work. In an age of mass extinction and climate change, no vocation is nobler. Thank you to all of them. For these travels in particular, a special thank you for the personal attention and work of these scientists and conservationists: John Payne, Cynthia Ong, Marc Ancrenaz, Anna Nekaris, Sharon McCabe, Hélène Birot, Zulfi Arsan, Terri Roth, Rosalind Kennerly, and Jose Nuñez-Miño.

A tip of my hat to all the therapists over the years for your many hours, your daunting work, your compassion, and your guidance. A shout out to Charles Depies, who has been my unwavering therapist in chief for many years and many trips. Thank you for helping keep this ship steady even in rough seas.

For my brothers, Karsten and André, for their love, support, and friendship. To my parents, Ed and Erva Hance, who always supported my writing, my creativity, and my myriad healthy obsessions, thank you for guiding me through not only turbulent early years but also those when I was knee-deep in mental illness.

My father died after a long illness while this book was in edits. Prior to that, I'd slip my mother rough copies of chapters so she could read them aloud to him; he never missed an opportunity to tell me how proud he was or how much he loved me. Thank you, Dad. I miss you so, every day.

And finally, of course, to Tiffany and Aurelia. For all those nights you let me work. For all those conversations about "the book." For all the sacrifices and all the patience. Without your love and support, this book wouldn't be. Thank you.

Author's Note

This book is a work of memory. But memory is fickle, impressionistic, seductive, and often robed in layers of emotion and color not present in the moment. So, some of the details in this book may be factually iffy. For example, some of the journeys may have been longer or shorter than I recall. Some events may be slightly out of order. Some peoples' faces and physiques may be different from how I conjure them out of the past. Some meals may not have been as delicious as depicted. You get the idea.

Where possible, I have relied on journals, itineraries, trip notes, photographs, Tiffany, and a million Google searches to fact-check myself. But more often than not, I have had to rely only on my memory and the stories I came to tell myself in the years since. This doesn't mean any of this is untrue—all the events happened—only that it's as true as my memory can make it. So don't sweat the small stuff too much.

In many places, I have made up names. Sometimes I did this to cloak the person's real identity but more often because I simply could not recall his or her name. (I've always been terrible with names. If I bump into you and don't recall yours, don't take it personally.) When I have used the person's real name, I have received permission.

The animals, to be honest, are probably better remembered than the people. If my memory is good for anything, it's for recalling thieving monkeys, banana-eating tapirs, and singing rhinos.

Finally, I do curse in this book periodically. I know it may offend some readers—and I get that—but do consider that it's difficult to write an accurate book about the awful hilarity of mental illness and the wild splendor of nature without a few choice words.

So, all in all, take the book for what it is: a memoir by someone on Ativan with a shitty memory.

Prologue

SEPTEMBER 2017

Thirty thousand feet in the air, there is only one place to find privacy: the toilet. I slide the lock that turns on the light, sit down on the white seat, put my hands together, close my eyes, breathe deeply—take in the nearly overpowering smell of bleach—and try with every ounce of my rational being to stifle the rising panic. But it's like trying to stop myself from throwing up.

One thought keeps ringing in my head: *You can't do this.*

Only a few minutes before, I was sitting in my seat trying to pick a movie, so many choices. I happened to glance at another passenger's screen a few seats down and across the aisle. It was *Moana*—the scene where the titular heroine is attempting to put the green-spiraled heart back into the angry, volcano-spewing god, Te Fiti. Having a six-year-old at home, I was more than familiar with the film.

But it was at that moment—Te Fiti flinging boulders of flame—when my impish brain decided to inform me, *You can't do this. You know you can't.*

With that single thought, something exploded in me. My heart started pounding, my hands beaded sweat, my thoughts coiled and rolled down the rabbit hole. I knew this sensation all too well.

But.

Oh no, not here—not when I'm alone. Not now. Not *on a plane.*

We'd been flying only a few hours, which meant I still had ten hours to go on this flight to Tokyo. Then the layover. Then another flight, the third leg, an additional agonizing eight hours to Jakarta, my final destination.

You can't do this. You know you can't.

It wasn't like this was my first time flying—I did that when I was five. Since then I'd been to five continents, more than thirty countries. I couldn't count the numbers of planes: from packed 747s to prop planes into the Amazon rainforest, planes diverted by North Channel winds to smooth landings on one of the most dangerous airways in the world. I'd done this route before, too: the United States to Tokyo to Jakarta.

I'm even working on a book about travel, for Christ's sake.

I escape Te Fiti and hurry to the bathroom, nearly bumping into my flight attendant, a pleasant young Japanese woman with a reassuring smile.

Many people fear the airplane lavatory because it's as claustrophobic as a tomb. But to me, it's the best place on a plane because it's the only option to escape the unrelenting humanity of coach. In the flight just before this, I sat next to an elderly woman who spent the three hours quietly throwing up in bags, which I stoically handed off to the flight attendants.

Once I have taken a few deep breaths, I attempt a good pep talk. *Okay, Jeremy, this is your OCD talking. Everything's fine, it's all good, it's hunky-dory and peachy pie. Just pick out a movie and get your mind off the panic. One day at a time... or, in this case, one minute.*

"You know you can't do this," the voice in my head says again. "This trip will definitely kill you. You need to find a way home, or you or your family will die." The voice is Steve's.

Steve is the name I've given to my obsessive-compulsive disorder. I did this to try to create some distance between my chronic mental illness and my daily self. I named my depression Malachi because he's a badass in a biblical kind of way. Steve and Malachi, I tell myself, aren't me. They are the disease.

But at least Malachi is interesting; Steve is unpardonably boring. He says the same thing over and over again. He's a busted grandfather clock, chiming every minute; he's a bored elephant in a zoo, pacing the same path until his footpads bleed; he's the friend who tells the same anecdote on every occasion. It's almost like Steve is obsessed.

This is what OCD is: It's the same song stuck in your head, playing forever.

Unfortunately, Steve and I can't stay in the bathroom the whole flight, debating. The vacuum flush of the automatic toilet startles me, making me imagine what it would be like if something struck the plane. Always keen to help, Steve reminds me that there's nothing between myself and the atmosphere but a few sheets of aluminum. Like a magician, he conjures up the image of another plane colliding with ours midair, the whole craft opening up as I'm tipped into the frigid emptiness.

It isn't the fact of death that alarms me so much as the terror of plunging thirty thousand feet, powerless.

I head back to my seat, pretending I'm still alone. I get out the rather enormous pillbox my wife sensibly sorted for me and take lorazepam, an anti-anxiety drug. I put it under my tongue and taste imminent serenity. The texture is chalky and the taste actually mildly sweet. It's one I know well.

Let's say I succeed today. Let's just say for a moment I survive the next twenty-plus hours to make it to the hotel in Jakarta and the sweet release of sleep. Then it's twelve days in Indonesia, without my wife and my child, but with a hundred thousand things that could go wrong. Snakebite, car wreck, rabies via stray dog or cave bat, a ferry capsizing, a volcano blowing, an earthquake cracking and swallowing. Or I could catch any one of a cavalcade of tropical diseases, be stampeded by an elephant, crushed by a falling tree, or maybe eaten by a tiger—they have those. There are just so many ways to die when you're not at home.

I buzz the flight attendant, hoping her smile will bring me back to reality. When she arrives, I order a glass of wine. My psychiatrist would scold me —mixing wine with a tranquilizer. But I don't care. I'm fucking desperate.

I finally pick a movie: It's called *Manchester by the Sea*. I don't know anything about it, only that it is critically acclaimed. A third of the way in and I'm sobbing now. This movie should come with a warning: *Not suitable for those experiencing in-flight panic attacks*. I try to switch to something else, something lighthearted—*Planes, Trains and Automobiles* (who picks these goddamn movies?). At this point, I'm too deep into this horror show of a film, and I force it down.

I miss my daughter and my wife; I miss them like a physical ache.

I want to talk to someone—my therapist, my wife, a friend...even this flight attendant who seems as chill as an ice cube as she's riding in this death machine.

Steve in my head continues repeating his mantra: "You know you can't do this. You know you can't."

I suddenly feel hot, clammy, my stomach twists. *Oh, Christ. Not here, not now.* I'm getting sick, and we're in the clouds somewhere above the ocean—hours away from Tokyo. I ring the flight attendant again and ask for a thermometer. She brings me one. I put it in my mouth.

"No, no," she says. "For here." And she motions to her armpit.

Oh. I slowly remove the thermometer from my mouth. I smile and nod as if I totally knew that...and was just nibbling on this armpit thermometer because that's the kind of hilarious guy I am. I wipe it off on my shirt and shove it under my arm. I'm certain it's going to come out saying 102 or 103. I imagine the smiling attendant picking me up and carrying me into First Class, bundling me in blankets; she strokes my hair through the rest of the flight, sings songs I don't know because they're in Japanese, and spoon feeds me ice cream.

I fantasize about landing in Tokyo and getting a hotel—a nice room with a big bed, a hot shower, and room service with housemade ramen—and then taking a flight home tomorrow, essentially calling in sick on my two-week reporting trip on Sumatran rhinos.

My temperature is a perfect 98.6.

The kindly attendant, my only anchor to sanity at this moment, returns with some Tylenol for me. I take it and ask for another glass of wine, trying to hide the tears strolling down my face.

I cover my head with a blanket and think, *This is just a dark night of the soul...just a dark night of the soul. This too shall pass...*

And Steve says, "You know, you're totally fucked right? Why are you so stupid to keep doing this to yourself? Why don't you stay at home where people like you belong? You're not going to win this time. You're going to die, and it's going to be awful."

Twelve days later, I walk off a different plane into the Minneapolis airport. I gather my luggage and head toward the exit where my wife and child are waiting to pick me up.

Screw you, Steve.

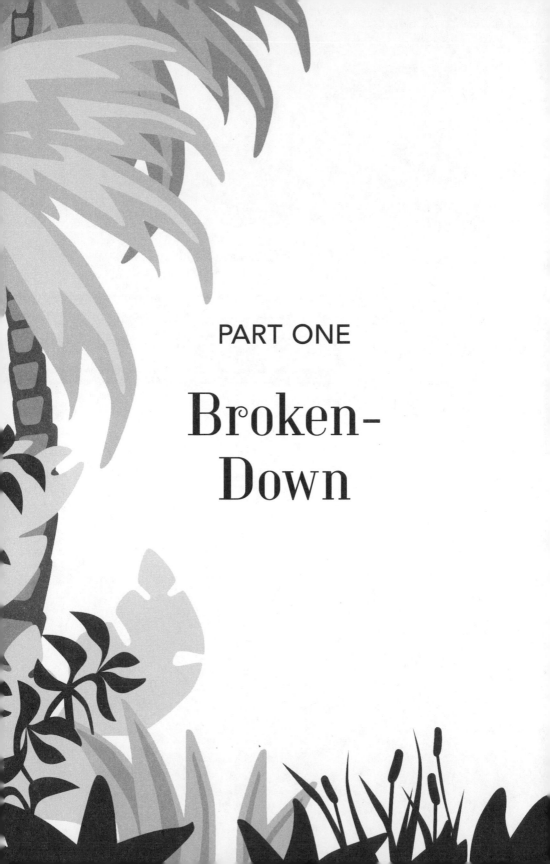

PART ONE

Broken-Down

Chapter One

Crazy for Peru

SPRING 2006

Five months before I was first diagnosed with OCD, I sat eating lunch in the basement of the Corner Bookstore on Madison and Ninety-Third in Manhattan. I was the Children's Book Buyer, a glorified title for whoever ran the children's section. It had proved a busy Sunday in the city's richest, snobbiest neighborhood, and I was glad of the respite. The tidy basement was filled with boxes of books—my favorite things in the world—and a couple of makeshift desks for the store's managers. I stole one and luxuriated in the darkness, the quiet of solitude, and *A Time of Gifts* by Patrick Leigh Fermor. But most of all, I offered blessings for the break from the Upper East Siders being their self-important, clueless, one-percenter selves.

This brief reverie, so rare in my life lately, was interrupted by my cellphone ringing.

"Hey," I said, mouth stuffed with sandwich.

"Will you bring home a book about Peru?" Tiffany asked.

"Huh?"

"Will you bring home a travel book about Peru?"

"Why?"

3

"Because we're going there this summer. And I'm going to book it by this time tomorrow."

Tiffany and I had met doing community theater in our home state of Minnesota in the last year of the millennium. Six years later, in a fit of post-college optimism, we moved from small-town Minnesota to New York City. It didn't take long for us to realize, though, that we weren't New Yorkers. With all due respect to Ol' Blue Eyes, we were going to try to make it elsewhere. We were young (me, twenty-six, and she, twenty-three), newly engaged, planning on quitting our jobs, and had nothing better to do that summer. So, while a trip to Peru was news to me, I couldn't really find a reason to argue.

True to her word, Tiffany bought the airline tickets within twenty-four hours—only for six weeks instead of four. Because why not?

Still, I felt anxiety blossoming like a giant flower in my brain as I took the subway home that evening—*Lonely Planet: Peru* stuffed securely in my backpack—south through Manhattan, under the East River like some mecha-sea serpent, and deep into Brooklyn until finally emerging from the abyssal tunnels into the spring sunlight fading over Crown Heights. I could not have guessed then that this trip would change the course of my life.

Instead, I was pretty sure it would end it.

Our plane circles like a great bird of prey before landing at Jorge Chávez International Airport outside Peru's smog-filled capital, Lima. The plane didn't crash, and we aren't dead, which I'd anticipated every night in those quiet, hazy moments before sleep in our apartment in Brooklyn. But that means I still have to go through with the next six weeks.

Earlier that day, it took all my willpower not to run around JFK in figure eights, screaming that all the planes were destined to fall and burn. I couldn't tell Tiffany that I'd become certain I'd die on this trip, not after months of planning and thousands of dollars spent. And I could hardly admit to myself that I might not be a good traveler.

Hadn't I roamed the byways and alleyways of London on my own when I was eighteen? Hadn't I undertaken a solo and impromptu trip to the Kenyan bush, sleeping in a tent beside Maasai warriors to the unsettling roar of lions? Of course, I'm a good traveler. Just look at my track record. I'm a modern-day Herodotus, James Cook, and Ibn Battuta all rolled into a skinny white boy with a penchant for exaggeration. Marco Polo, eat your fucking heart out.

A piece of me, a big one, is elated to see Peru, to walk the Inca Trail to the airy palace of Machu Picchu, to glimpse the Andean condor soaring above Colca Canyon, to explore the ancient city of Cuzco, to drink pisco sours and eat quinoa soup and chew coca leaves, to live in some other land for just a little while. To dwell fleetingly in novelty and to forget for a moment my mortal pettiness—that is, after all, why we travel.

Most of all, I ache to see the Amazon rainforest, the shadowed locale that haunted my childhood dreams alongside dragons and giants.

But another piece of me, growing more potent daily, is sick with fear. The mere thought of the trip makes me want to check myself into the hospital, put on a straitjacket, and lock the door, letting the cool and dark keep me safe.

Mental hospitals are not unfamiliar territory. At the age of ten, I was diagnosed with depression and anxiety. I was put on every psych medication available until I began to feel like a lab rat. I spent a considerable portion of my youth not in arcades or gyms but on therapists' couches. Twice I ended up in psych wards.

But none of the dozens of therapists and psychiatrists I saw with numbing regularity during those years noticed that another beast may have been lurking beneath the surface.

A few months after we moved to New York City, I began visiting doctors regularly. I was twenty-five and healthy; I'd even been off psych meds for years. However, I would realize I had cancer, so I visited a doctor who told me, "No, you don't have cancer." And then I'd feel free, beautiful, powerful, alive. Until a few hours later when I'd realize I had AIDS. I'd return to the doctor. "No, you don't have AIDS." Whew! But hours later I'd discover my lymph node was actually a lump of cancerous death cells. And the cycle would repeat. Terror, relief, terror, relief, terror again. And as winter turned to spring, the gaps between doctor visits became shorter.

I couldn't tell Tiffany any of this, though she knew something was wrong, because I could barely understand what was happening myself—why the doctors couldn't see all the cancer clusters dancing in my body and why, wherever I went, everyone seemed to look at me with a strange sort of pity.

It wasn't mental illness. I was sure of that. I had managed those irregularities for more than fifteen years. I didn't feel depressed. I felt more like I was on a constant caffeine kick, like my brain was running a race that didn't end, not even during sleep. I didn't cry myself to sleep or call on God to strike me down. Sure, I was anxious about the various diseases eating my body—but those were *real*. This wasn't mental illness; this was self-knowledge of the deepest and most mystic kind.

So, when cancer didn't kill me, I became convinced my death lay elsewhere. Why not Peru? The closer the trip came, the less doubt I felt. Yes, I would die on this trip.

Just apparently not on the plane ride.

Lima, the capital of Peru, is a two-headed creature: grand colonial buildings on one side and vast slums slipping down dunes on the other; sprawling views of the Pacific Ocean and pollution thick enough to make you feel like you're breathing oatmeal; Western-style shopping malls for the rich and crumbling street corners for the begging poor. Lima is a living, pulsating city with a vibrance, color, and adventure lacking in most American cities today, but also possessing a desperation, despair, and chaos that rivals the most impoverished parts of my homeland.

My favorite part of this dual-brained dragon is our hostel because here I can close the door and lock Peru out. I feel like a tortoise who likes the inside of his shell a little too much. I prefer the hostel's little courtyard to the entire city. Here unknown tropical flowers bloom, strange birds chirp and flit in the shadows, and a menagerie of little ceramic statues hide among the foliage: white Jesus in a brilliant blue robe holding a lamb, Mother Mary trying to pray but her hands have chipped away, and an angel with a mottled face where the paint has peeled. I feel secure here, inside the classically Peruvian white walls with a literal gate between me and the city.

Outside is the cancer-causing smog. Outside are the guard dogs that slam themselves against gates, trying to get at you; cabbies who drive like they are characters in *Alice in Wonderland* and whose cars (as if to punctuate the joke) lack seat belts; the poor who hold out bronzed, wrinkled, suffering hands, muttering all the despair of the world in Spanish; and adroit thieves who are capable of taking your wallet or purse while you sit on it in a café (this nearly happened to Tiff).

Oh, and the fake money.

Ever since our arrival in Lima, we tried giving money to people—cabdrivers, museum staff, waiters—only to have them shove the bills back in our face, declaring, "*Falso.*"

"*Porque?*" we say. And try handing the money over again. They'd shake their heads and say more emphatically, "*Falso!*"

Please, just please, take our money, we thought. And sometimes they did. Sometimes they'd take our money without a breath of *falso*, and we spewed *gracias* so effusively they must have thought Americans were very appreciative folk. Oh, we hated paying for stuff. We argued over who should be the one to try, dreading that *falso*.

The final straw came when we tried to enter the Lima Zoo, and the woman at the entrance took out a black marker and wrote FALSO on our bills before shoving them back at us.

This was a sign, I thought, an omen like a blood-red moon or a forest that goes marching. This *falso* was really Spanish for "Get out now! Get out while there's still time." I even went so far as to say aloud to Tiffany, "Maybe we should just go home?" Abandon our six-week trip on day three. If Tiffany had said yes, I would've been on the next plane out of this madcap city.

Instead, we head to our hostel and spread all of our Peruvian cash out on the bed and peer at it with the scrutiny of natural philosophers.

"Okay," Tiff says. "I think this one is fake."

"Yeah...but maybe not."

"No, I'm pretty sure. Look at it. Closely. It matches this one, which we know is fake," she adds, pointing to the bill with FALSO written on it.

Honestly, they all look the same to me: colorful bills with the countenances of Peruvians I'd never heard of. But Tiffany sorts the suspected wheat from the chaff, and then we cart the whole wad over to a bank and ask a teller to confirm. The young woman looks terrified, as if she expects us to yell at her for being born in a country that isn't America. But we just want to know: What's real? What's not?

Tiffany has turned expert; every single bill she picked out as fake is indeed counterfeit. We'd changed our money in the airport with two women who shouted and gesticulated enthusiastically behind an old card table but who wouldn't lift their heads to meet our gaze. They'd swindled us out of about sixty dollars. Not chump change to two young backpackers on a strict budget, but better than we feared.

Weeks later, we tell this story to fellow travelers while eating a scrumptious lunch overlooking the vast blue waters of Lake Titicaca. A young man who's been traveling across Ecuador and Peru for three months exclaims, "Really? I've never run into that."

At that moment the waiter shows up beside him, hands him back his cash, and says, "*Falso.*" We feel bad, like we jinxed the dude, but he takes it good-naturedly. He is, after all, a good traveler.

My happiest moment in Lima is leaving Lima, the dingy bus pulling away like a long exhale.

We now begin our journey down what's become known as the Gringo Trail. This is what the vast majority of white, privileged tourists do when they go to Peru: they start in Lima, head south through various towns along the Pacific coast (Pisco, Haucachina, and Nazca), then pursue a sudden change in elevation for the Andean city of Arequipa and the Colca Canyon, with maybe a stop at Puno and Lake Titicaca, before finally descending into Cuzco for the Machu Picchu climax. Being about as gringo as possible, this is our route, too—only veering off at the end for the Amazon. But that remains a month away. *A month.*

Once beyond the outskirts of Lima—a seemingly endless run of gas stations, billboards, and precariously positioned slums—the landscape reveals its yellow, water-parched earth beneath an undulating flatness resembling the ripples of a prairie but without the grass. Through the dirty windows of the bus from Lima to Pisco, it feels like we're watching footage of an alien world. Here the Pacific meets one of the driest places on the planet with topography that resembles Tatooine or Arrakis: Sand dunes and rocky barren lands stretch to such lengths that it wouldn't be surprising if God had sent a second flood of sand, rock, and heat.

Incredibly, great civilizations rose and fell here with the regularity of desert rain. They had names like the Norte Chico, the Chavin, the Paracas, the Nazca, and the Huari—names most of us have never heard of. But people lived here, loved here, died here. They even, at times, thrived here, like terraforming astronauts, for thousands of years (the Norte Chico is one of the oldest civilizations on Earth, flourishing at the same time as Mesopotamia, and if that fact doesn't blow your mind, I got nothing).

South of Lima stands the Pachacamac, a temple and palace complex that thrived for six times as long as the United States has been a thing and, today, is as impressive as anything you'd find in Rome. One of the temples housed the Virgins of the Sun, local girls selected for their beauty, who lived in an all-female mansion. Held to chastity, they cooked, wove, and kept the fire for the emperor and his priests. A small minority would be eventually selected, highly honored and famed until garroted by a cotton noose and sacrificed to the sun god. Grisly, sure, but no more so than the Inquisition's burning of so-called heretics during the same period or the mass horror of the slave trade instituted by "civilized" countries just as the Incan Empire crumbled.

Along the roadside, the Peruvian government has planted palm trees as if to pretend anything green could survive here. Eventually, though, even those fade away, and the trip becomes four hours of exotic monotony but for the few times when the bus turns a corner and suddenly there's the Pacific Ocean, and I realize how much I've missed it, how cheering the golden sunlight on the blue, and how welcoming the motion of the rolling swells.

We arrive in Pisco in time for lunch. Although it's a bustling town of almost 100,000 people, it feels nothing like the unnavigable madness of Lima's 8 million denizens. It feels doable. Tiffany and I celebrate that night at the otherwise empty hostel bar, overlooking the also empty swimming pool, by repeatedly indulging in the town's eponymous drink, the pisco sour—lemon juice, syrup, bitters, pisco (a special brandy made from local muscat grapes), and raw egg whites—which leaves me hungover the next morning when we get into a motorboat. Tiffany is fine. She can hold her liquor like a sailor; I'm more like a wilting flower.

With about twenty fellow tourists, all wearing bright orange vests in case of sinkage, the boat heads out into that great blue vastness known as the Pacific, just one little corner of our planet's most notable feature: the global great blue.

We scheduled the tour the day before, not knowing how delicious pisco sours would be and how much I'd need to self-medicate. Still, as the boat runs farther into the sea and the equatorial sun beats down, I sober up. And, fortunately, the Pacific is living up to its name. So far, the ride is smooth, and the fear of losing my breakfast passes as our destination comes into view, the Islas Ballestas, or crossbow islands.

These crumbling, implausible peaks rise out of the marine waters like desiccated shells left out in the sun too long. Their outlines seem to squiggle. It is only as I grow closer that I realize that this isn't a mirage brought on by overindulgence in the sun; these are birds, their number uncountable. As we pull in closer, Guanay and red-legged cormorants—the latter unmistakable due to their carrot-colored legs—peer down over the cliffs at us like little condescending lords. Their wings splay wide to dry off in the light and the heat.

The boat slows and bobs as the driver steers us around the islets' edges where waves curl and end in white froth. Every time the water descends, sea stars and many-colored anemones appear, clinging just below the tideline, living lives wholly unimaginable to two-legged hominids.

Suddenly a Peruvian booby, which lacks the sea-blue feet that makes the other unfortunately named seabird famous, dive-bombs into the water a mere two yards away. It pops up moments later, having missed the fish it spied from above. But more boobies plunge into the sea from the sky above, like shafts of arrows sent from a heavenly army. Some hit their mark, gobbling up the living. Others bob on the clear marine waters, breathing momentarily after their exuberant, though unsuccessful, attempts.

They fill the air with their cries, as does the heavy smell of ammonia from their guano that covers the islands in a whitish powder, almost like dirty snow.[1]

Our driver takes us deftly under an island archway, and we see our first group of Patagonian sea lions. They lounge on slick rock, soaking in the tropical sun, seemingly unperturbed by our presence—this is, after all, a daily tour. We drive through a little cavern, and there, with his harem, is the king: Pepe. He is as big as a goddamn grizzly bear and sports the thrifty mane that gives sea lions their common name. The rascal towers over the females like a Great Dane over a pack of yapping corgis, his voice booming against the cavern's walls and drowning out the cries of all others, including our own *ooohs* and *ahhhhs*.

Turning another corner, we encounter a bizarre sight: penguins. Yes, penguins chilling—pun intended—on the jagged, sunny, rainless islands. I've never seen a penguin in the wild before and would not have expected it here, of all places. But four penguin species inhabit the tropics, including these well-dressed Humboldt gents.

For the first time since landing in Peru, I spend several hours feeling no anxiety or trepidation, only wonder and awe. And on the way back to port, dolphins appear suddenly, their blue backs sliding up through the surface before disappearing again, paralleling the ship and guiding us home.

In the years to come, this morning excursion will prove to be one of those travel memories that becomes a jewel in my pocket I can take out anytime, even decades later, to lift my spirits or remind me of the beauty of our little planet, third from the sun.

I feel like maybe I might make it out of Peru alive after all.

A year after we leave Pisco, the town is hit by an 8.0 earthquake. The San Clemente Cathedral in the center of town collapses, killing 187 worshippers attending a memorial service for a much-beloved Piscoan. The town itself falls: 85 percent of Pisco, mostly made of adobe buildings, is in ruins. Across the region, 540 people perish.

Even in my morbid imagination, it's difficult to square my memory of our twenty-four hours in Pisco with the reality that must still exist today, more than a decade after the earthquake: the heartache, the rubble, the shattering of so many lives.

But here is the luxury of travelers: We are ghosts, here one moment, there another, never around long enough to become truly intimate with the places or the people who pass their lives there. Our experiences are fleeting, our familiarity only superficial, our connections momentary and illusory. It conjures up one of my favorite lines from *Pride and Prejudice,* when Mr. Bennet confesses the heaviness of his sins as a father: "I am not afraid of being overpowered by the impression. It will pass away soon enough." Here is a brutal condemnation of the human species, but an honest one.

Indeed, Tiff and I are soon climbing the stairs of another bus headed for Haucachina. And as we do, Pisco recedes into memory, devastation still a year away.

I'm not a lifeguard. If I were, a lot of people would drown. But here I am, perched eight feet above the ground in a lifeguard's chair overlooking a lagoon in parched coastal Peru.

Below me is a stray dog. It's one of those ubiquitous canines of the developing world that looks like no breed whatsoever but somehow still resembles the quintessential canine, Plato's perfect dog. This one is peering up at me with bright eyes and wagging its tail frantically. It almost seems to be smiling. But I know better than to trust that. Sure, the dog looks amiable now, all sugar and sweet, but it's been haunting my steps ever since we left our hostel in this desert resort town of Haucachina.

This dog wants to give me rabies.

The whole bright-eyed, wagging tail thing is just an act before he bites me, injecting the virus into my muscle. From there, it will travel over a series of months through various nerves until it reaches its terminus: my brain. And then I'll die. Oh, how I'll die in fearful agony.

I know this dog has rabies because I wouldn't be so afraid of it if it didn't. If I've learned anything from sixty-seven close readings of the Health Section of *Lonely Planet: Peru*, one should always be consumed by terror where rabies is concerned. Better to scramble up an empty lifeguard's chair than to perish in pain and delirium.

At first sight of the little town, I thought Haucachina looked like an old postcard depicting a world away, an oasis in the Arabian Desert with a natural lagoon of purple water and lush palms surrounding it like a prayer circle. And just as in this postcard, everything is slightly yellowed, and a tad faded.

But now it feels like death, like, okay, I get it, so *here* is where I'm going to die.

All those people down there impressed into the sand of this Peruvian well-spring, taking in the wintery but equatorial sun, drinking cocktails, slipping into a midday nap, reading their books, or seeking the shade of the palm trees around the still lagoon. They're the crazy ones, risking rabies from this monster for just one afternoon of leisure. Their lackadaisical attitude will cost them their lives, but not before costing them their fondness for water.

From time to time I see their perplexed faces looking up at me, perhaps thinking, *What is that white boy doing sitting up there? He's not a lifeguard, is he?* No, he's definitely not; not unless you want a lifeguard who has perfected the doggy paddle and can't see properly through his water-smeared glasses. Fortunately for everyone, it's winter and too chilly to swim.

One of those perplexed individuals is Tiffany. She's watching me as I sit glumly in this tall seat, hoping I'll eventually come down. But I'm not going anywhere. Not until that thing stops stalking me with its mortal slobber. Self-sacrificing Tiffany does her best to steer the dog away. But for some reason, Rabies the Dog has no eyes for her. Only me. So I'll have to wait out Rabies. I don't care if I sit here all day. I don't care if the sun sets and I'm still up here, fiancée-less. It's better than death by four furry paws.

After about twenty minutes, Rabies finally tires and abandons me for some gringo dudes with sandboards climbing the hill-sized dunes that surround Haucachina.

I crawl down the lifeguard chair onto solid ground, but adrenaline still shoots through me like some electric shock. I'm actually shaking. Having just left our party-hard hostel to take in the delights of Haucachina, Tiffany and I return deflated. I lay on the moist bed in our dim room and try to shut down my mind. But I can't, given the optimistic, nauseating beats of Euro dance music that penetrate every nook of this grubby hellhole.

I refuse to leave our hostel again, even with the *thump-thump-boom* of the insufferable music, until Tiff checks and double-checks that Rabies the Dog is not sitting outside the door, come to finish the job. He isn't, but as we emerge a few hours later into the dimming day, we spot him far away, just a tiny silhouette now, at the top of the sand dunes, trailing the group of sand-surfing dudes who are to prove as disappointing as us.

Still, I win. I beat the dog, and I beat all those naysayers staring at me. I deserve a fucking medal. I don't have rabies. And that's all that matters.

Tiffany and I quickly discover that there isn't much to do in Haucachina, especially if you don't find the idea of dune buggying or surfing down sand hills appealing. What's left is eating, drinking, sleeping—and avoiding dogs. We move out of the party hostel for a more expensive place but with the luxury of quiet, along with wing-clipped parrots and wooden statues of ancient little head-dressed fellows sporting giant, erect penises. We eat at the same pasta place every night, read the same books, take the same naps, and enjoy dessert at the same café overlooking the still lagoon.

It's at the café one evening that we meet Cute Kitty, years before *Felis catus* would become a global internet sensation that defied explanation. The café's black-striped kitty has the playful disposition and big, expressive eyes that would've made it an internet star if fate hadn't dropped her in Haucachina. Indeed, she strolls about the tables in the twilight looking for a handout with the brazenness of a being that knows gringos will *oooh* in her presence. The baristas allow the behavior, probably understanding that Cute Kitty's irresistibleness increases gringos' tips.

We, too, enjoy watching her striped form curve its way under the tables, chasing shoelaces, baristas, and birds.

But one evening, Tiffany makes the fatal mistake of wearing a long swishy skirt. It's scientifically proven that kittens can't resist swishy skirts, and Tiff's is of the swishiest kind. As we share a caramel crêpe, Tiff acquiesces to Cute Kitty's playfulness. Under the table, the feline chases the fabric, jumping and clawing and maybe, oh just maybe, nipping. In its exuberance, Cute Kitty tears at one of Tiffany's legs, breaking the skin. Just barely.

"That's really, *really* not good," I say as Tiffany lifts her skirt to show me.

"It's just a scratch," she replies, shooing the kitten away.

"Are you sure? Maybe it was biting you, too? We couldn't see underneath the table."

Her voice takes on a familiar tone, one she's been employing with increasing frequency over the last few months, "*Jeremy...*"

To counter it, I pull out *Lonely Planet: Peru* 5th edition and read aloud from a dog-eared page. "Rabies virus is carried in the saliva of infected animals and is typically transmitted through an animal bite," I stress the next bit, "*though contamination of any break of the skin with infected salvia may result in rabies.*"

"That seems really crazy. I doubt she even bit me."

"Yes, but she *could* have, you know. Licking can do it. Sometimes just a scratch can prove fatal," I, with my PhD in rabies, insist. "*Seriously.*"

I then begin to lecture, for the umpteenth time, why rabies is the world's most psychologically terrifying disease. How by the time you become symptomatic you're dead. No one and nothing can save you. How you have to get treatment *before* you get symptoms, without even knowing for sure whether you have it. And how the symptoms are infamously bizarre: frothing at the mouth, delusions, giddiness, and, best of all, fear of water. Yes, at the end, you will literally spasm when the nurse brings you a glass of H_2O.

Even if you're lucky enough to realize you might be infected, treatment isn't exactly accessible, cheap, or pleasant. It's a succession of five injections over several weeks (not long ago it required twenty-one shots in the stomach, a thought that kept me up at night as a child, and sometimes still does).

"*Jeremy...*"

I flip the page and read the practically memorized words, which have been going around in my head like a mantra. "Any bite or scratch by a mammal...should be promptly and thoroughly cleansed with large amounts of soap and water, followed by application of antiseptic...Local health authorities should be contacted *immediately*"—I stress that bit because it suits my urgency—"for possible post-rabies exposure treatment."

Tiffany heads to the café's bathroom either to wash the scratches or to get some peace from me—probably both.

But my pontificating continues even when we return to our new-and-improved hostel, have a drink at the bar, and retire to our room. I tell Tiffany, not for the first time, about a newspaper story from Minnesota where a man showed up in the hospital with inexplicable symptoms. The doctors were baffled, running test after test until finally the patient remembered being bitten by a bat months before. By then it was too late. Too, too late.

Now Tiffany is an incredibly strong, vigorously independent, and willful person, and I love her for all these qualities I largely lack. But even the toughest personality can withstand the withering horror of rabies for only so long, and that night I succeed in spooking her. The last thing she hears me whisper to her as she falls asleep, "Rabies, rabies, raayyyyyybeeeeeeeessssss..."

After breakfast the next morning, Tiffany heads to the internet café to do her own research on the *R* word. This is 2006, after all, when no one has smartphones but every tourist town on the planet houses at least one internet café jam-packed with travelers trying to upload thousands of photos on a wheezing connection.

That afternoon we return to the scene of the crime, Tiff wearing jeans, with a new mission: spy on Cute (Killer) Kitty.

For all my mansplaining, Tiffany hasn't fully accepted my perfectly reasonable explanation that this perky feline is infested with the rabies virus, which is surely making its way through her kitty nerves toward her vulnerable mammalian brain.

Drinking our coffee, we watch from just above the rims as Cute Kitty plays under the tables (whenever she gets close, we shoo her away), the purple waters of the lagoon lazing in the background. Employing her Spanish skills, Tiffany tries to ask the waitress about the cat but can't get any real information on its origin, its general background, or how many times rabid bats have bitten it in the night. My guess is about fifty-two.

After an hour or so, cups emptied and Tiffany bored, I begrudgingly admit the cat seems fine but emphatically add that an animal can carry rabies for months without showing a single outward symptom. Still, in the undiffused sunshine of daytime in Haucachina, Tiffany is less convinced that the rabies virus is kayaking its way up her bloodstream.

Tiffany never would get those five injections. In the end, it turns out she wouldn't contract rabies, though I watch her vigilantly for the symptoms for months. And let me tell you, it's exhausting waiting to see if your fiancée dies from rabies.

After all this relaxation, escaping Haucachina feels like breaking out of Bedlam. We pay extra for a luxury bus, so-called because it has air conditioning and a TV at the front, which plays Steve Martin's remake of *The Pink Panther* in *español* against a landscape as empty as the end of the world.

And then we see them: lions floating above the highway. Ahead of us, a flatbed truck for a traveling circus carries an iron-barred cage containing two lions, a lithe female and a big-maned male. As we pass them, the male stands and roars while Steve Martin stuffs hamburgers into his pockets.

Perhaps the lions are a positive omen because we finally begin to settle into a travel rhythm. We are becoming accustomed to the voltage of culture shock until it feels like only a slight tingling on waking every day. In Arequipa, arguably Peru's prettiest city, we stay in a hostel that serves a scrumptious breakfast on the roof while Misti, an active, snowcapped volcano, dominates the horizon.

It is also here where we have our first cups of coca tea and where I feel I can breathe again. And what air! It's crisp, clear, thin, sharp, and refreshing as ice, probably because there is less of it at 7,600 feet. As we tour the sites, we break for more cups of coca tea, down coca candies, and even chew fresh coca leaves. And instead of fearing that Misti will blow, ending us all in a sulfurous hell, I admire her curvaceous slopes. Coincidence? Peruvians view the coca leaf as a cure-all; the Incas thought of it as a sacred gift from the gods. Today we bastardize it by transforming this humble-looking leaf through various chemical processes (think acid and ammonia) into industrialized cocaine for yuppies to snort. Illegal in most of the world now, coca leaves, in their unprocessed, natural state, may be a potent therapeutic for a whole slew of ailments.

After a few days in Peru's Ciudad Blanca, we head into Colca Canyon. To lessen altitude sickness—we would peak at 16,100 feet, higher than the summit of Mount Rainier—our guides show us how to lick the coca leaves and stick them onto our temples. In Colca we watch the world's heaviest flying bird, the Andean condor, soar on rising currents of air; hike through the idyllic scenery around the village of Chivay; catch a momentary glimpse of the planet's biggest hummingbird; and spend one inebriated night dancing with very attractive locals (who are very much paid to do so since we're on a tour). Then it's on to Puno and the world's highest navigable lake, Titicaca, where we slumber on an island that feels like a hundred-years-ago time machine. My good traveler daemon is back, and I couldn't be more relieved.

We begin to take pleasure in the small things that characterize Peru: roasted corn nuts at every restaurant table; mega-theatrical Peruvian soap operas; a ridiculous number of starches with dinner: fries, roasted potatoes, and rice on one plate; roasted *cuy*, guinea pig, sold on the side of the roads; beautifully simple clay crockery; touches of artwork and craftsmanship on doors, windows, tables, seeming to say that life is meant to be surrounded by beautiful little things.

We are nearly halfway through our trip when another bus drops us off in Cuzco. For me, the Cuzco region, or Qosqo, stands out from our itinerary like letters in Braille because it's here the Incan imprint remains the sharpest. Having been educated in America's wondrous public-school system, I'd never heard a thing about the history of anywhere south of the Rio Grande. It took me weeks in New York to sort out the differences between the Maya, the Inca, the Aztec, the Olmec, and the dozens of other groups that filled up the rich and dramatic history of Central and South America. At least until Columbus showed up with his whole hemisphere's worth of disease, violence, and slavery, upending innumerable civilizations and more than ten thousand years of largely independent history.[2] It was as if he'd taken a spaceship and despoiled an alien world.

This lost world fully emerges, complete with tactile impressions, in Cuzco, the metropolitan heart of the Incan Empire. They built the whole city in the shape of a puma—as seen by the gods above. Walking in the heart of it, I run my fingers along stone walls—monstrous, impossible stones in a New World cyclopean style—that Incan children once played ball against. Without the use of wheels or mortar, the Inca people, as well as those they ruled, set these stones, some of which weigh more than an African elephant. This is known as dry ashlar (what a beautiful term!) masonry, and it produces a city that seems straight out of Tolkien or, conversely, Lovecraft.

By now Tiff and I have learned to take things more slowly—leaving time every day for doing nothing much. We spend pleasant hours at cafés overlooking the Plaza de Armas and its magnificent baroque churches—a symbol both of the country's faith and its bloody colonization.[3]

But Cuzco is also the launching pad for the Inca Trail, our planned four-day, twenty-eight-mile hike climbing five thousand feet from the Sacred Valley to every gringo's highlight: Machu Picchu. Given the understandable popularity of this guided trek, we'd booked it minutes after buying our plane tickets five months prior.

The evening before our start date, we have an informational session during which we meet our guides and fellow travelers. As Tiffany and I walk slowly back to the hostel, savoring the twilight, the lamplit streets, and the great stone blocks, we talk over little details about embarking tomorrow, one of those innocuous conversations that fill up so much of travel.

When we reach our room, Tiffany heads to the bathroom. Ten minutes later she opens the door and utters the words I've been steeling myself against since we left New York: "I think I'm sick." A few minutes later she is huddled over the toilet, vomiting. We've made it twenty-one days without either of us getting ill. The jig is up.

Peru and rabies are alike in one important way: They both make you terrified of water. In Peru, you learn quickly to fear ice cubes, lemonade, showers, and even washing your hands. You're warned repeatedly never to drink the tap water and don't accept water at restaurants if it's not bottled. Don't open your mouth in the shower and keep showers short. Don't order fruit juice. Never ever use tap water to brush your teeth. Don't drink anything with an ice cube in it. Don't eat fruits or vegetables you can't peel—who knows what they were washed with? And if the seal on the cap of a water bottle is broken, don't put it to your lips.

Peru's water is notorious, failing miserably at various World Health Organization standards and routinely landing Peruvians themselves in the hospital. Not only is the country's water home to a whole menagerie of bacteria that cushy Western guts have a hard time stomaching, but it can house dangerous parasites, E. coli, and a horror show of heavy pollutants, a concern that

Americans have successfully combated through the Clean Water Act. Well, so we thought, until Flint, Michigan.

Tiffany and I have been obsessively careful about water. One couple we met in Haucachina told us that on their first day in Peru, they ordered lemonade. It was only after they both started drinking that they looked at each other and said, "Oh, shit." And shit they did. Shitting and vomiting away the next few days. A study-abroad student we met decided to do something reckless on his last night in the country: brush his teeth with tap water. He ended up in the hospital and missed his flight home. When you visit Peru, you really need to schedule about two to three extra days to the vomit gods.

As Tiffany lies on the bathroom floor, we figure that somehow, despite our best efforts, she'd consumed everyday tap water. But maybe we can still do the Inca Trail? By dawn, it might be out of her system.

Then I feel my stomach heave. And I think, *Oh no, oh no, it's come for me now*. The monster is here. I feel heat like a fever steal up my body and fear clench my heart. I steal the toilet from Tiffany, but try as I might, I can't throw up. Once I poop, though, I feel eminently better. It's a false alarm. I'm fine. And Tiffany gets the bathroom back just in time to continue heaving.

As the night winds on, it becomes obvious that we are not going on the Inca Trail. Tiffany is still on the bathroom terra-cotta floor, now heaving up bile and growing weaker by the hour. Before dawn appears over the mountains, I walk to the departure point to inform our guides we are out.

Heading back, where Tiffany lies exhausted in bed, I feel a mix of relief and trepidation. The decision is made, but *now what*? Tiffany shows no signs of improvement over the morning. She can't even keep (bottled!) water down. On arriving at the hostel, I noted an advertisement for a travel clinic. I go to the hostel desk and have the clerk make the call. Less than an hour later, a young, well-groomed doctor knocks at our door. After watching Tiffany vomit up all the PediaLite he gives her, he recommends that we head to his clinic on the outskirts of town. I have the hostel call us a cab.

Until this day, Tiffany has been our translator. She'd had Spanish instruction in both grade school and high school. Though by no means fluent, she could get around. I, however, never learned any Spanish. And even if I had, it wouldn't have made a difference. I have the uncommon talent of being completely incapable of pronouncing foreign words, many domestic ones, too. I have a tendency to just make up whatever pronunciation sounds right in my head and then stick to it, often embarrassing myself when I open my mouth. But with a few weeks of careless listening to get by, I attempt enough Spanish to get us from point A to B.

Miraculously, my butchered Spanish makes *just* enough sense to the driver. Even more miraculously, Tiffany makes it through the whole thirty-minute drive without puking all over the seat belt-less taxi.

The clinic, it turns out, is a big suburban house in an upscale neighborhood. On arrival, Tiffany is admitted immediately and seen by another doctor. She's the only patient. As two Americans, we are privileged enough (and flush enough, it just so happens) to go to this traveler's clinic, complete with a shaded arbor and view of Pillku Urqu rising like a wall.[4]

The doctors, who specialize in the ailments that strike down gringos, want a fecal sample. They also want blood. But on seeing the needle, I halt them with cries, incomprehensibly pronounced but sufficiently loud, of *"Nueva aguja!"* I'd read (and reread and reread, sometimes late at night under the cover of darkness, like a teenager who'd just discovered their dad's *Penthouse*) how one should be careful of needles in Peru—how sometimes they are, how shall I put this? Used more than once.

So I pipe, *"Nueva aguja! Nueva aguja!"* like a one-note trumpet. Tiffany tells me to calm down and explains to the perplexed doctor, who doesn't understand my deft Spanish accent, that I am only concerned about whether the needle is clean. He laughs at my arrogant stupidity and assures us it's brand-spanking-new (though I'd remain convinced that it's really something he picked up in a ditch somewhere and wiped off with a bloody rag).

An hour later we have a diagnosis: This isn't just your basic traveler's diarrhea.

"You have parasite," the doctor tells Tiffany in English.

"What? How?"

"Bad food. Bad water. It happens. Easy. Very easy."

It turns out the microscopic Cyclospora parasite had been incubating in her body for at least a week. While we would never know what caused it, Tiffany suspects a particularly unappetizing portion of chicken salad. The doctor says she'll recover in a couple of days with medications, but they want her to stay overnight until she can keep water down. Overnight? We're just trying to wrap our mind around the word *parasite*, a little living beastie that has been feeding off and growing in Tiffany for some time. (This was, of course, before we had a child.)

As the doctor talks, I begin to sweat and feel a chill up my spine.

"Do you think I have the parasite, too?" I ask.

He looks at me coolly. Tiffany wears her familiar exasperation.

"Do you have diarrhea?" he asks.

"Er...no."

"Vomiting?"

"No."

"Blood in your stool?"

"No."

"Then you don't have parasite."

"Do you think you could just test me to be sure? I don't mind tests."

And Tiffany says, "*Jeremy . . .*"

The doctor looks from her to me and then shakes his head. Still, he takes out a thermometer and puts it in my mouth. It comes out perfectly normal.

"But I read in my guide book that you don't have to have a fever to—" I stop when he gives me that barely masked look of pity I'd seen so often in New York doctors, as if I were a deformed puppy that had been run over by a lawn mower and now could only grow hair on its left side.

"Okay," I acquiesce. But in my head, I think, *I'll show 'em. I'll prove it to them when I die horribly. Then they'll say, "Wow, we really should've listened. He was right after all. And now he's just dead. Really dead."*

The doctor changes the subject. "Before we show you room, you need to pay. Only cash."

Tiffany and I look at each other. We don't have much money beyond what we budgeted for this trip, and neither of us has a job in hand when we return to the States. We have traveler's insurance, but that would only *maybe* reimburse us after the fact. So we wait with bated breath as he writes down a number and passes it to us. The doctor has itemized everything, and I follow the long list down until I hit the total: $300. I almost laugh. *Three hundred!* You can barely see a doctor in the States for that, and here we were paying for a house—er, hostel—call, a consultation, lab tests, medicine, an IV, and an overnight stay in a private room with a stunning view of the mountains.

An hour or so later, when I arrive back at the clinic with the cash, they tell me they'd moved Tiffany upstairs to her room. Just as I open the door, I see the nurse with a little white dog (surely rabid) at her heels, preparing to set an IV into Tiffany's arm. Again, I interject, *"Nueva aguja! Nueva aguja!"*

"Calm down, Jeremy," Tiffany says. "It's okay. It's okay."

The nurse, who must have been warned that there was a gringo who would shout, *"Nueva aguja!"* at her, shows me the wrapper the needle came from. Still, I grimace even more than Tiffany as the needle is stuck through her skin and into her bloodstream.

As dusk creeps up Pillku Urqu, the doctor returns. He brings with him a Quechua friend in traditional dress and a bedframe in pieces. *Quechua* refers both to the indigenous ethnic group, direct descendants of the Inca, and their language. Our doctor introduces the man, whose face, lined with wrinkles, sports that immensely powerful Incan look, as a spiritual leader in the community, a kind of shaman. Indeed, he seems at once stern and gentle, wisdom emanating from his presence, even though we can't understand a thing he says. His eyes are bright, and he laughs easily. I am reminded of the millennia-old descriptions of Socrates.

The young doctor and the direct descendant of the Incan people get to work, quickly assembling a bed so I can stay with my parasite-ridden fiancée. And I feel I've entered some weird dream world where shamans build beds for pitifully panicked Americans.

We both sleep soundly after a day that seems to have gone on forever. Cradled by the mountains surrounding Cuzco, we slumber underneath stars that shine just a bit brighter because of the altitude.

The next morning, with Tiffany able to keep down fluids, the doctors discharge her. We decide to splurge and stay at a hotel, a real and proper one for once, with air conditioning, TVs and hot showers, and, most luxurious of all, a real bed. For two whole nights we get a respite from beds moist with humidity or smelling of mold, or those that fold over you like a taco shell, or are so small we're forced to sleep apart.

Just as we settle in for a well-deserved respite, thoughts begin to bubble out of my brain's abyss. I sit on the toilet and think, *What if I'm next? What if I have diarrhea? What if I start vomiting everywhere?* The thoughts accelerate. *Likely, this isn't just a parasite but something worse. I am bleeding from the inside. When I look down into the toilet, there will be blood everywhere, buckets of it. I'll die before they can helicopter me home.*

When I emerge from the bathroom, I tell Tiffany, "I think I need to see a doctor." She is pale and exhausted from her forty-eight-hour battle with a real parasite. "I feel terrible. Really terrible," I say. "I think I might be sick, too."

"*Jeremy*…"

"I feel all hot. And kinda queasy. And I was looking at my poop in the bathroom. And it looks kinda weird. Maybe there's blood in it. Do you want to see?"

What woman wouldn't want to drag herself out of her sickbed to look at her betrothed's shit? But Tiffany, not knowing what else to do, follows me into the bathroom.

"It looks fine," she says after we both peered into the bowl like ancient diviners scrutinizing tea leaves.

"Really?"

"Honey, you're not sick," she says after flushing it away. "If you were, you'd have symptoms by now. Look, you never had that—God, I can't even think about it—chicken thingy. Let's just get back in bed and watch some TV. I'm so tired."

I want to argue with her, to get it through her thick head that *I* am in imminent danger, that *I* need desperate medical attention. But she looks so pale, I shut my mouth.

"Let's see what's on…um… *White Chicks*?"

The movie's unapologetic ridiculousness lulls me enough that, by the end, all I want to is to sleep away most of the day. And that's what we do.

The next morning, however, I decide my symptoms require an extra trip to the internet café. I spend a good portion of our last full day in Cuzco researching tropical death.

Years later, Tiffany would confess there was a moment in Peru when she considered leaving me. During our last day in Cuzco, as I was in the internet café thinking only about myself and my imminent death, she sat outside alone on a bench watching Cuzco bustle by, worn down by the parasite, but even more so by the three weeks of traveling with me. At that moment, she thought, *Maybe I can't spend my life with someone so crazy.*

Tiffany and I eventually make it to Machu Picchu. Only instead of climbing the twenty-eight miles of the Inca Trail, we simply take the train from Cuzco to Agua Calientes, spend the night, and then take the bus up to the site as dawn flows down to meet us. There we run into our hiking troop, just finished with their arduous, once-in-a-lifetime adventure. As we stare at one another, the group and us, we wonder what might have been. Now strangers, we could've been companions but for a bunch of rogue protozoa that made a home in Tiff's intestine.

Machu Picchu is more amazing than expectations could make it, but by this point, we are so tired and run-down, it feels more like a dream than reality. We are there for a couple of hours and then we aren't anymore, and the lost city disappears again into the mist, vanishing like a phantom from a past that will never be again.

On arriving in the United States, I would finally see a psychologist for the first time in years. To them, there wasn't much mystery about my behavior: It took them less than an hour to diagnose me with obsessive-compulsive disorder. It was the first time anyone noticed Steve whispering in my ear. Manifested in my hypochondria over cancer, AIDS, rabies, parasites, or whatever disease you want, OCD had insidiously taken over my life. I could look back now and see its beginnings in my childhood with a terror of doctors and hospitals and needles, an uncanny ability to fixate on things, and then its casual resurrection throughout my adolescence and college years until we ended up in unrelenting New York City. Here, my brain finally totally betrayed me.

OCD is an affliction of exaggeration. This is what it does. It catches on those little fear-laden thoughts that crowd everyone's head and pushes them to the front of your brain until you hear only one discordant note. It is a disease of waste: wasted time, wasted efforts, wasted living. You become a servant to its endless, crippling thoughts and circular whims. OCD made me swing from one panic to another with barely an hour off; it made me so self-involved that I pretty much ignored the needs of the person I love most; and it made me, someone who once went to Kenya solo on a whim, a really bad traveler.

Now, when I think of that dog that I flew up a ladder to escape—and I do with far more regularity than one might expect so many years later—I feel regret and a kind of lingering melancholy. Poor Rabies just wanted my attention. He wanted to bound after my heels and lick my face. He wanted to be petted and patted and scratched in that place just behind his ear while I cooed, "Good boy, good boy, good Rabies." Really, he just wanted what we all want: a little love. And, sure, maybe some of my dinner.

As I write this, Rabies is most surely dead and gone, the great sand mounds surrounding Haucachina an ossuary for his malnourished bones. I imagine he spent a lifetime trying to find love around that picture-perfect oasis and never succeeding—and I wish I hadn't treated him so shabbily. He was just one victim of my OCD.

Still, giving something a name doesn't destroy it. Things got worse—much worse—before they got better. After returning from Peru, I spent the next few months digging through my poop looking for blood. I became obsessed with finding a sign, a confirmation that I'd picked up some deadly tropical disease or was succumbing to colon cancer.

Oh, Tiffany and I were young yet. And, yes, we had jobs to get, a wedding to plan, and a future stretching long beyond the horizon. But I could think of nothing except shit, disease, and death. I was a prisoner still, but at least I knew the name of my jailer.

Before making it back to the States, though, before the countless hours of therapy, going back on psychiatric drugs for the first time in years, and Steve's exposure, we would have our date with the Amazon.

It's a good thing no one ever died horribly there.

Chapter Two

Into the Amazon

SUMMER 2006, CONTINUED

Between me and instantaneous death is nothing but air. Just a bunched-up mush of nitrogen, oxygen, water vapor, argon, and carbon dioxide. It would do little to slow me as I plunged off the cliff until striking the ground below, bludgeoned into Jeremy-oatmeal.

Despite being en route to the Peruvian Amazon, the most life-infused place on the planet, the world doesn't feel enlivening this morning. I'm riding in a red twelve-person tourist van that winds up the gravely, dry western slope of the Andes. There are no railings, no fences, and no rock walls to stop vehicles from sliding off the cliff, into the open air, and down a thousand feet. Like so much of Peru, our vehicle has no seat belts. This poorly maintained road, more like a dust-choked track, is barely wide enough to fit our van.

Tiffany is next to me, fully recovered from her bout with the parasite. Other travelers fill other seats. Our guide, whom we just met this morning, sits up front near the driver. The driver, the only thing standing between us and the opportunity to meet St. Peter at the pearly gates, is a goddamn superhero, navigating the road like a thread through a needle's eye.

There are only two ways to get to Manu National Park, in the heart of the Peruvian Amazon. One is overland on this road, up one side of the Andes and down the other; the other is via a small airplane that lands in a thin airstrip cut out of the rainforest canopy. I'm not sure the latter would have been preferable, but at least it would've been quicker. We'd know by now if we were dead.

The road up the mountain is so narrow you can only go one way, and that way depends upon the day. Seriously. Monday, Wednesday (the day we left), and Friday you go up the western side of the mountain and down the eastern, while Tuesday, Thursday, and Saturday you go up the eastern, down the western.

On Sunday, the road is open to anyone traveling in either direction—aka the suicidal.

At times, the right side of the van brushes up against the rock mountain, scraping the side. When the road narrows further, the driver gets out, pushes in the side mirror, and then inches forward, ever so slowly, forward and reverse, forward and reverse, rubbing against the rock in what seems like a weird mating ritual with a mountain, until finally the road widens and everyone breathes a sigh. And our driver lights a well-deserved cigarette.

But it's not hard to imagine it all going differently. The wheel going off the edge, a rock breaking free, the van tilting, and then...well, it's Toonces the Driving Cat in Peru. It's not the death so much that winds up my brain but the imagining of the few moments of terror beforehand, the realization that I'm going to die now.

"Just don't look out the window," Tiffany tells me.

It's good advice. But hard to heed. The window is just so goddamn *clear*.

If I weren't so white-knuckled, I'd enjoy looking out the window. We are, after all, driving *up* a mountain. The landscape is typically western Peru: brown, tan, and desert dry. Small scraggly trees with more branches than leaves, some brush and bushes, a nearly clear view all the way down, should you choose to stand at the edge and look. But why would you?

At 9,500 feet, we stop for a snack break in the small mountain town of Paucartambo, but we keep it short because we are behind schedule. We had to wait an hour at the airport this morning for a fellow traveler named Jane. Jane is from California and in her fifties with the endearing face of a squirrel and the energy likewise. Jane missed her flight out of LAX yesterday.

The group's conversation with her went something like this.

"See, here's my ticket. It says six ten."

"Yes, but that means six ten AM, not PM. If it was six ten PM, it would have been eighteen ten, that's military time."

"No, no, they didn't put AM or PM."

"Military time doesn't need AM or PM. It's a twenty-four-hour clock."

"The airline got it wrong. It should have said six ten AM, not PM."

"But there is no PM."

"When you see six ten, what time do *you* think of?"

Collective sigh.

"But airlines go by military time just to avoid this kind of mistake."

"But they got it wrong."

"No, you just mistook the time."

"But it's the airline's fault."

"Hey, look, a mountain!"

The whole group spends nine days trying to convince Jane that, however understandable (kinda), the mistake was on her side. But Jane can't bear defeat.

Jane is a birder, with the equipment to prove it: a high-powered scope, the best binoculars on the market, and brand-new books with glossy images of the 1,700-plus bird species in Peru (nearly twice as many as the entire United States in a country seven times smaller). Jane is a birder, just check out her birder bling.

She is also the only other American in our group, a motley crew of tourists from all the rich corners of the world: the Australian couple and the Danish couple, the Swedish grandpa and grandson, the Canadian girlfriends and the trio of Dutch gals.

As we drive higher, the road gets bad—hey, everything's relative. Sometimes, we all have to clamber out of the van to lighten the weight so the driver can maneuver it out of a depression. Other times, our guide gets out, pulls out planks from the back, and sets them down over scars in the road, and the truck rolls, slow like a turtle, over the planks. Signs of landslides are everywhere, debris shuttled across the road as if a giant had swept it there but forgot his dustbin. One landslide at the right (or wrong) moment and we'd all be Toonces.

And then it happens. We crest an ascent at 11,581 feet and the exhausted van lurches to a stop. Our guide announces lunch and we all pile out like obedient school children. Just in front of us is a plateau of the same dry, scraggly, dust-choked landscape sporting occasional plants that have evolved over eons to eke out an existence on atmospheric spittle. But when we walk to the edge of the plateau, the mountain pass, before us is a vision that will lie within me the rest of my days: two mountains swaddled in riotous jungle and rolling between them an unbroken blanket of cloud.

This is my first encounter with the Amazon rainforest, the biggest explosion of life on our planet—maybe in the universe. After weeks of dry brown-and-tan western Peru, here is an ecosystem drowning in water, dancing with photosynthesis, sucking up carbon dioxide, breathing out oxygen, manufacturing its own weather, and supporting the dramatic lives of millions of species, trillions of lives, most found nowhere else but in this great green garden.

The terror of the drive pours off me as if I've been baptized, and I can't keep my eyes from the scene before me, from the sublimity of this thing.

I never actually believed I'd make it to the Amazon rainforest.

After lunch, we are herded back into the close-pressed van and onto the road, only this time, instead of going up a mountain we begin down the other side, entering a new world.

Green is everywhere, chlorophyll on steroids. Trees buck and bend against each other, wrestling in slow motion for space, their green leaves splaying, desperate for light. Ferns rise from the floor like green crowns. Moss and lichens cover all available surfaces like a Magic Eye rendered in every shade of green.

And not just greenery, but water, too. It spills from the cliffs in shallow falls; it drips from the edges of ferns; it collects in mini pools created by epiphytes; it likely caresses a hundred orchids hidden just beyond our view. The air smells of bursting, blossoming, unfolding life.

Rapidly we descend into clouds. Cloud forests, like fairy-tale castles, are nearly always blanketed in cloud cover, providing constant moisture to a distinct ecosystem with hundreds of thousands of critters found nowhere else.

The road doesn't improve. In fact, it gets worse because water is everywhere, as if God had kicked over a bucket, creating puddles, mud, waterfalls, streams, slipping and sliding. Yet, I stop caring, my adrenal glands no longer flooding my system with cortisol, because I am *here*.

I love nature. That's putting it lightly. Nature is where I find God. When I'm in the woods, my breath feels like a prayer. A grove of old trees is a church. Animals are sanctified beings.

Even when I was a child, the Amazon rainforest always felt like my Mecca, my Jerusalem, my Bodhi tree.

I have come to believe that every human born is implanted with the seed to love nature. It's an evolutionary, existential, almost metaphysical reality. It's layered somewhere deep in our double helix. Scientists have come to call this seed "biophilia," first coined by Erich Fromm in the 1960s but popularized by the inimitable E. O. Wilson in 1984. Like all the best scientific terms, *biophilia* is a Greek word and translates to the love of life or living things, or as Wilson calls it, "The urge to affiliate with other life-forms."

But like everything with humanity, variety is the order of the day. I think some of us are born with larger seeds than others. And many simply don't have the experiences anymore to water those seeds and allow them to grow. If you are born in a high-rise apartment and only ever see concrete and television, is it any wonder that nature would seem anything but alien and terrifying at first?

I grew up surrounded by forty acres of Midwestern farmland and forests. Well, not forest really. As a child I believed it a forest, a woods of light and shadow, but it was just a few treelines between the neighbor's property and a couple of small groves. Still, it was large enough to immerse and impress a small child.

Nature was also in my blood. My maternal grandfather, Leon C. Snyder, was a botanist at the University of Minnesota and the founder of the Minnesota Landscape Arboretum. By the time I was born, he was already a touchstone for the family, with his children treating the unruly white-haired elder as if he'd been sanctified. On the other side, my father was born on our family farm in 1942 and never lived anywhere else. His family raised cows and crops, and by the time I came around, my parents had turned the land into a hobby farm growing raspberries, strawberries, and azaleas, a distinct variety, developed by my grandfather.

My childhood was pretty idyllic, with fields, forests, and friends—until my mother's collapse. She went from being my rock—well, more like my boulder—to eroding away in the geological span of a single day.

I'm ten, and it's good to be ten. I'm running down a trail so well-known it's practically a member of the family: down through the long straight rows of strawberries, over the dike, along the pasture where the cows graze languidly, through the treeline and the raspberry bushes, and into the Victory Woods (named after an infamous party on V-E Day) that line our local lake.

My little black dog, Chip, is by my side. I hold a stick in my hand, but at this moment it's a sword and I'm chasing down a quest, fighting off some goblins or maybe seeking a jealous dragon. The sun is on my back and the sky is clear. At the edge of the forest is the lake, and here is where the drama concludes under a canopy of still-green leaves. Still green, but not for long.

Victorious, I head back toward home, taking the long way around the pockets of forest interspersed amidst our neighbor's cornfields. In one of these pockets, I lounge on a log, kick up my feet, and set my sword by my side. There are birds singing here. I don't know the species and I don't really care. Butterflies are dancing in the pockets of sunshine—ditto for them. But I am happy they are here. This place, this trail, this land that rolls away from my house like a swelling sea is almost a physical extension of myself, a partner in my story. In the little grove, surrounded by corn, I feel a child's peace that is difficult for any adult to understand, even when looking back from twenty-five years away.

Memories are like this. Moments are bled into by what came before and what came after; context matters after, even when it didn't give a fuck in the moment. At that moment in August 1990, I was still free.

Two months later, my mother would have a mental breakdown.

Lady cock-of-the-rocks must like their men beakless because the males' orange crest successfully hides the beak under its neon feathers. In profile, this odd bird looks like an orange plate with a single eye.

As the sun descends behind the trees, we mutely watch a group of cock-of-the-rock males enact their most important ritual. Every dawn and dusk of every day of every year, these beak-defying dudes come out to dance in the same lek for the females, squawking and prancing in a display that is less gracious than, well, horny. If a female shows up in her drab brown gown, the males go nuts trying to out cat-, er cock, call one another. When the last rays of the sun splay through the trees and touch them, the bright birds—scarlet and tangerine orange—burst like jewels.

Alas, for us and the dudes, a female doesn't show this night.

Over dinner, our guide Tomas entertains us with tales of the forest over the warm glow of kerosene lamps and the night sounds of innumerable insects humming, buzzing, strumming, and violining all at once. Little frogs, clinging to trees or lying in a tiny bath of a bromeliad, chirrup from the distance, and night birds sing their epoch-old songs, all in a chorus that could not have but helped inspire our ancestors to invent music.

The conversation quickly turns to what species we might see over the next eight days. Indulgently, Tomas (who's ridiculously handsome) asks everyone at our table what they'd most like to see. A jaguar, of course, is the most popular answer. He cautions us that the Amazon is not like Africa or the American West. The animals, especially the big ones, usually remain deep in the forest and slink away before you ever come on them. You can't expect to see animals like jaguar or tapir or anteaters or anacondas. What you can expect is a mind-boggling, ridiculous variety of birds and insects. Being in the Amazon isn't a safari; rather, it's full-on nature immersion.

Still, when it comes to me, I say, "Capybara."

Tomas is surprised. "A capybara?"

When I was a kid, I had a book on the Amazon rainforest, and on seeing the photo of the capybara,[1] I thought, *Could there be such a creature in the world?*

"Well, a capybara is pretty likely, Jeremy," Tomas says with a charismatic smile that has undeniably melted the hearts of many a lonely tourist. "They often hang out on the riverbanks."

The capybara is the world's largest rodent, weighing up to two hundred pounds. If you've never seen one, it looks like a space beastie from *Star Wars*. They have the head of a guinea pig, the body of a giant dog, and the legs of a hairy pig. On their snouts, they sport a large scent gland known as a *morillo*. It looks like a monstrous engorged tick. Capybaras are so at home in the Amazonian floodplains that these rat-hippos can sleep in water with just their snouts—and morillo—chilling above the water. Come on, who hasn't dreamed of meeting a capybara on a moonlit night?

Over dessert, Tomas regales us with a story about how he recently did ayahuasca with a shaman and then went for a midnight walk.

Used by some indigenous groups as a component for spiritual rituals or medicinal practices, ayahuasca is a potent hallucinogenic made out of boiling the caapi vine. Tomas had done ayahuasca before but felt nothing. This night was different.

He followed the shaman through the night-sheltered rainforest, sensing all of nature coming to life. He heard the leafcutter ants chewing and felt the flowers closing up shop for the night. He perceived the mushrooms growing and smelled the peccaries' musk far off. The hike culminated with a harpy eagle, the largest bird of prey in the Amazon, flying down to a low branch to peer at the two men.

He smiles after he tells the story, downs a glass of whiskey, and looks at all the gaping gringo faces staring at him. I'm pretty sure if Tomas were forced to compete in a lek, he'd win. I mean if Tiffany leaves me for Tomas on this trip, I'd be devastated...but I would also *totally* understand.

The more you travel, the more you appreciate adept guides. A guide is an entertainer, an encyclopedia, and a babysitter all rolled into one. We are fortunate in Manu, for Tomas is one of the best we've ever had.

In bed that night, slightly drunk, I read a bit of *Bleak House* and then the kerosene lamp is turned off and the sounds of the cloud forest enclose me like a blanket. No car alarms, no police sirens, no shouting drunks disturb the night, only the songs of a multitude of wild things.

The night feels less heavy, and I sleep in deepness for the first time in months.

✧ ✧ ✧

At dawn the next morning, we get back into the van and drive farther down the mountain. We eat breakfast en route to make sure we get to the direction-change gate on time.

A couple of hours later, and about 3,300 feet down, we leave the cloud forest behind and finally enter the world's greatest lowland rainforest. The Amazon basin stretches over 2.9 million square miles (nearly the size of the continental United States) with the vast majority of it covered in forest. This is nature's greatest performance on its biggest stage.

But as if to punctuate the Amazon's current troubles, our first views in the lowland area are of rough homesteads and small crops of coca carved out of the protected forest, evidence of people trying to make a living off the notoriously infertile and nutrient-poor jungle soil. Within a few years, they will have exhausted the soil and will cut more of the forest.

We finally cross the direction-change gate. Already, vehicles sit there waiting to take the perilous trip the other way. Good luck, y'all!

By noon, we reach the village of Atalaya, a hesitant grouping of ramshackle houses and buildings. In the tiny town, the main thing I remember is a cute puppy the group cuddles and passes between them. I don't touch it, but I also don't scream "rabies" at our fellow travelers. So…progress?

Amid the graffiti of Atalaya hangs a sign that's deliberately hard to miss. To one side of a silhouette of a long-haired man with a bow and arrow are these words:

¡CUIDADO!
Zona de tránsito de indígenas en aislemiento
Evite Conflictos
No intentar contactarlos
No entregarlas ropa, alimento, hierramientas u otras
No fotografiarlos (podrían interpretar a la cámara como arma)
En caso de occurencias, comunicarlo al Ministerio de Cultura

If you're like me and understand about as much Spanish as astrophysics, here's a translation: "Warning! Transit zone of isolated indigenous people. Avoid conflicts. Do not try to contact them. Do not offer them clothes, food, tools or anything else. Do not photograph them (they could interpret the camera as a weapon). In case of occurrences, contact the Ministry of Culture."

Manu is home to the Mashco-Piro, one of the world's last uncontacted indigenous tribes, and the Yora, a tribe one could call only hesitantly contacted. When officials use the term *uncontacted*, it doesn't mean these people are wholly isolated; they do have some contact with other tribes, but they have so far avoided any kind of long-term contact or integration with the modern world. A more accurate term may be *voluntary isolation*. These people know the modern world is out there. They see airplanes, they have run-ins (sometimes violent) with illegal loggers and drug traffickers, and they will sometimes chat and trade with other indigenous people who have more fully met the modern world, but they will kill to keep their independence and security. The Mashco-Piro have learned over the centuries that their best security depends on almost total isolation.[2]

The presence of the Mashco-Piro is one reason why it's illegal to enter Manu National Park without a guide. While Peruvian officials don't want a bunch of dumb gringos getting themselves killed while treating Manu like Disney World, they also claim to safeguard the Mashco-Piro. Uncontacted tribes remain extremely vulnerable because they have little natural immunity to many of our most common diseases. When missionaries made contact with the Yora in the Amazon in the 1980s, respiratory disease led to the death of 70 tribal peoples out of just 200—and that was with emergency medical attention.

Of course, if the Peruvian government—or any Amazonian nation for that matter—really cared about their indigenous populations, they'd stop handing out concessions to oil, gas, logging, agriculture, and mining companies inside indigenous territories. A single sneeze from the common cold could wipe out most of a tribe.

After lunch in Atalaya, we gather on the transport that we'll depend on for the next eight days. It looks like a giant canoe, about sixty feet long but with an outboard motor and a cover to keep out the rain. The boat is large enough not only to fit our whole group but also several crates and barrels of equipment since everything has to be brought to our destination.

And then we're off.

My mother's devastation seemed to come out of nowhere, as though struck down by a bolt from the blue, thrown by one of the bored gods.

For months on end, she was resigned to a couch, intermittently sobbing and sleeping. Doctors stacked her with medications and put her on constant suicide watch. No one knew if she would ever recover. No one knew if she'd live out the year. She had gone from a healthy, optimistic, and capable person to wholly impassable overnight.

Of course, this was the perspective of my ten-year-old self. In reality, her breakdown stemmed from the buildup of years of stress, frustration, and pain, the way pressure builds inside a teakettle before finally the blow—the whistle a cry of pain so acute it shook the lives of all around her.

Up to that point, my father had often been distant and mercurial. Living with severe depression and anxiety, he struggled for years both as a husband and a father. In response, my mother would do anything to try to make him happy, including working nonstop to bring in more money. By the time of her collapse, she was not only raising three young boys but working three jobs. She had become ill and frail, the mental toll showing up first physically, with my father an unwitting accomplice in her fracturing.

Over the years, I crafted this mythology about what happened next. I don't know how much is true and how much is legend, but it *feels* true and maybe that's the best any of us can get from memory.

When the family shattered, I had two choices: Either I could break away from my mother and go on with my life, cutting myself off from her as if she were a tree limb I could do without. Or I could follow her down into what appeared a dark, twisted stairway to hell. So I decided to become my own little version of Dante, Odysseus, Orpheus, or whatever abyssal-dwelling hero you like and follow my mom into the depths. I'm not saying this was a conscious decision made at a particular moment but rather the unconscious, deeply emotional response of a ten-year-old.

I started skipping school to stay home with my mom. If she was going to be depressed, suicidal, and practically catatonic, then, by God, so was I.

Mental illness was all over my DNA. It was just waiting for a crisis to really pop.

In the months before leaving for Peru, I compiled a mental list of the ways the Amazon could kill you:

- bite from a venomous snake (forget jaguars, piranhas, and anacondas —those fears are overblown)
- malaria (still kills over 400,000 people a year)
- typhoid
- yellow fever
- spider (the wandering spiders have the deadliest bite of any arachnid)
- tetanus
- Oroya fever
- Chagas disease
- the plague (yes, the medieval variety)
- caiman (the massive black caiman is probably the most dangerous big animal in the region)
- falling branch or tree (seriously, probably the most likely murderer in the rainforest)
- fire ants (in the past, some native tribes used them as a punishment)
- rabies
- drowning

Still, contrary to all expectations, including my list's, the next eight days slip by in a kind of reverie. My OCD symptoms, which I don't know are symptoms at all at the time but assume are simply rational responses to imminent mortality, slip beneath the surface. Oh, they are still there (Steve and I will be together till death do us part), but once we enter the Alto Madre de Dios, the High Mother of God River, they've calmed and diffused.

Indeed, much of my memories of these eight days in the Manu Biosphere Reserve are of being on the water, either the Madre de Dios or the Manu.

Fed by the Andes, the Alto Madre de Dios is a wild, rapid-heavy river flanked by two-story-high banks and unbroken forest, with majestic godlike trees that reach up 180 feet into the sky. Above the river rises the Pantiacolla Mountain Range, a final strand of the Andes covered in verdant jungle fare.

On the Madre de Dios, you truly realize you've entered the green, wet, beating heart of the Amazon.

At first, I keep my eyes peeled for wildlife, hoping I'll find a jaguar on every beach or a tapir on every hill. But Tomas is right (and clever to bring it up on our first night). This isn't about the big animals. It's simply about being here.

After a while, I fall into a kind of waking dream. I no longer care if we see a giant anteater or capybara. I am no longer seeking. I am just being.

For the first time since arriving in Peru four weeks ago, Tiff and I have absolutely nothing to do: no hotel to find, no money to change, no restaurant to choose, no decisions to make. All we have is this: the turn of the river, the great canopy, the periodic heron taking flight, the sloping beaches, the turtles slipping into the water as the wake from our boat inundates their perches on fallen logs.

The scenery doesn't change, and the beauty doesn't diminish. Everything just is. After a few hours on the river, one begins to feel that they can comprehend, however naïvely, the vast size of this rainforest and the incredible scale of the world's greatest wilderness. One wonders if maybe this is indeed how we are supposed to be.

Manu National Park is larger than Connecticut. It's also a strong contender for the most biodiverse place on the planet, which potentially means that more species live here than anywhere else of similar size. More than in Sumatra or Papua New Guinea or the Congo (all the other candidates are also in the Amazon). According to UNESCO, the park itself contains over two hundred species of mammals, eight hundred species of birds,[3] sixty-eight species of reptiles, and seventy-seven species of amphibians. And here's a kicker: Scientists have identified fifteen thousand plant species in Manu. That's nearly as many as in the whole of the United States in an area 570 times smaller.

But the real wealth of any rainforest is the smallest things: the insects. Some have estimated that 2.5 *million* species of insects dwell in the Amazon basin, more species than we've named across the entire planet since Carl Linnaeus started his ongoing system of naming organisms in 1735.

The vast majority of life-forms in the Amazon (and on the planet) remain cryptic, hidden, unknown even in their most basic forms to science. We really have no idea what's out there.[4]

One cannot be hyperbolic about the Amazon; it's simply impossible. It's like trying to be hyperbolic about the genius of Shakespeare or the joy of ice cream or the birth of a child. The Amazon is drunken karaoke; it is hyperbole come to life.

Still, the going isn't exactly smooth. It's the dry season, which means the river has hit its annual nadir, but this year the Madre de Dios is lower than anyone on our crew has seen it. Our pilot, much like our van driver, has to have both a keen knowledge of the river's shifting course and nerves of steel to avoid grounding us or, worse, tipping the boat.

At times, the low river means we all have to get out, pull up our pants, and wade through the water until the boat is light enough to pick us up a few hundred yards down. You can see us all, the Americans and the Danish and the Dutch, high-stepping gingerly through the water, holding our boots or shoes above our heads.

Tomas and the pilot talk a lot about how they've never seen the river so low and mention climate change. Global warming, caused by all the greenhouse gases spewed into the atmosphere over the last century-plus, had already become omnipresent here. In 2005 and 2006, the Amazon was hit by a so-called hundred-year drought. In other words, a drought so severe under sane circumstances it should statistically happen once a century. But a *second* hundred-year drought hit the Amazon in 2010. Then a *third* in 2015. If this becomes the new norm, which looks likely unless we finally start treating climate change like the monster it is, the Amazon could change in ways we can't imagine. All this riotousness could be lost.

Arriving close to dinnertime at our first lodge inside the Amazon, Tiffany and I retreat to our cabin. This is what happens when we open the door:

"Whoa," Tiffany gasps.

"What?"

"Over there, above the bed."

"Ohhhhh… That's big. I mean really big," I say.

"Yes. Big."

The eight-eyed, eight-legged beastie is gray and brown with a broad abdomen sparkling with white dots. You could draw constellations on its belly. Researchers have named around 3,600 spider species in the Amazon, but we have no idea if this is one of them or something undescribed. It's quite possible when you're in the Amazon that you're chilling with things that have no names.

"Do you want to move it?" Tiffany asks me.

"Hell, no, I'm not touching that thing."

"Well, neither am I."

"So what do we do?"

We exchange a look, close the door, and run, calling, "Tomas!" like little children.

He saves us, of course. But we are heartened by the fact that when he opens the cabin door and sees the arachnid, he's sufficiently impressed. "She's *grande*," he says, as though he expected we were exaggerating like typical gringos. Although the size of a small dog—I'm a typical gringo—the spider is harmless. Tomas thinks it's a big-bodied wolf spider, pacific to humans but a friggin' horror show if you're a grasshopper.

It turns out that if a fifth grader starts skipping school regularly, adults are going to notice. Even ones like my father, who had enough on his plate trying to save his wife from total dissolution.

This behavior landed me in my first visit with a therapist. I don't remember it. I don't even remember who I saw first out of the vast multitude, their discombobulated faces hanging over my frontal cortex like those exploited by the Faceless Men of Braavos. But I do remember the therapists' building in my hometown of Buffalo, Minnesota. It was just two blocks from my elementary school.

I hated the short walk from the car to the building's door because I was terrified a fellow fifth grader would see me and discover my secret. It felt like the fifth-grade version of a perp walk.

The building was an old ranch house, meticulously landscaped as if to shove their mental tidiness into their patients' faces. The waiting room looked like something out of the late 1970s. The furniture itched and the placed smelled weird, a cross between an old folks' home and the sweet decay of dead mice in the walls.

Once in, I'd have to sit and talk to some strange adult—I have the vision of a black-bearded man with a serious, studious face (perhaps he was the first?)—about all my problems at home and at school.

I was a sensitive, artistic child, more interested in animals than trucks and guns; keener to live in a fairyland of my imagining than play sports. I'd always felt more able to be myself around girls than the typical rural boy. I never felt *boy enough* to be accepted by my small conservative town. A lingering sense of inadequacy plagued me.

Just beyond the sprawl of the Twin Cities, Buffalo is a difficult place to characterize. It's a cross between a small farming town and a bustling exurb. Today, it's known for antiquing and car dealerships. As a kid, it was wonderful to grow up in a land of fields and lakes and rural byways. But the older I got, the more I felt constricted by what I would call the town's Minnesota-nice rabid conservatism.

Politics were less talked about out in the open than they were an underlying force that decided who was worth something and who wasn't. The hierarchy of worth was clear even if unstated. If you weren't Christian, you weren't saved. If you weren't straight, you were broken. If you weren't athletic, you were a pansy. Some were welcome; others were not. And the mentally ill (which, according to a surprising number of people I grew up with, was a sign of not loving Jesus enough) were definitely not among the chosen.

I disliked everything about school. I was bored, restless, and terrified. The boys, especially ones I didn't know well, filled me with a sense of latent violence, as if they would pummel me without a moment's notice.

Worst of all was recess because suddenly the teacher's authority vanished, and we'd all be thrown out into a playground of unspoken hierarchies and unstructured drama.

It wasn't that I was overly enamored of structure, but I knew teachers were the best guardians of my security and certain boys were willing to take a swipe at it. It wasn't just physical safety but social inclusion as well. One knows where they fit in at recess, for good or ill. Corners, trees, and swings were all good places to hide, to keep away from roving boys who may want to vent their frustrations at the world on my small, fragile, inviting frame.

My school situation was odd in fifth grade. My class had two teachers: Ms. Laurie, who handled the mornings, and Mr. Craig, the afternoons.

Ms. Laurie, empathetic and kindhearted, was slight with curly black hair. When we brought my situation to her, she took the courageous step of telling me how she, too, sometimes suffered from deep depression and was willing to help in whatever way she could.

Mr. Craig, tall, blond, and handsome, viewed my whole situation with the skepticism of someone who has never experienced any kind of mental illness in his life but is certain he knows all about it. He thought I just wanted to stay home like a baby.

My teachers' polar-opposite reactions pretty much defined how adults responded to me for the next eight years. Some would be compassionate, generous, and nonjudgmental. They did their best to understand and mostly just treated me as any other normal kid. But many were like Mr. Craig, deciding I was taking advantage of the situation or making it all up or was just a rotten kid, skin to core. I stopped trusting that adults, even therapists, would believe me, take me seriously, or really listen.

I developed a chip on my shoulder, one that grew so big it sliced into my flesh throughout the years. I began to look at the world around me, the community, and see it as rejecting me, as twisting my story into one in which I played a liar, a coward, a weak thing that should've been left out in the cold to perish.

Much of this was unfair to all those who did try to help me, whether in my school, in our church, or in the community. But these feelings of a growing young man took root for a reason. I was simply trying to survive.

And to do so, everything must be hidden.

Our days are made up of either traveling downriver or hiking a trail.

On one day, dozens of squirrel monkeys, interspersed with capuchins, cross over our heads, chattering loudly and sending a flurry of leaves, seeds, and debris down upon us. Tiffany calls it our "monkey shower." On another, the group stops, motionless, and listens to the telltale cracking of a herd of white-lipped peccaries, over a hundred strong, just beyond the impenetrable trees. Though we never see them, we smell their pungent skunkiness. One night, long after the sun goes down, we find the only species of salamander in the park, the alien-looking (and wonderfully named) Nauta mushroomtongue salamander clinging to a leaf.

Instead of a place of death, I find one of never-ending wonder.

Jane the birder, it turns out, is about as good at identifying birds as she is at telling time. Tiffany is quick to pick up some of the basics: woodpeckers fly with a distinct dip-and-up-dip-and-up, macaws fly high and straight and always in pairs. But Jane, no matter how much of a birder she is, can't seem to bird. She confuses her parrot with her macaw and her woodpeckers with her toucans.

I'm not the argumentative type. Usually, I'm the poster child for Minnesota Nice, but one day, deep into the trip, I snap.

"A heron," Jane sings out from the boat at an avian silhouette standing on a branch above the water still a ways away.

"I think it's actually an anhinga," I say. An anhinga, also known as the snakebird, is a type of water-hunting bird with an exceptionally long neck. It's the giraffe of the order of Suliformes and common in Manu.

"No, a heron," Jane says.

"Anhinga, I think," I repeat as Minnesota Nicely as I can.

"Heron."

"I'm pretty sure—see the neck—it's an anhinga."

"Heron."

"Okay, I think anhinga."

Silence for twenty seconds until we are considerably closer, and she says, "See, Jeremy. Heron."

"Anhinga," Tomas corrects her.

Jane doesn't speak again for several hours, much to everyone's relief.

I've met a lot of birders in my travels and I respect their dedication and devotion, but if you're a birder, stop reading now, okay?

All you non-birders beware because birders be crazy. I've met birders who if they were to see an elephant humping a rhino, they'd just move on because what they're really seeking is a Tanzanian tailorbird. I've met birders who travel thousands of miles via airplane, hundreds of miles on terrible roads, and when they finally reach their destination, hear the song of a particular warbler, tick a box on their *Life List*, and say, "Well, that's it then. Might as well go home early." I've met birders who routinely—routinely, mind you—wake up before the sun does to find a bird. *It's still dark!*

Don't get me wrong, I *love* birds, and the more I travel, the more I appreciate our global avian diversity (who doesn't obsess over tiny flying dinosaurs?), but calling myself a birder would likely force me to do several things I'm incapable of. Like getting up at 4 AM.

One morning, not even on a hike, but just heading the few hundred feet from our lodge to the boat, Tomas motions quickly but quietly. There's something here. He points above us in the trees. We tilt our heads. And there, just six feet from us is an animal that looks like a cross between an alien and a teddy bear with nearly orange fur. A gasp, almost the sound of a long sigh, escapes the group collectively. About the size of a toddler, the animal moves precisely and slowly through the trees, its four-clawed forelimb grasping on branches and pulling it forward, its snout, shaped like a handheld vacuum, quivering.

"Tamandua," Tomas whispers in suitable awe.

A tree-dwelling anteater. We likely caught this one on its way to bed, as they are nocturnal.

The tamandua appears wholly unconcerned with our presence. Some animals in Manu have lost their fear of humans after going unhunted for so many generations.

Unfazed and steadily, the tamandua tree-crawls just above our heads to find slumber among the morning light.

Halfway through the trip, we leave the white waters of the Alto Madre de Dios and turn onto the Manu. Unlike the Mother of God River, the Manu is a slow-moving, sediment-filled waterway the color of chocolate.

Shortly after arriving in Manu, we stop and check in with forest guards. We are now entering what's known as the Reserve Zone of the park, an area that is only for brief tourist stays. Beyond it is the Intangible Area, which is an option only for scientists or archeologists with special government permission. It's there the uncontacted tribes still dwell.

One morning while deep inside the Reserve Zone, we slip onto a lake in a catamaran. The water is still, the clouds above perfectly mirrored. The whole world is silent but for the rhythmic sounds of our guides paddling.

We are floating on Lago Salvador, an oxbow lake[5] with its own community of wildlife. Rufescent tiger herons stalk the shadows, prehistoric-looking hoatzins roost low in the shore trees, furry bats snooze on tree trunks, and a small caiman suns itself.

But the real star here is the giant river otter. For hours we watch a family swim, play, and feed on their lake. True to their name, these animals are huge, growing to five feet six inches, exactly my height. With big eyes, dashing fangs, and handsome white splatters that look like Rorschach tests on their necks, these carnivores are both regal and beautiful. Intensely social, they do everything together, even taking on the Amazon's biggest predators, such as the black caiman and jaguar.

I remember a photo of one taken years ago in a *National Geographic* beguiling me. And here I am, surreally, a brief guest in their lake kingdom.

"You sure you're not coming?" Tiffany asks me as the boat drops anchor at a shallow portion of the Manu.

"There's no way I'm getting in *there*," I tell her.

We've had this conversation before, several times. Just because I'm generally less anxious than Peru 1.0 doesn't mean I'm stupid. I'm not going to *swim* in a river in the Amazon.

There's a good reason, and it's not piranhas or black caiman. Nope, it's the candiru. Or as I like to call it: the urine hell beast. The urine hell beast (UHB) is a tiny parasitic catfish, also colorfully known as toothpick fish or vampire fish, that allegedly, very allegedly it turns out, can invade your urethra and stay there, hanging out in your piss stream. The story goes that when someone pees in the water, the candiru, aka UHB, swims up the urine stream and then latches itself inside the urethra, using backward-pointing spikes. I can't even write these words without my crotch going numb.

I've heard this story from various people, which goes back centuries as related by indigenous people. But it turns out it might be a little bullshit. There are various claims of candirus invading the urethra but, to date, very little direct evidence. Most of the stories stem from the nineteenth century, and the most reliable of those involve candirus getting stuck not in urethras but vaginal canals. Careful ladies. There is one modern incident in 1997 when a young man had to have a candiru cut out of his urethra, but even that has been called into question. It may be such incidents are just wildly unlikely but still possible, like the stingray attack that killed Steve Irwin.

Still, even if I would have known all that, I don't think I would have made the descent into the calm waters of the Manu. Instead, I become the group photographer, documenting the fun had by everyone else.

That evening, Tiffany and I lie in separate hammocks an arm span away from each other.

"If you could have anything to eat right now, anything in the world, what would you like?"

"Hmm." Tiffany, invisible inside her hammock, draws out her musing. "My mom's crab salad."

"Your mom's crab salad? That's what you'd have? Out of anything in the world?"

"Yes, what's wrong with that?"

"Nothing. It must be *some* crab salad."

"Imitation crab."

"That's a selling point?"

Below us is the bank of the river, the water rolling slowly past. A fallen tree with green leaves still blooming floats by, a kingfisher swoops low.

"It's the only thing in the world I want right now, aside from a good cup of coffee. I'd murder you for a coffee." Almost all the coffee we encountered in Peru was Nescafé—perhaps due to our budget hostels.

"Hmm."

"What about you?"

"I don't know. Pizza, maybe, tacos. Any meal that doesn't have potatoes. Or tea. Strong English breakfast tea. No more Lipton."

"Did I mention coffee?"

"You did."

Several hours later, we've sufficiently gone through each of our cravings, which have built up like scabs that require itching after six weeks of unvaried Peruvian tourist food.

On our final day on the river, I stand suddenly in the boat (not advised). I point and yell, "It's skimming! Look, it's skimming!"

Everyone's attention turns to me. And I shout again. "See, it's fucking skimming!"

In front of the boat, a black skimmer, a bird with a lower beak that is several centimeters longer than the upper, has just opened its black-and-orange beak with the bottom half now cutting through the water like a plow in a field. Behind it, another skimmer opens it jaws and follows the first.

We've seen hundreds of skimmers on the river, odd-looking birds with their giant beaks and black eyes that disappear into black feathers. We've witnessed them sometimes flying, sometimes chilling on the beaches, but never *skimming*, a feeding behavior in which they stick their lower mandibles into the water until it pierces a small fish or insect. I'd so longed for some skimming!

Most of the crew chuckles at me. They have become well acquainted with my *very* enthusiastic response to wildlife. A few of the other tourists pull out cameras, at this point almost as though out of obligation, but most just smile and watch lazily. Not even Jane, birder extraordinaire, looks at all interested. But I am beyond pleased as punch.

Later that afternoon, just as the sun makes its descent, casting a fiery glow across the canopy, the boat slows. Tomas taps me on the shoulder. I look to where he's pointing. Just on the bank is a family of capybaras. One set of eyes meets mine, and then they're gone—swallowed by the forest into which they've escaped.

"Capybaras, Jeremy," Tomas says. "I got you your capybaras."

The next day, I fall into a hole.

It's not in the dangerous jungle, but in a little street heading back to Cuzco. I step then fall through the air until one leg and my backpack catch me. I perch there, one foot dangling, the other perpendicular to the street. It's only after Tiffany and one of the staff pull me out that we notice a jagged rebar sticking out from the hole like a spear. If I'd fallen just slightly differently... I still imagine it, the broken rebar going through my crotch. I bleed out in an Amazon town.

Perhaps in another dimension that's exactly what happened. I died in Peru and Tiffany married Tomas. Could I blame her?

But here, in this one, I'm left with little more than a sprained ankle.

That afternoon Tiffany and I fly back to Lima. The next day, our last in Peru, we hit the Lima Zoo. But this time, instead of *falso* our soles are accepted. I request a wheelchair because I can do little more than hobble. Between the seals and the crocs, I'm greeted by a poor Peruvian man forced into a Teletubbies costume, the red one, Po. And even though he is the one who looks like a space pedophile, he has the gall to feel sorry for the glum gringo in the wheelchair.

Tiff can't stop laughing as she snaps the picture.

A month later, in my parent's bathroom in Minnesota, I've torn up a cardboard toilet paper roll and am poking through my shit in the toilet bowl, looking for blood.

In a back room of my brain, I know this is a lunatic and disgusting activity, with potential connotations for the state of my sanity. But in the forefront of my brain, I know it's absolutely necessary. If I do not dig in my poop, I won't find the blood. And if I don't find the blood, I'll be terminally ill without knowing I'm terminally ill. The only thing that can save me from this *unknowing* is finding the disease in my poop.

Located on the ground floor of our centurial farmhouse, the bathroom is no bigger than an airport toilet stall. It was added in the 1950s when the farm moved into the future with indoor plumbing. The flower and bird wallpaper, the aroma of the particular soap, and the quality of the light are as familiar to me as my mother's face and voice.

Tiffany is knocking on the door. She knows I've been in here too long. She suspects what I'm up to. But I need to discover proof that even though we left Peru, Peru hasn't left me. It has given me the gift of typhoid or malaria or yellow fever or Oroya fever or the plague or some as-yet-undiscovered killer disease. And even if it's not Peru, I *definitely* have colon cancer.

Tiff is knocking with more urgency now. My mother has come to the door, too, and they are both calling my name. With a tremendous burst of effort, I flush the toilet and open the door. My face is ashen, my body trembling.

"I need to see a doctor," I say.

To be honest, I hadn't thought much about life post-Peru. I was too certain I was going to die there to give much credence to the future. I expended all my energy on getting through each day and had little left for a hazy, indistinct homecoming.

But Tiff, ever the organizer, had. We were moving back to Minnesota to be near family and friends again. Tiffany had already secured a new position with Teach For America and tasked her brother, Chris, with scoring us an apartment and a very used car. When we land at the Minneapolis–St. Paul Airport—miraculously, to my mind, not dead—he picks us up in our "new" car. Driving down the freeway, looking out over the all-too-familiar skyline of Minneapolis, I remember thinking, *Well, what the fuck now?*

It turns out that I don't have much agency over that. As we try desperately to settle into our new lives, I start looking through my shit for blood. And I can't stop. All the relief and relative calmness that I'd felt deep in the Amazon fled away like a spirit scared by the urban clamor.

I know with that special kind of knowledge given to the clairvoyant that I'd picked up something in the forest, a hitchhiker in my body that is slowly killing me. One day I'd shit and there'd be nothing but blood, blood emitting from the stool like steam.

For months this was our routine: I'd come out of the bathroom, shaking, heart pounding, sweat pouring, and I'd tell Tiffany that I was dying. And I didn't understand why she didn't believe me. It'd take me hours to come down. I stopped eating anything vaguely red in color—no more tomatoes or strawberries or raspberries or peppers. I'd force Tiffany to take me to doctors. I'd bring them samples of my shit. They'd run tests and tell me, "You're all clear. You're fine. No parasites. Nothing wrong."

But I didn't believe them. Whatever it was, it was just waiting for the right moment to reveal itself and say those three magic words: "You're fucked, dude."

It may seem that it's easy for me to admit all of this now because I'm writing about it somewhat matter-of-factly. Nothing could be further from the truth. When you have mental illness, you learn very quickly and adeptly how to hide things from family, friends, coworkers, and even therapists. Madness can make you do mad things, and the last thing you want is for others to know what mad things you have done. Madness made me, for months, dig through my shit. And even when you can begin to accept that it is the illness making you *do* those things (it was Steve!) the stigma of shame, fear, and revulsion at your own actions doesn't vanish. It lingers. Probably forever.

Thinking of that time now, more than ten years later, my immediate knee-jerk reaction is *Christ, Jeremy, you're a pathetic and disgusting human being.*

It's only by sitting with it a little longer that I can find a bit of forgiveness for myself.

"Okay, Jeremy, why don't you tell me what's going on?" the psychologist asks a few weeks after we arrive in Minnesota from Peru.

It's the first time I've seen a therapist in years. And doing so, admittedly, feels like a failure, an admittance of my weakness, a bending toward my family and my past, encased by mental illness.

In truth, I'd become complacent, almost arrogant, thinking (hoping, really) that maybe I'd never again need to deal head-on with mental illness. Maybe college and growing up and getting out into the world had done it for me. Maybe I'd solved that whole thing, and it would, in later years, become just memories of a misshapen youth. But sitting here, looking at this stranger before me, I know that dream has been decisively proven an illusion.

Still, if there is one thing I'm good at, really freaking good at, it's therapy. From the chair, I describe the last year in more candid detail than I could've to my parents or even Tiffany, from doctors in New York City to puppies in Peru to digging through my shit in Minneapolis.

In the end, the therapist looks at me. "Well, it's clear you have obsessive-compulsive disorder."

"Okay." Deep breath. "I've heard of that. What is it?"

Mental illness is much more common than we think. According to the National Alliance on Mental Illness (NAMI), around one in five adults experiences mental illness in a given year in the United States. So if you have five friends or five family members, chances are that one of them, at the very least, has struggled with mental illness. Why isn't this more evident? Because those of us who live intimately with mental illness become so goddamn good at acting, at pretending, at smiling through the pain or laughing through the fear. And the longer you live with mental illness, the better you become at throwing a veil over it. Most of my friends, even close ones, know I've struggled with mental illness because I'm casually open about it now, but only a handful have ever really witnessed its manifestations.

But get this: Nearly half of the homeless people in the United States suffer from a severe mental illness, while nearly a quarter of prisoners have had a recent mental illness. Worse still, 70 percent of juvenile offenders suffer from it. Is it any wonder that some have called this a mental health crisis?

After my new diagnosis—which piles on my previous ones of severe depression, anxiety, sleep disorder, and post-traumatic stress disorder—comes months of immersion therapy. I have to force myself to watch medical shows like *Grey's Anatomy* and *House* and follow my spiking anxiety. I have to ascribe numbers to my feelings: Gregory House running a scan for multiple sclerosis, that's a four; a patient dying from a record tumor on *Grey's*, yeah, that's a niner. I have to force myself to look at my poop until I grow bored with looking at my poop, something that takes longer than you'd expect. I have to read memoirs from cancer survivors. I am supposed to go for walks in hospitals to see people who are, you know, actually dying. But I lack the courage to reach this final step.

I go back on the psych med Escitalopram, the first time since the millennium. It helps with my OCD and depression (which had reared its head since landing in Minnesota) but makes me about as interested in sex as I am in Advanced Calculus. I also want to sleep *all the time*.

And I have to meet Steve formally. I have to say, "Hello, Steve."

"Hello, Jeremy."

"I see you now. I know you're not *me*. I know you're something else. An imp. An imposter. A disorder. I know your weapons and your tricks."

"Cool man. Cool, cool. But your stomach feels a little upset, doesn't it? Have I told you how stomach cancer is the worst of the cancers?"

"Oh. Okay. Oh…uh…Tiffany?…Tiffany! Maybe I should call the doctor?!"

I still have a long way to go.

Even as I am trying to crawl out of the OCD abyss, I have to find a job and health insurance. In America, just because you're daily digging through your shit doesn't mean you can't hold down a full-time job.

First things first. I need health insurance—badly. I couldn't find any paid private plans to cover me because I have preexisting conditions (no shit, Sherlock) called depression, anxiety, and OCD.

To solve my insurance problem pre-Obama Care, Tiffany and I have to get creative. We get married in city hall with just our parents present. We call it our "fake wedding" because we are planning our real wedding for the following summer. But sometimes in America you have to marry someone to get health insurance.

As to my other requirement, a job, I start working at a bakery, making bread and muffins and cinnamon rolls. I like the work. It has a meditative quality. But waking at 3:30 AM is unsustainable for someone on Escitalopram who also needs ten hours of sleep a night to stay sane (around 2 percent of people require ten hours per night—why? blame our genes). So one still-dark morning in December, I wake up in a full-blown panic attack. Tiffany has to call my employer and tell them I'm quitting during the holiday rush. I try a bookstore next. It goes okay until I start noticing the fumes. The bookstore is next to a tobacco shop, which has a smoking lounge. As I sort books, I think about nicotine. I think about cancer. In places, it *smells* like cancer. I have to lock myself in the bookstore bathroom to try to talk my OCD down on a daily basis. I remember that bathroom keenly. I call my boss and quit one sunny day in spring.

As spring turns to summer, I finally begin to stabilize. The combination of intense therapy and medication sedates Steve just enough that I can sometimes step outside myself and catch him at his nasty tricks before they go too far.

I start working part-time from home, allowing me more time to focus on taking care of myself. I can't stop the obsessive thinking, but I can, at least, see it for what it is for the first time in my life. It's not me, but Steve. Not rational, but irrational.

Lying in bed before sleep, I often think of the Amazon rainforest. The countless butterflies aggregated on the river's beach, the leafcutter ants marching undeterred across our path, the birds I'd never heard of flitting in the gloomy canopy, the shadows of the trees on the river, the glint of sunlight on the oxbow lake.

I begin to search out news about the region and stumble on a website called Mongabay. At the time, it is run entirely by its founder, Rhett Butler (yes, his real name, and don't ask him whether or not he gives a damn). I read the site daily—obsessively. When a couple of days go by without Rhett updating, I find myself disappointed.

Just before Christmas, news hits that the baiji, a 20-million-year-old denizen of the Yangtze River, has gone extinct. I've never seen a baiji, I've never been to China, but the news strikes me like a blow. I have to do something. So I write an article and email it to Mongabay. Rhett responds and says he will publish it. It's my first environmental article.

Summer comes, and on a clear day in July, Tiffany and I are married in our real wedding. For many of our Catholic relatives, it's a weird one. We get married under the sun and blue sky by Tiffany's brother and his husband in a ceremony I wrote, combining elements from various traditions as well as stuff I made up. My "best man" is a woman and the food is Greek-Turkish because why not? Afterward, we all dance ecstatically in a community barn, celebrating in the midst of a bonfire and sheep and baklava and so many proud homosexuals.

Two weeks later, Tiffany and I are driving across the country to start a new life. Again. Our third attempt in two years. I'd been accepted at St. John's University for its Great Books Masters Program in Santa Fe, New Mexico.

Even with six months of improvement, I'm pretty sure we'll crash and die before we get there.

PART TWO

Meeting
Nature

Chapter Three

The Good Traveler

WINTER 2002

Asound enters my slumbering brain. It's someone knocking. "Go away," I want to say. But the knocking continues. I wake up in a strange bed, in a strange room. For a moment, I panic. Where am I? Minnesota? Ireland?

Oh. I remember. I'm in Kenya.

Africa.

Approaching my fourth Christmas, my parents spent a lot of time in the basement. After dinner, my father would head downstairs, and the echoes of tools floated up from below. On the weekends, he'd disappear for hours at a time and return for a glass of milk and an exchanged look with my mother.

On Christmas morning 1983, the outcome of their toiling was finally revealed. They had built me, their youngest of three, a nature diorama on a four-by-four plywood square, with one end cut out, creating an L-shape.

Even though long gone, I can still conjure it up before me. Starting at one end is a jungle habitat, verdant trees rising from a floor painted dark, shadowy green, the kind of color animals can disappear in. After about eight inches, the jungle transitions to a savanna, where the trees are sparser and the green of the grass sun-tinted. Splotches of yellow prove where the vegetation fights against drought. A lake, a disk of glass glued onto the board, lies at the end of the savanna. Reeds, tall and willowy, line one portion of the shore where a river flows down from the lake to the edge of the world. At sunset, the lake quickly falls under the shadow of an adjacent mountain chain. The mountains, a purple-blue, rise to an altitude where the snow, white paint, never melts. Ascending from where the diorama angles, the mountains separate the driest habitat, the desert, from the rest. Here sand dunes rise and fall as if children are playing beneath a blanket. A few cacti stand precariously, slightly tilted, as though even their ability to survive desiccation may not save them this season.

When I saw the mystery of the basement revealed, I honestly didn't know what to say. What do you say to such a display of love? And what do you say, when at this time in our relationship, my father was often distant, remote, touchy?

But, boy, was he smiling this morning.

"Get your animals," he said.

I ran to my room. Up the stairs, right at the top, another right down the hall. Here I kept the small plastic animals I had purchased with my allowance at the local Ben Franklin.

When I returned, I set them up, something I'd done countless times before. But now they had proper ecosystems. Tapirs in the jungle, elephants in the savanna, camels in the desert, crocodiles along the lake.

I can't remember a time when I was not obsessed with animals. I wanted to be a zookeeper years before I ever wanted to be anything else. I knew thousands of species already and where on the earth they were found and how threatened or abundant they were.

Aside from my family, animals were my first love. Not so much the farm animals that were common in our small town. I wasn't all that interested in cows and horses and cats. No, it was wild animals that pulled me. And the stranger, the more exotic, the better.

As I grew older and discovered new loves—dinosaurs, girls, books, theater —my first love of wildlife went into hibernation. As a teenager, I tested being an environmentalist and animal activist for a year or two. It was a weird thing to be during the early 1990s in small-town Minnesota, but I wore T-shirts about the Amazon rainforest (and how it needed to be saved), I wrote letters asking cosmetic companies to stop testing their products on animals, and I donated my allowance to conservation groups instead of buying small plastic animals for play.

My dad would become furious. "Why are you throwing your money away like that?" He'd lost his father at the age of fourteen and spent years, along with his mother and younger brother, doing everything they could to save the farm from bankruptcy.

Later in life, he apologized, more than once. My father never did or said anything just once. "You were right," he'd say. "It was the best way you could've spent your money."

After a year or so I dropped my activist phase. I became exhausted under the weight of the sins of the world, tired of trying to convince others to care, cynical in waiting for companies and politicians to do something. I had enough to deal with at home—my mom in-and-out of debilitating depressions, my dad busy fighting his demons, my brothers in high school (and acting weirder than usual), and my daily struggles to hide my depression and anxiety from everyone.

So I let my early love of animals and nature fall into a long dormancy, like a turtle digging beneath the lake bed, hollowing out a cocoon of mud, its body temperature plunging to forty degrees, soaking up oxygen from the water, and slumbering through the long winter to come.

But it's the animals that bring me *here* this morning, eighteen years after my parents built me a "jungle." I finally get out of bed and make it to the hotel room door. I groggily open it to reveal a big black man.

"Jeremy Hance?" he asks with an accent I'm not used to.

"Yes."

"I'm from the safari company. I'm here for your payment." He seems a bit bemused by my clearly just-out-of-bed appearance. It's probably, like, noon here.

I tell him to wait a minute, then walk back into the dark room and find my shoe. I take out an envelope from the lining and pull out $800 in cash, how the safari tour operator requested it. Well, not in a shoe, but in US dollars, crisp cash. The shoe part was because I figured that was the safest way to carry so much over thousands of miles. I hand him the money.

He counts it and says, "We're good, Mr. Hance." He tells me that I'll be picked up tomorrow at 6 AM for my nine-day safari.

Then he's gone.

I sit down on the bed, my brain still waking up. I'm in Kenya, I remind myself. Nairobi. A last-minute solo trip to Africa before my study-abroad time comes to a close. Because why not? Because I'm twenty-two and I'm a good traveler: I'm spontaneous, I'm adventurous, I'm smooth like a laxative.

I open the shades. Raw hot sunlight leaps in, so different from the sunless winter I'd left behind, the near-constant rain refracting the lights of Galway where I'd been studying abroad. I look five stories down onto central Nairobi. Cars are driving improbably around an intersection as if they are stuck in a Wonderland tea party and all moving "one place." A man, perhaps the cause of the traffic confusion, single-handedly pulls a horse cart behind him in downtown traffic.

I suddenly feel scared, intimidated. Almost like a child. Okay, I could stay all day in the comfort of this nice hotel in Nairobi. I could watch some TV, eat at the restaurant downstairs, and then start the real deal tomorrow. I could hide from this adventure I'd kick-started, which suddenly feels a bit like a wasp nest.

But it's 2002, four years before my OCD diagnosis and the enlightening Peru trip. And while I linger on this temptation, I eventually force myself out, like how you have to force yourself to go to the dentist. I have only one day in Nairobi. I'm not going to spend it in a stupid hotel. I get dressed and take the elevator down to the lobby.

The air outside is heavy with humidity. Skyscrapers rise above me, shimmering in some of the most intense sunlight I've ever seen. The city, sleek and modern, also looks as if it's run-down, a garden let to grow wild.[1]

The only thing I've seen so far is the highway from the airport to the hotel where multitudes of men walk up to vehicles, selling newspapers, candies, cigarettes, pretty much anything and everything. A mobile 7-Eleven.

Now, I walk aimlessly a few blocks and end up at a central city square, where I stand and watch all the people around me. Everyone else looks different from me, their skin a thousand different shades of brown while mine is the color of blanched almonds with a rosy hue.

For the first time in my life, I'm a racial minority. It's so strange, I think, how so much of human history over the last thousand years has been domination, slavery, conflict, and mass death based on concentrations of melanin.

From the throng, a man approaches me. He's in his thirties and well dressed. His face is friendly and open. He waves as if we're already old friends.

"Hello, I'm Charles," he says.

"Jeremy," I say.

"I saw you—I work at the hotel as a—" I miss the word here as I'm having trouble following this newly encountered accent.

"Oh. Okay." I don't know if he's telling the truth.

"American?"

"Yes."

"I love America. So sad about 9/11."

The terrorist attacks were four months prior. "Yes, terrible."

"First time?"

"Hmmm," I say straining to understand and conflicted about whether to disengage or not.

"First time in Nairobi?"

"Oh, yes, yes. I was studying abroad in Ireland, and then well…it's a long story, but I decided to do *this*." I wave my hand, as if that explains it. "I'm going on a safari, you see. I love wildlife." I have no idea why I'm telling him all this, other than it's the truth.

"Oh, you'll see so many wonderful things. Elephants, lions, rhinos. Big five. Kenya has all the big five. When do you go?"

"Tomorrow."

"Good. You'll have a great time. Would you like me to show you around Nairobi now, brother?"

"Show me around?"

"A tour. I'll give you a very nice tour of the city, brother. You'd like that, right? Nairobi means 'cool water.' Comes from the Maasai language. You know the Maasai? They are one of many tribes of Kenya. I'll give you a wonderful tour. Teach you all about the Maasai and our history."

A pause.

Then I say, "Okay, why not."

You see, I wasn't always a bad traveler. For a brief period of my life, circa ages eighteen to twenty-five, I was pretty good, and by good, I mean I got around without panic attacks or unfortunate fecal incidents or kitty terrors. (I even accepted an impromptu invite for a guided tour from a total stranger. Take from that what you will.) One might even go so far as to describe me with the adjective of "adventurous." *Might.*

Whatever I was. Whatever I am even today, I've always had a wanderlust I couldn't shake, a curiosity about the grass on the other side. I blame this on my mother and Walt Disney.

My mother raised me on her stories of backpacking around Europe. Not a rarity today, but she and a female friend did it in 1968, at age nineteen. She hung out in remote villages that had never seen Americans (not even during the war), befriended a gigolo to stave off the ravenous attention of Greek men, and nearly died from a severe allergic reaction to red wine.

She explored a Europe now lost forever, one not marked by mass tourism or globalization, where Italian men could speak English only through the lyrics of *The Beatles*, and any traveler's route abruptly ended at the Iron Curtain. It was a life-defining experience for her, as her stories and slides would be for me later. I never understood the bad reputation of vacation slides because I loved it whenever my mom pulled hers out of the closet. As each image winked, her stories poured forth like an offering.

The other culprit: Walt Disney World. When I was eight, my parents saved up enough coupons cut out of cereal boxes to get free airfare for their three kids to Orlando. I sat open-mouthed as a fake boat took me through the Jungle Cruise and a submarine into the depths of the sea. Even then, I hated rides with any intent to physically thrill or scare, but these two allowed me a safe adventure through biodiverse, animatronic bliss.

Still, they were nothing compared to Epcot World Showcase, a kind of "World's Fair" celebrating various cultures. I got a massive prepubescent crush on a belly dancer in Morocco, saw Norway's history through the Maelstrom ride, and marveled at the faked architecture of China. It was all illusion, of course, but what's that to an eight-year-old? By the time we left, I wanted nothing more than to see the world, which still felt young, exotic, and full of possibilities.

It's what I feel, even now, when I wake up in a foreign city for the first time or hike down a trail in the Amazon or take a boat in the Okavango Delta. Anything is possible.

So I spend my only day in Nairobi with stranger-turned-friend Charles, going from one wild adventure to another. I get offered my first prostitute (I very much decline); watch dozens of dancers go through the entire, mind-blowing repertoire of Kenya's spectacularly diverse forty-plus tribes; and eat so much meat at the restaurant Carnivore I consider early vegetarianism.

"Good morning, Mr. Hance." The voice pronounces my name funnily. "This is your wake-up call."

It's 5 AM the next morning in Nairobi. And I'm leaving for the Great Rift Valley to see … well, *everything*.

The drive that day, all five hours of it, is largely obliterated by time (seventeen years) and my crappy memory only returns, like the opening of some movie *in media res*, at the moment when the van finally pulls into our destination, Lake Baringo in the Great Rift Valley.

I get out and the driver tells me to wait while he fetches my guide, Walter. As I do, I hear something like a giant clacking its teeth. Crack, crack, crack. I make my way toward the sound, to a small grove of acacia trees standing near the edge of the lake. Escaping the heat and sun, both searing and suffocating, I enter the grove. I turn my head up and see two massive bird bottoms perched twenty feet off the ground.

When you say the word *marabou stork*, an image may be conjured of a long-legged, elegant bird. But the marabou stork is *much* better than that. It's a giant, ungainly nightmare. Its beak is a monstrous needle-point plier. Its face is mottled and ugly, a giant vulture's red, raw head, on the body of a stork. Unkempt strands of old-man hair curl about its head, and its eyes are small, round, beady. It looks like it's walking around with several gaping head wounds.

I'm in love.

One of them above me ruffles its wings, and the sound and scale are astounding. The wingspan is wider than any man's height. Indeed, the marabou stork nearly rivals the wandering albatross for the world's longest wingspan.

The name *marabou* may come from the Arabic word *murabit*, meaning a religious teacher or holy man. Perhaps the silent (but for the clacking), stoic bird reminded Muslim traders of Islamic hermits. But locals also call it the undertaker bird for its somber dress, grim visage, and hunched manner, as though always searching the ground for the dead. In truth, it's more coroner than undertaker, for it likes to pick apart the newly deceased with immaculate precision. Perhaps it's trying to find the secret of life, or maybe it's just hungry.

I wonder as I stand below this clacking beast how I could have lived twenty-two years without hearing of this magnificent bird, this ungainly avian death eater.

We err when we say dinosaurs went extinct. Most of them did but not all. Some never left. Today, their direct ancestors are everywhere. Sixty-five million years ago, a few small, feathered, two-legged maniraptoran theropods survived the unimaginable asteroid blast. They probably had small dragon-shaped heads with wings, tails, and feathers like crows. Some may have even been capable of flight. Perhaps they lived in the hollows of old dead trees or took up residence in caves—as the cave swallows of the Americas or the cave swiftlets of Indonesia—allowing them to hold out during the long aftermath of the world-ending blast.

When you eat a chicken, you're eating a dinosaur with 60 million years of extra evolution lumped on top. But, hey, it's still a dinosaur.

After my introduction to this African nightmare, the driver returns with Walter, my guide. He's fortyish, sweaty, with a bit of a beer belly and an LA

Lakers hat that I never see leave his head. His smile is large, like himself, and genuine. He seems immediately bemused by me, a young solo white dude who can't stop pointing out to him a pair of marabou storks.

Once the pointing is clearly at an end, I follow him to the campsite, where I meet our cook, Albert, wry and wily, in his sixties, always with a ready smile. Albert uncovers an impressive meal prepared entirely over the fire.

I bought one of the cheapest safaris possible: an $800, nine-day camping safari. I'd be sleeping in tents, eating over fires, and getting a cold shower when available, sometimes with a praying mantis for a bath mate.

Just as Albert is laying out lunch, in come two other tourists: Anna and Rens, a pair of freelance illustrators from Holland. I'm very lucky. Just three of us with one guide, one cook, and one safari van.

Rens and Anna had started their trip a week before me, so I was essentially crashing their party, but both are warm and welcoming. Anna takes me under her wing as if I were her little brother and spends a generous amount of time listening to my lady drama, the fling I left behind and the girl I love back home who's now dating someone else (that would be Tiffany—later I'd win her back).

The only reason I'm here in Kenya at all is because of a car accident in Ireland.

A few months prior, a couple of study-abroad friends and I were spending the weekend in the tiny village of Glencolmcille, day-trekking while visiting ruined towers and standing stones. As night descended, we decided to hit a local pub and have a pint (or two), as a trio of twenty-somethings nearly always will in Ireland.

Leaving Dooey Hostel, the street was dark and, like so many rural paths in Ireland, tightly bound by stonewalls. We weren't in a hurry, so we strolled. No curfew, no parents, no rules. Then out of the darkness careened a car. The first and only thing I realized before time stopped was that the car didn't have its lights on despite it being full night. I scrambled up the rock wall to try to escape its charge. I can still conjure the image of it, like some wild beast from antediluvian times. It swiped one of my friends. I heard her cry out, and I felt the juggernaut of steel and motion cuff my leg as it scraped against the stone, the sound of cutting steel, a spark of lightning. The car only stopped when it struck my second friend, throwing him forward half a dozen feet.

After the accident, confusion reigned. Screaming. Moaning. Crying. A night so innocuous, shattered so quickly. Two young women emerged from the car. There were renting apologies and recriminations. To this day, I don't know if the women were drunk or high or both, but it took a special kind of stupid to drive down a dark Irish lane without the car lights on. The friend who was thrown was miraculously uninjured, but my other friend believed her leg was broken. I escaped with little more than a scrape.

Given our remoteness, we waited an hour for the ambulance to show, and then another hour to travel to the closest hospital in Donegal. Fortunately, my friend's leg wasn't broken but badly sprained. We'd all been miraculously lucky.

Weeks later, an insurance rep showed up in Galway. He offered me USD $1,200 as compensation, and my friends more (but not much), given their injuries were greater. He said we could take the driver to court, but it would drag on for years.

He was very convincing, and all three of us agreed to take the money. We were young, none of us seriously injured (at least not physically), our parents (who might have advised differently) were far away, and our ill-will toward the two women was not long lasting.

Psychologically, however, something like that doesn't just disappear. I can trace the beginnings of my hatred of cars and driving to that day (it's only been increased given several accidents since, including one in which the car blew up).

At twenty-two, I had $1,200 burning a hole in my pocket. I could have used it for something sensible like, oh, I don't know, paying college tuition. But I thought about it like this: What happened was so terrifying (but miraculously un-ruinous), why not use the money for something really cool? I was already in Europe, I'd already seen a lot of it, but from here I could go freaking *anywhere*.

I began researching. I considered trips to Kenya, Tanzania, Nepal, or India. A week or so after Christmas, I finally found just what I was looking for. The flights were around $400, and the budget camping safari was $800—I booked it just a week before it was to start. I knew when I did, I risked kick-starting my childhood obsession with animals and my adolescent environmentalism, something, at the time, I wasn't sure I wanted.

I was happy at college studying English literature and history, embracing my introversion, and largely ignoring the contemporary world by escaping in novels written by long-dead people. I knew that caring more broadly—about forests far away, people I'd never met, species no one else knew—risked new pains and sorrows. I remembered well the sting of caring as a teenager and watching nothing change, in which giving a shit about the destruction of the Amazon and the extinction of species had left me feeling only more isolated.

But here was a chance to see the Serengeti. So, screw it.

Sometimes life requires risk.

I settle into my sleeping bag framed by the canvas folds of a tent, reading a copy of *Harry Potter and the Prisoner of Azkaban* that I picked up at Gatwick Airport. I like it because it has the British cover. The hippogriff (which doesn't look cartoonish like in the American version) is soaring with Harry and Hermione over a full moon.

Suddenly a voice comes from outside the tent. "Yes?" I ask, not expecting anyone.

It's Walter with a staff member of a nearby lodge. A young man probably a couple of years older than me motions shyly for me to follow him. I put on my shoes and do.

Walter winks at me as I pass.

We cross down the shoreline, heading toward the lodge. It's a new moon tonight, the sky about as black and seemingly empty as it can be. As we walk up to the lodge's porch, I see a group of tourists standing together. Anna and Rens are already there. Just beyond them, at the edge of Lake Baringo, is a herd of hippos mowing the lawn.

"Don't go too close," the young man whispers, as if he needs to point *that* out.

I halt next to the other tourists and gape. The young man turns on a flashlight, or as they call it here a "torch," and aims the beam on the hippos. They are nonplussed. One of the hippos is a calf that stays close to its mother and crops the greens like her.

"You must stay here. You should never get between a hippo and open water," the young man whispers to me. "If you block their escape route, they will run you down."

(Days later at Lake Naivasha, I'll watch a big-tusked hippo charge a couple of fishermen who narrowly miss being capsized by the furious purple beast. The men paddle for their lives as the hippo, mouth agape, rears behind.)

A hippo is pretty much a replica of how nineteenth-century paleontologists imagined the first discovered dinosaurs: a weird cross between a plump, overweight reptile and a monster pig. And it's fucking huge. Regularly weighing over three thousand pounds, hippos are the fifth largest land mammal on Earth, only bested by Africa's savanna and forest elephants, Asian elephants, and white rhinos.

But the hippos here, out of the water and meticulously cropping the grass, appear strangely gracile (a word, I admit, that's probably never been used to describe this species), almost delicate, beautiful creatures. The darkness shines off their smooth purplish skin; their mouths move with a fastidiousness rarely attributed to hippos. At this moment, I can almost understand why the Greeks named them *hippopotamus*, which means "water horse." The first use of this moniker is by Herodotus who saw them while visiting Egypt in the fifth century BCE.[2]

Perhaps Herodotus and other Greeks first encountered hippos in a fashion similar to this nighttime adventure, while touring the flood plains of the Nile. Perhaps these ancient Greeks also noticed a certain dignity and beauty of these bulky animals, not unlike horses. Or perhaps the Egyptians already called them "water horses," and the Greeks stole the name from the people who knew the animals much more intimately. The Greeks were notorious for stealing things from other cultures: gods, stories, technologies, philosophies, whatever was at hand. It was one of the keys to their success.

Either way, Herodotus's description of hippos is notoriously strange, but then these are notoriously strange animals. And how you see a hippo is probably dependent on how the people around you talk about them.

By the time I get back into bed, I can't read Harry Potter anymore. I feel as though I've just witnessed something far more fantastical and wonderful than wizards in London and hippogriffs above Hogwarts—a dozen hippopotami chilling out and chewing some grass under the plunging dark of the moonless night.

It's day two and I'm pretty much already in love with this place.

We only call this continent Africa because that is what the ancient Romans called it. Why they did so is a mystery. One theory is that the name came from a now extinct tribe in northern Africa; another is that it stems from a lost Phoenician or Berber word. But no continent on Earth is arguably more misunderstood by outsiders than the African one. For one thing, Africa is not a monolith as it's so commonly portrayed. Anything said about Africa will inevitably be a gross and inaccurate generalization.

Currently, the continent, the second largest on Earth, is broken up into fifty-two countries, more than South and North America combined. Over a thousand languages are spoken from the southern shores of the Mediterranean to the Cape of Good Hope. Three thousand historic tribes, each with a distinct culture, history, and identity, inhabit the world's second-largest continent.

Outsiders' common perception of Africa is that of a continent mired in poverty, corruption, and conflict, but that is gravely misleading. Desperate poverty can be found here; corruption lurks in many countries; some areas are conflict prone. But I've also been in a grocery store in Botswana that resembled an uber fancy Whole Foods in America; I've visited world-class museums and eaten what I'd describe as five-star meals. This is not to argue that this is somehow the common experience in Africa (it's not—nothing is), or that it is "good" that Africa should fall into Western ways of materialism and consumption but merely to point out the sheer diversity of living on the continent where humanity was born.

If there's any common characteristic I've witnessed in my personal experience of visiting four countries in Sub-Saharan Africa, it is a general joyfulness at being alive, even in situations some Westerners would consider impoverished.

Community, the art of living life together, seems to blossom here more than anywhere else I've been.

The Great Rift Valley is bonkers. Running from the Afar Triangle (abutting Ethiopia, Eritrea, and Djibouti) to Mozambique, it is the line where Africa is tearing itself apart. Here, the geologic plates that make up the continent are actively splintering, although only a few millimeters a year.

Still, sometimes the volcanic and tectonic forces here can be dramatic. In 2018, a massive sixty-five-foot-wide crack opened up in Kenya, dividing a highway and collapsing a house. Scientists believe that rains had exposed the crack, or large gully, filled in by nothing but volcanic ash.

In millions of years, maybe tens of millions, Africa will be sundered into two distinct continents, essentially slicing East Africa in half, where the Nubian Plate and the Somalian Plate reside, with seas filling between. Can you imagine the day the ocean rushes in, dividing the land forever? Give it a few more million years after that, and who knows how the animals and plants of the new continent will differ from those on the old. Tiny hippos? Twelve-foot-tall marabou storks? Hyenas that look like Paul Giamatti?

Most of my safari follows the Great Rift Valley, a truly wild landscape of dormant volcanoes, potential earthquakes, boiling geysers, and some of the most splendid scenery on our fair little planet.

At the edge of Lake Bogoria, we watch a fishing eagle defend its flamingo kill against three marabou storks. The bold eagle keeps them at bay with snapping and flapping, turning over the broken body, a pile of bones and feathers, wielding its beak at one of the storks while twisting again to push away another. The marabous pace ankle-deep in the muck, little phased, creating circles around the eagle. Finally, the raptor tires of this dance over death; it grasps its kill in its talons and takes off. The only thing left to the marabous is a single flamingo leg and a few pink feathers floating in the air. Quickly, the coroners go to work dissecting.

Behind the drama, a few hundred flamingos alternate between standing and marching in unison in that way only flamingos can. At times one or two will dip their heads to feed on the cyanobacteria that is one of the only life-forms capable of surviving this alkaline soda lake.

The geysers and hot springs scattered around the lake are so scorching that if a flamingo flies into one, it's boiled alive, evidenced by the bones we discover of one such unfortunate avian. Indeed, the whole shoreline of Bogoria is a flamingo mausoleum: feathers, bones, skulls picked or boiled clean.

Lake Nakuru, our next destination, ends up being my favorite. It's the African savanna as any faraway child might imagine it. A pride of lions sleep next to the haunch of a young zebra, killed the night before. Herds of African buffalo a thousand strong move over the hills. Impala males stand over their harem of females in the bright morning light, and hornbills excavate a termite nest in the dark. White rhinos, the biggest land mammal in the world after elephants, chase a couple of tourist buses. A family of vervet monkeys invades our campsite, infuriating Albert, who takes after them with swinging pans. A lone waterbuck stands aloof, its two scimitar horns carving against the pink of faraway flamingoes and the blue of the lake.

Kenya is truly a land of wonders.

After lunch one day, I sit in the heat of the afternoon, when most of the animals have sensibly taken refuge, and pull *Harry Potter* out of my backpack. I'm near the end, where it's difficult not to be transfixed, when suddenly I feel the presence of someone next to me. Someone slightly alien and unknown.

I look up and meet the eyes of a massive male baboon.

The two of us, primates both, sharing more than 90 percent of our DNA, stare into each other's eyes for a moment. And then the baboon shoots its hand into my bag and yanks out a Kodak film cartridge. It's 2002 and I don't have a digital camera, few do, so I'm lugging around dozens of film cartridges. Treasure in hand, the baboon makes his getaway into the nearby vegetation. But he's soon followed by another larger primate. Rens, who saw it all with his keen eyes, decides to play the hero. As he runs after the sixty-plus-pound monkey, Rens is yelling, jumping up and down, motioning wildly. Apparently, his apish antics work because a few yards off, he finds my film canister lying in the grass where the baboon had thrown it.

The cardboard wrapping is bent, having been bit by the baboon. Once he realized he can't eat Kodak, he probably thought better of it all.

"Got it," Rens says as he returns to me.

That night, as the fire dies down and the Tusker beers are passed around, Albert sits and regales us with stories of lions killing people. He tells us how there's a Tsavo lion at Lake Nakuru. "Man-eating," he says, "runs in its blood."

The original Tsavo lions were a pair of maneless males that worked in concert to kill and devour dozens of people in Kenya (at the time, the claim was 135 victims).[3]

"It's only a matter of time," Albert says.

This is all fun and shivers until I have to go to bed in my tent, alone, nothing between myself and the bush except easily torn canvas. Nakuru is where I first see lions, nimble females climbing trees and big-maned males sleeping in sun-splattered grass.

As I fall asleep, I hear the guttural roars of one, the sound setting the reptilian section of my brain on speed. I think of our ancestors, tens of thousands of years ago, falling asleep to lions' roars every night, not knowing if tonight was the night when Africa's greatest predator would bring down upon them doom and despair, a violence-infused death.

There was one destination I was not looking forward to when I read the safari itinerary in an internet café: Hell's Gate National Park. The description probably read something like this: "Enjoy a day out biking in Hell's Gate National Park, one of only two parks in the country where you can bike among wildlife. The park is a fascinating slice of the Great Rift Valley, including wild cliffs and deep gorges. Scenery so memorable, it inspired *The Lion King*!"

The problem: I don't bike.

Okay, I know what you're going to say. Something like, "Jeremy, you grew up on a forty-acre farm [admittedly, I'm surprised you remember the acreage!] in rural America during the 1980s and you don't ride a bike?"

Let me be clear, it's not like I *never* learned to ride a bike. Well…actually, yes, that's it. I never learned to ride a bike. My older brothers learned readily enough, and my parents repeatedly tried to teach me, but it just never took. I remember riding around our circle driveway, starting slow, going faster, and falling over. Giving up.

As a kid, when my friends biked into the fields and forests, I'd run alongside. Eventually, my small frame fell behind as they sped ahead and reached our destination long before I did. Huffing and puffing, I made up the whole rear guard. Their bikes, hateful things, leaned against the trees as I stumbled in, holding my side, my breath like a bellow's.

"Hey," I panted. "What y'all up to?"

Bikes always remind me of inadequacy. It's the same sense of inadequacy that rises to the surface whenever I sleep twelve hours or can't work more than a couple hours in one day; whenever I feel so despondent for no reason that I can do nothing but go to bed, or when the mere mention of cancer in a casual conversation causes me to run to the bathroom to escape. Perhaps it's a human condition to always be falling below one's expectations, to judge oneself by what others have achieved, to feel somehow that the love one receives isn't quite deserved—or maybe I'll just blame it all on friggin' bikes. After all, it's not like Jesus ever had to deal with this two-wheeled silliness.

On the second day of the safari, now that I've gotten to know Walter a little and trust him as a convivial sort of man, I approach him after dinner. "Hey, Walter, about the cycling trip in Hell's Gate National Park…"

"Oh, it's beautiful," he says.

"Yes, I'm sure. It's just…well, I don't really feel comfortable biking."

He peers at me closer.

"I mean, I can bike. I totally can." I lie. "I biked all the time as a kid. All my friends were impressed." Why did I say that? "It's just I haven't biked in a few years, and I was just wondering if there's something else I could do?"

"Something else?"

"Yes."

"You don't want to bike?" He employs his hands as if holding imaginary handlebars.

"Yes."

He shrugs, smiles as if he knows. "Sure," he says. "You want to walk instead? I could probably find you a local guide to walk with you there, but it would cost a little extra."

"Oh, yeah, that sounds great!" I say with more relief and enthusiasm than I wanted to show. "I don't mind paying extra."

Walter smiles a private kind of smile, something he does frequently when he's bemused by us strange Americans and Europeans. So bizarre we are, like fragile and neurotic birds he must keep safe and happy. "Leave it to me," he says. "I'll figure it out."

Of course, when Anna and Rens discover this, they hound me. The Dutch are basically born on bikes. Their mothers birth them onto little two-wheeled infant bikes with no training wheels, and the nurses of Holland send these hour-old newborns down the halls at incredible speeds. The ones that crash into one another or topple over are thrown into the canals as sacrifices to the Dutch gods, the names of which are unspeakable and unwritable. This would have been my fate had I been born in Echt, Nijkerk, Hoogeveen, or any other ludicrously titled Dutch settlement.

"You sure you don't want to come with us?" Anna asks me in her impeccable English. "You never forget how to ride a bike."

I don't tell her that you *do* forget how to ride a bike if you never got it in the first place.

"Naw, I'm okay."

"You can bike with us the whole way. We don't mind going slow."

"Thanks. But I'm happy to walk. I feel like I'll see more walking."

She eyes me oddly, then shrugs.

The night before the hike at Hell's Gate, Albert mentions casually over the firelight that there are lions in the park.

"Lions?" I say. "In Hell's Gate?"

"Sure." Walter nods. "A few."

"And they let tourists walk and bike there?"

Walter shrugs in a way that clearly means "Yup."

"Why?" I ask.

"There aren't that many, and they tend to shy away from people. But that's why you can't just go walk in there on your own. You have to have a guide. Don't worry; he'll bring a stick."

"A stick!" I practically shout.

"Oh, Jeremy," Anna says. "You're such a worrier."

The next morning my guide shows up with a stick, indeed. But instead of the two-hundred-pound ex-Army officer I expected for such a perilous journey, my guide is a sixteen-year-old boy named Simon. He's lanky with a charismatic smile. He leans on his stick, really a staff, as if he was born with it.

"Simon will take good care of you," Walter says.

We begin trudging together down the dusty track, our eyes alert for wildlife. We see impalas and zebras and giraffe, the last running across the horizon. We've all seen a giraffe in zoos, but to see a giraffe and not see them run is like drinking non-alcoholic beer. It's a little bit pointless.

Simon asks what America is really like. I try to answer honestly. I ask him about himself. He's reticent for a bit but soon opens up. He has dreams. He wants to be a tour guide like Walter one day, maybe have his own company and spend all his time in the bush. He wants to go to school and study biology. He wants to help his country conserve its natural splendor. He wants so much.

And I wonder now, as I wondered then, if any of this happened for talented and bright Simon, who grew up in a poor country beset by political upheavals and a booming population.

We find the skull of an African buffalo lying in the grass. It's white with black horns, massive, like how you'd imagine the skull of the minotaur lying in the labyrinth a few thousand years after Theseus's sword rang true.

"Here," Simon lifts it off the ground and holds it in front of his face. "Take a picture."

I do.

"Now give me your camera and I'll take a picture."

I raise the horned skull over my face and Simon snaps it.

"What happens if we are attacked by a lion?" I ask Simon.

"We climb a tree," he says. My gaze falls over the landscape. There aren't many trees. And none of them close enough for a quick and desperate climb.

"Uh...Simon?

"Yeah?"

"What happens if there aren't any trees?"

"Then we must accept it is our time to die."

I look at his face, assuming he's kidding. But it's clear from his expression he's not. He's fucking serious.

Simon is so much better at being a human than I am.

It would take about two years before my mom would make something of a recovery from her breakdown. The moment is enshrined in family mythology with my mother getting out of bed one day, still in her nightie, and dancing to Bobby McFerrin's "Don't Worry, Be Happy."

She was saved from suicide by two things: Lithium and six miles a day.

Doctors tried every medication on my mother, but nothing worked until she took Lithium. It was only that chemical element, the lightest metal on Earth, atomic number three, that allowed my mother to dance again.

Around the same time, another particularly prescient therapist told my mother that if she wanted to survive, she needed to do just one thing: walk six miles outside every day. Everything else, her job (from which she was on extended leave), parenting, partnering, could wait. But she *had* to walk six miles a day. She did. And to hear her tell it, walking on the outskirts of a small town through farmlands and around lakes for six miles a day did save her life.

Still, my mother was never the same. She never worked outside the home again. She still suffered periods of debilitating depression and terror. She never got off medication and ended up in psychiatric wards more than once. But in the intervening years, she had learned the need to take care of herself and the strategies to do so.

She learned the value of exercise and the value of nature. She learned resilience, an increasingly vital area in mental health research today. My mother became an example to all of us of how to survive mental illness, how to live with demons.

Meanwhile, only months after my mother's collapse, mental illness would begin popping up among the rest of the family like pissed-off groundhogs. My father eventually was diagnosed with severe depression and at times crippling anxiety. One of my brothers received a diagnosis of bipolar and schizoaffective disorder. He underwent electro-convulsive therapy. My other brother struggled with depression and anxiety. It was like a goblin had crept in from some subterranean catacomb and began savaging us all.

Years revealed that a good chunk of my mother's family had also suffered from some mental illness or addiction, while my father's side included those who liked to pretend mental illness isn't real or is visited on one for some sin against God, which pretty much means they suffered from it, too.

It seemed as though the whole story of my family, near and far, was being rewritten by a ghostwriter with a penchant for melodrama.

In the Maasai Mara National Reserve, the grasslands that form the Kenyan section of the famed Serengeti Plains, I shout a lot. "An elephant!" "Look, a lion!" "Hey, there's a bird! What is it, Walter?" My unflagging enthusiasm must be grating on Anna, Rens, and Walter, but they treat it with levity.

"You're so excited all the time, Jeremy," Anna says to me, grinning. "I wish I could summon the energy."

I want to shout, "Because we're in freaking Africa, and this place is so nuts! Giants are everywhere, megafauna never went extinct here, there is a full suite of carnivores and herbivores, everything is so big and beautiful, the world is—hey, look! A Nile crocodile pulling a giant fish out of the river. Holy shit!"

But I also think I keep it up for another reason. It's lonely traveling solo, and the months abroad are beginning to weigh on me. I know the fateful day is coming all too soon when I'll be heading back home to Minnesota after five months of studying abroad. So I shout when I see an elephant, I trumpet for a cheetah, I point and holler when I see a lion because it's the best thing ever and because, for a moment at least, it keeps my brain from mulling on what the future holds.

It's in the Mara where we complete the big five: innumerable elephants and one leopard added to the rhinos, lions, and African buffalos we've already seen. The "big five" is *big* in African tourism, but it's a stupid, silly thing. The term comes from big game hunters of yore (read: white dudes with money and guns). Elephants, lions, leopards, rhinos, and African buffalo are referred to as the "big five" because they are the most dangerous animals to hunt on foot. I'm surprised the hippo isn't included, but I guess that manly hunters just shot them dead from the security of shorelines. Today, the big five is primarily used to entice tourists and turn safaris into some kind of inane checklist that puts undue and unreasonable pressure on guides.

I startle awake in the middle of the night. Something is against the tent. Something large is lying on the canvas, and whatever it is, it is breathing. Earlier in the night as I put down *Harry Potter* and closed my eyes, I heard the occasional roar of a lion in the valley.

The sound of a lion isn't a normal thing. It's not a big *roar* as it's often portrayed. It's much more fucked up than that. It's a guttural call that rises, crescendos, and falls. It's almost like the keening of an avenging demon. It's a spine-tingling, sweat-producing, Paleolithic horror that not even Lovecraft could adequately describe. It sounds like the lion is saying, "Come here. Come here. Come here."

And we all know why it wants you to come.

The sound still echoes in my frame when I wake in the middle of the night and notice the mystery body pressing against my tent. "It's not a lion, not a lion, not a lion," I keep telling myself. "I'm sure it must be one of the dogs. If there was a lion in camp, the dogs would be going crazy. They'd have barked their heads off, and everyone would be up."

Our campsite in the Mara is guarded by a few yellow scruffy dogs. They are here to do as they have done for the Maasai people for eons: raise the alarm if a lion prowls too close and, if necessary, sacrifice themselves for the sake of their "pack," the Maasai. Located on a hill overlooking the rolling savanna of the Mara, our campsite, with its permanent tents and full kitchen, is managed by Maasai people on land that the British took from them.

I toss and turn, the rational part of my brain unable to fully convince the antediluvian brain that anticipates lions. I debate yelling, calling out, but know it would probably lead to ridicule. It's almost surely a dog. And if it *were* a lion and I yelled out, wouldn't that only alert it to my presence? Can a lion smell a man through a thick canvas tent? Of course. I try not to move too much, not to make sounds. I try to keep my breathing soft and soundless. I try to disappear.

At one point the animal rolls over, and I flinch back, dragging my sleeping bag to the far corner as quietly as I can.

Finally, while debating, I slip into a kind of half-tortured sleep, and then full slumber. When I wake again, the inside of the tent has grown humid with the rising sun.

The shape is gone. I step outside cautiously and there, stretching his forelegs, is the yellow Maasai dog. Its expression seems to say, "Don't worry, tourist dude, I got you."[4]

Later that morning, we stumble on a mama cheetah with three cubs. They share a flat rock, bathing in the rising sun. The mother is lying down while the cubs play over her lithe body. Walter has the driver stop at a respectful distance, as he always does, and we watch in a quiet hush. Time seems no longer to matter.

The mother rises, stretches, yawns, sits on her haunches, and allows the cubs to tumble around her. For a while, she appears to be watching the horizon languidly, not all that interested. Then her body stiffens; her ears go up. She smells something or perhaps spots it with her burnt-yellow eyes, adapted for seeing wide and far.

There seems to be some communication, the mama telling the cubs, "Stay here, I'll be back soon. I'll fill your bellies." The cubs stop playing and stand in a row, watching their mama as she slinks off the rock and into the tall grass. She moves with the precision of being built, over millions of years, to do just this. Slow, smooth, steady. A herd of impala is grazing just down the hill. We lose her for a minute, and then see her again, that same motion, so quiet, so smooth it's almost still. Then she stops at a crest of grass obstructing the view of her from the impalas.

She waits. We wait. Time drifts.

As if a starting gun has gone off, she springs forward. She's already picked out the impala that will die this morning. Her body tilts as she turns like the keel of a ship in a storm.

As their enemy explodes into terrible view, the impala panic, busting into flight in various directions, leaping eight feet over the ground. She runs among them. Her forelegs flash out. She bounds and then she's on her target, dragging it down to the ground. Her jaws cling to its neck. Silence. When she looks up again, a life has been snuffed.

Our driver has moved our vehicle a little to get a better view, but we still keep back, giving the murderous mother plenty of space.

But, a stationary vehicle in the Maasai Mara attracts others like vultures spotting one of their own on a kill. And suddenly another van appears, then another and another. They drive right up, parking just a few yards from the mama. Walter is cursing. We drive up to one of them and tell the guide to back up—give the cheetah some space. He pretends he doesn't hear. Rens starts writing down the license plate numbers of the vehicles. More tourist vans are arriving.

The cheetah, in the confusion, turns around-and-around her kill while looking for her cubs. She cries out plaintively, trying to find them. Cheetahs don't roar; they chirrup like birds.

Within minutes, the vans encircle the cheetah and her kill like a wreath. Dozens of cameras are going off as people talk in hushed voices.

The cheetah continues pacing around her kill. At one point she picks it up in her mouth and tries to move it, but she's surrounded. She stops and calls again for her cubs. She wants them to come and eat, but with all the vehicles, the cubs stay back, hidden in the grass. And then it happens: She gives up. She abandons the kill and slinks back to her cubs, even as the cameras continue flashing.

The tourists, most of whom had probably flown thousands of miles and spent thousands of dollars to see such endangered animals, had just further endangered this one. It's not hyperbole that the loss of that single meal may have meant the difference between life and death for one of her cubs.

It takes a mother cheetah a tremendous amount of energy to attempt a kill, and on average they succeed in bringing down their prey only about half the time. Worse still, given their slight size, cheetahs are always on the lookout for the bullies of the savanna: lions. Tremendous killers in their own right, lions also get a lot of their meals by thieving from smaller predators, like the cheetah and hyena.

There are tourism rules in Maasai Mara. Vans are to keep a distance of twenty-five meters from all animals, and they are never to pursue an animal but to let it go its own way. In addition, only five vehicles are supposed to aggregate in one spot. To his great credit, Walter adhered to these rules the entire trip. The guides and drivers all know these rules but, unlike Walter, rarely follow them because of the immense pressure from the tourists to find the big five and show them every animal in every imaginable situation. (A guide's tips may depend on it.) All of these vehicles, which numbered more than five, were closer than the twenty-five-meter limit.

But the Maasai Mara isn't a fucking zoo or *Planet Earth*. We, the tourists, are entitled to *nothing* when it comes to wildlife watching. Everything is an honor and privilege. Guides should take the time to explain the rules and why they are so important. And tourists should respect them.

Walter reports the incident to the park's rangers and hands over the license plate numbers of the offenders. But whether anything ever came of it, I don't know. The fate of the mama and her cubs is beyond the knowledge of us all.

On our last night in East Africa, a few Masaai warriors gather behind the evening fire. The stars burn behind and above the men's tall, lanky frames, their ochre-dyed Shuka robes, and their long, plaited black-as-night hair.

One steps forward and calls aloud; he is the *olaranyani*. The others follow their choirmaster with a call-in assent. And then the song begins, the olaranyani taking the melody, the other four the harmony in a call-and-response.

And then one of the men steps forward, toward the fire, and the dance begins. Effortlessly, it seems, his heels bounce up, his sole goes nearly vertical, his toes lift off, and he's in the air. For a moment, his body appears suspended—arms straight at his side—like a moon around our planet's gravitational pull. And then he drops; his hair, however, stays momentarily where he was, rises, lengthens as if it wants to linger just a little longer among the stars.

After a few vertical leaps, the dancer returns to the group and another takes his place. And he, too, enters the sky.

I find myself drawn in despite knowing it's just a show, not an authentic ceremony. These men are leaping into the night on land that was once their own and not a nature reserve so they can make a little money to feed their families (the great travel-writer Peter Matthiessen warned in 1972 of the Maasai becoming a "human zoo for tourists").

The Maasai have managed, against incredible pressures, to retain a significant portion of their heritage, culture, and language. But the pressure to "modernize" and "assimilate" is only growing. I know all this. And a bunch of foreigners gawking at these men as they perform their highly ritualized adamu dance, which marks the transition from adolescence to manhood, rightly feels exploitative. These aren't professional dancers but simply men doing something for us that they have done with a ritual purpose in their villages for hundreds, perhaps thousands, of years.

Despite this, there is a moment when all these concerns pass away, and all I can do is marvel at my species, its diversity and beauty. These men, at the height of youth, remind me of the ancient Greek word *arete*, which means a kind of excellence or fulfilled potential. Here, behind a fire one night in Kenya, is a momentary encapsulation of the beauty of our species.

And if tourism is one way in which the Maasai can balance the pressures of the modern world and still maintain their culture and identity then, while it may not be the best of all worlds, it may at least make the best of the one we currently have.

I didn't know it at the time, but my ten or so days in Kenya would be the peak of my travel powers. We always think that how we are in our youth will last forever.

I was a bloody superhero of travel. I actually *enjoyed* the airplanes. Flying over the Sahara Desert at night, knowing that thirty thousand feet below me fennec fox hunted in the dark, felt novel and wonderful. I thought little about death. I didn't worry about car crashes despite the recent one in Ireland. I didn't fret over snake bites or malaria or some unspeakable never-known ailment. When I got my vaccinations in Ireland, I felt as though I'd gained some superpower—lord, how I love vaccines! No disease could touch me now!

It's been pretty much downhill since.

Perhaps surprisingly, I didn't leave Kenya with a sudden desire to drop my English degree and major in environmentalism. In many ways, the hibernating turtle still slept within me, wildlife and ecology still waited patiently in the wings, and it would take the Peruvian Amazon to fully awaken it. But the trip to Kenya proved something to me: I could manifest my wanderlust. I could see the world.

In the meantime, I'd get back together with Tiffany, we'd graduate college, move to New York City, spend five hilarious weeks in Peru, move back to Minnesota, get married twice (once for health insurance), then onto Santa Fe for graduate school and something wholly unexpected called Suriname and Guyana.

Chapter Four

I Hate the Sun and Other Tales from Suriname

SUMMER 2008

When we tell an acquaintance in Santa Fe we are traveling to Suriname and Guyana, he says, "You're going to Africa?"

"No, it's in South America. At the northern end of the Amazon."

"I'm pretty sure it's in Africa."

"Nope, South America."

"Really, I don't think so. I *know* it's in Africa."

Yeah, okay, douche beans. I think we're pretty friggin' positive which continent we're flying to. In general, Americans are about as good at geography as we are at doing anything about climate change.

After settling into our new home in Santa Fe, I find myself with time on my hands. I'd started my Great Books program at St. John's College, where I would read lots of books written by really dead white dudes (ever heard of

Titus Lucretius Carus? That's okay, I hadn't either) and then talk about them ad nauseam. I was very good at the talking part. But the days were long, and I wasn't working. I wanted to do something useful with the memories of the Peruvian Amazon that still float up from my subconscious like bubbles.

So I approach Rhett, head of Mongabay, and ask if I can start writing some articles. Truthfully, I don't have much to offer, I have zero science background and have taken fewer journalism classes than I have physics, which is to say none. I was your typical English major: obsessed with Shakespeare and Jane Austen and the Brontës. My skills were largely superfluous in an uber-capitalist society in which depth of thinking and love of words are about as valued as philosophers and puppet makers.

Despite my lack of experience, Rhett agrees. I think my eagerness wins him over...*and* the fact that I am totally willing to write for free. So in September 2007—just over a year after the Amazon—I start my unofficial, unpaid internship. Rhett sends me scientific papers or press releases to cover, and I write articles. At first, I'm doing one article every couple of weeks. But as I dig deeper into the subject matter and get better through good old-fashioned trial and *lots* of error, I begin writing more and more, eventually putting in enough time to constitute a part-time job.

About six months into this partnership, Rhett sends me an email. "Hey, you want to go to Suriname this summer?"

Apparently, the Association for Tropical Biodiversity, a global scientific organization, has organized a conference in Paramaribo, the capital of Suriname, of all places. I guess these biodiversity nerds had heard of Suriname.

Rhett writes something like, "Hey, want to check out this conference? We could meet in person *for the very first time* (emphasis mine). I'll cover your airfare, hotel, etc."

I think this is his way of paying me back for the last six months. I'm more than happy to trade in my writing for a trip to Suriname, wherever that is.

I have to Google it.

Obscure to most of the world, Suriname is the smallest country in South America, both in population and landmass. It's also host to one of South America's most diverse populations, and the only one to speak Dutch. It's a triplet, bordered on the western side by Guyana and the eastern by French Guiana. Together, these three tiny countries make up the Guianas, which cover about half of the Guiana Shield, a 1.7 billion-year-old geological formation rising out of the north portion of the Amazonian Basin. It is technically not part of the Amazon rainforest, though both ecosystems house many of the same species.

At the time of his invitation, Rhett doesn't know my past mental health history or my current diagnoses. He doesn't know about my OCD, anxiety, depression, fear of flying, fear of stray dogs, fear of stray cats, fear of cars, fear of airplanes, fear of raw chicken, fear of malaria, or fear of fear. You gotta hide that mental illness. Hide it from friends, potential mates, and especially employers and anyone mad enough to offer to send you to Suriname.

So I do the only thing you can when such an incredible opportunity crosses your Gmail. I say, "Hell, yeah," with the postscript, "But can my wife come?" Because I very much need someone to hold my hand.

The thing is, I'm not only terrified of everything above but also of snakes. And Suriname has *a lot* of snakes. Okay, you're right to ask why I didn't mention my paralyzing, crippling fear of snakes when I was bumming around Peru. The answer is simple. I wasn't terrified of snakes *then*. I probably would've hugged and played footsie with a snake just for fun (though the latter would have been challenging). But I am terrified of snakes *now*. Steve's decided.

The thing about living every day with OCD is that you quickly discover your obsessions aren't fixed. In fact, the more you beat back one, the more likely, at least in my noggin', a new one will rise like a demented Highlander (only in this case there can be *way* more than one). I'd spent the last two years in intensive therapy working on my obsessions about cancer and other potentially fatal diseases. But Rhett's invitation to Suriname spurred Steve to whisper something new to me. "Snakes, snakes, snakes."

This sudden phobia around the suborder *Serpentes* probably stems from a story Rhett told me about a recent close call he had with two fer-de-lance in Belize. Rhett, who's pretty much been everywhere, has lots of stories, like almost being killed by a forest elephant or charged by a gorilla or coming down with some unknown, unspeakable, ungodly fever that lingers in his body like a hobbit at home.

Rhett even has a photo of armed men touting guns and bows and arrows who are blocking his path in Indonesian New Guinea. This means while three dudes were pointing weapons directly at Rhett, he was *taking a picture*. This is the kind of guy Rhett is. This is *not* the kind of guy I am.

Rhett's snake tale takes hold in my brain, and suddenly I become convinced a snake will probably kill me in Suriname.

Obsessive-compulsive disorder latches on to the simplest anecdote (or even just a single word), which can turn on the obsession switch. It's like I have marbles rolling forever in circles in my brain, and one word—snakes, cancer, rabies, elephants, airplanes, motorcycles, snow, dessert, cookies—provides the initial velocity to send it rolling down a seemingly never-ending spiral of fear and despair and pointless bargaining. There is no rationality in OCD, so stop looking for any.

After saying yes to the trip, I make an amateur OCD error. Rather than fight back against my new best friend—snakes—I begin to research fer-de-lance.

The internet is pretty much the worst thing that ever happened to OCD sufferers. Having instantaneous access to the most horrible, god-awful, soul-crushing things that can happen to a human being is like OCD catnip.

Via this Google hell pit, I discover that a fer-de-lance is a pit viper. Unlike most snakes, the fer-de-lance, which means "spearhead" in French, bites first and flees later. It's the Billy Budd of the serpent world. This skittish snake is responsible for nearly all serpentine bites in South America. One estimate puts it at 90 percent. It also doesn't just inject venom but *shoots* it. It can spray venom up to six feet. Left untreated, a fer-de-lance bite spreads necropsies, basically killing your flesh, leading to gangrene, which requires either amputation or, you know, a coffin.

I start looking at pictures of gangrene like some twenty-somethings look at porn.

"Well, crap," Tiffany says as we step into a grocery store in Paramaribo, the capital of Suriname. It's our first day here, and we'd just been informed by our driver that we have half an hour to purchase enough food to last us *two weeks*, with no chance of deliveries or re-ups once in the coastal jungle.

"How much food do you think we eat in two weeks?" I ask.

"I have no idea."

"Remember, he said no refrigeration."

"How could I forget—"

"Do you think they have alcohol?"

"God, I hope so."

With our usual exuberance, Tiff and I felt we couldn't go to a place like Suriname and spend the whole time in hotel and conference rooms drinking tea out of Styrofoam cups and chatting with other like-minded Westerners. So we signed up for a fortnight of volunteering with an organization dedicated to the care and study of sea turtles on the coast before the conference and one whole week in the rainforest of Guyana after. We still hadn't learned the lesson of Peru: shorter trips are saner trips.

This Surinamese grocery is full of colors, smells, and shapes that are delightfully unexpected. We should be enjoying the experience as few things define a culture more than what's in a grocery store. But it's not so fun when there's a time limit or when your diet for the next fortnight depends on diligence.

"Let's split up," Tiffany says.

Twenty minutes later, she returns with boxes of crackers and cookies, mini-packs of plantain chips, fruit, both recognizable and not, a dozen cans of beans, a few bags of Basmati rice, six boxes of pasta, and so many jars of tomato sauce we could bathe in 'em, grape jelly, instant coffee, tea. And she even found peanut butter.

I picked up bread but got sidetracked by the pig faces and the pomtajer and the tayer and the table full of stacked dried fish.

"Jesus, Jeremy, what would you do without me?"

"I got chocolate!" I brag, showing off a bunch of bars tucked under my bread-laden arms. "And I found the alcohol."

"Show me."

We dump bottles of wine, a couple of six-packs of beer, and a bottle of whiskey into the cart.

We push the overloaded vehicle to the clerk, her eyes-wide, at these two gringos who look like they're hoarding for the zombie apocalypse. As she begins swiping the foods, Tiff turns to me: "Do you think—"

"I'll get a couple more bottles of wine," I say, finishing her thought.

After our shopping triumph, our driver takes us east toward the Marowijne River, the natural border between Suriname and French Guiana, where we will switch to a boat that will bring us north to the site of our fortnight marooning.

Once out of Paramaribo, the road is rough, pockmarked, and flanked on both sides by thick vegetation. Sometimes a colorful house stands on the roadside or a woman sits on a blanket selling fruits and vegetables. Chickens run free, and toddlers toddle in nothing but diapers on the side of the road.

There are two regions in Suriname: the sliver-like coast where 90 percent of the people live, and the interior. All we have to do is turn our heads to the right to see the beginning of the latter, dense tropical rainforest. Indeed, Suriname is the greenest country on Earth if you take forest cover as the standard. An astounding 98 percent of the country lies within the shadow of a nearly unbroken canopy.

Little do we know at the time that the highway we're on had been the site of vicious fighting during a civil war just two decades earlier.[1]

It's amazing how a few hours on a plane can bring you to a land where you are utterly ignorant both of its past and present. You don't need to know a thing about a country to show up there one day and walk its streets and interact with its citizens. Traveling is a journey through our ignorance.

Most of the people we see from behind the windows of an air-conditioned car are direct descendants of maroons, the slaves who had escaped their bonds and built distinct cultures deep in the rainforest. Today they live on the edges of one of the only highways in Suriname, with nothing but miles of rainforest behind them.[2]

By car it takes us just two hours to cross nearly half the country and reach the Marowijne River, which forms the natural border between Suriname and French Guiana. Here we meet our two guides, Amerindians from the local Kalina, or Carib, tribe, and ditch the car for a small canoe-shaped motorboat.

As we motor down the Marowijne, we enter the lands that the Carib people have inhabited for thousands of years. They were there when the first Europeans showed up, bringing guns, steel, and germs—epidemics untold.

We can barely talk with the pair because they speak minimal English and we speak zero Dutch or Carib. Communication for the next few hours is largely devoted to pointing, nodding, and smiling. But I feel good, I really do. Actually, at that moment I feel *great* being back in the world's grandest wilderness. Somehow, by some wild fancy of the gods of fate, I've made it to the Amazon rainforest twice in three years. Child Jeremy would be very proud of me.

Tiff and I put up our feet and watch the scenery scroll by, an unbroken wall of towering rainforest trees underneath an expansive sky. Large strands of boulders creep out from the bank from time to time, looking almost like severed fingers of a stone giant. Birds fly the width of the river, their shadows rippling on the water.

Time itself drifts along like a cloud. We have no idea how long the journey will take or what our destination will look like at the end.

In 2008, there are no guidebooks devoted to Suriname. Believe me, I looked. I have a guidebook fetish. I like to know which restaurants to eat at, what museums to visit, which diseases I might contract, and how quickly I can get to a hospital from every location. Even if I'm going for only a few days, I want that sweet, sweet *Lonely Planet* in my carry-on so I can read the History Section en route (a kind of totemic ritual for me). But I couldn't even find a guidebook on the Guianas, i.e., Suriname, Guyana, and French Guiana. You know a region has to be way off the beaten path when Anthony Bourdain never did a single show there. How I would've loved to see Bourdain bring his signature stature to the bizarre streets of Paramaribo, the sea always beckoning, the sun ever-shining, the wooden Dutch buildings rotting, and the Greek-style statues slowly being consumed by tropical mold.

After a long search, I was forced to concede by purchasing Lonely Planet's giant *South America on a Shoestring* instead, which had very brief sections on Suriname, Guyana, and French Guiana but hardly enough to satiate my compulsion.

An hour in and our Carib guides point excitedly. They are trying to tell us something, but we can't make it out. They turn the boat around and head back to a little beach at the edge of a mangrove forest. Are we there? Is this where the sea turtles come ashore?

"I think they're saying 'anaconda,'" Tiffany says.

At the word *anaconda*, I do what any normal human would: I stand up in the boat.

One of our guides moves his hand up and down energetically, which translated means "Stop trying to capsize us, white boy." I obey, but by then we can see its shape even sitting. The anaconda is lying on a beach under the cathedral-like roots of a mangrove.

But the anaconda is missing its head.

The guide lands the boat and we all jump out (of course, had it been alive I would've stayed in the boat). Even in eternal repose, though, this green anaconda is *huge*. I'm not as taken aback by its length—one expects an anaconda to be long—as its width. It's less palm tree and more oak. This is partly due to gases released after its death, but it also shows how a snake like this could swallow a capybara. It is huge, magnificent, with a beautiful pattern of black spots, some with yellow blossoming out of them. It is utterly awful, meaning full of friggin' awe.

The green anaconda is the world's biggest snake in weight and potentially the longest. Our guides tell us later that they thought the dead snake was just short of twenty feet. The largest confirmed anacondas run between twenty-three and twenty-five feet, though there are tales of much, much bigger animals. Perhaps such a leviathan is still out there, or perhaps they were out there not long ago but have been wiped out in the wake of human destruction.

After I returned home, I would try to uncover the mystery of why the snake would have had its head cut off. But like so many encounters when we travel, there was no proper end, no bow tied over this paradox box. Jaguar will sometimes eat the head of an anaconda, but the cut looked too sharp and clean for that. Possibly someone chopped off the head to sell as a trinket to a tourist. If so, what a sad and pointless end for a creature both terribly beautiful and beautifully terrible. Its life cut short and its giant genes left to perish.

We leave the animal on that beach. The jungle would soon consume the rest, bringing sustenance to thousands.

Down the river, we pull in toward shore again, only this time not to gawk at a murdered snake but to get some gas at a native village. While one of the guides disappears to buy fuel—alas, there is none here—the other heads over to a tree and shimmies up it. He brings us back a newly plucked mango and shows us how to peel it. No mango since has ever compared. Still warm with the tropical sun, the juice drips down our fingers as the boat makes its way farther downriver toward the sea for another chance at fuel at the next village, Galibi. In addition to being the name of this village, Galibi can also refer to a member of the Kalina tribe.

While one of the guys disembarks to track down gas, four boys swim near our motorboat as a young one sits on the shore. He wears a shirt but is naked from the waist down. Their mother, shoulder-deep in the water, holds on to one of the moored boats.

Part of me wants to say hello or make some gesture of greeting, but why interrupt their reverie? They are showing off for strangers, as children do everywhere. They do underwater handstands, somersaults, and smile as though onstage. A brawl begins as two of the brothers fight over I-can't-remember-what.

The younger of the two, fey throughout, laughs and laughs as his older brother repeatedly attempts to drown him, launching on him like a killer whale on a seal but always missing. While these two tussle, the third swims up to show us a river creature he's caught in a Coke bottle. The tiny arthropod scuttles around its prison like a trapped djinn. The mother beams, and we can't help but beam as well at these young boys undulled by television, video games, phones, and the endless sensory overload of the world we left behind.[3]

The siting of Warana Lodge is like something out of another millennium: on both sides, nothing but miles of undeveloped beach. You could pretend you were a Polynesian wayfinder thousands of years ago stumbling on an unknown, unmapped shore, a true tropical paradise.

But the first humans we see at Warana are not Amerindians but old white women, as if we'd pulled up to an Old Country Buffet rather than a remote Amazon lodge in a country only 2 percent of Americans have ever heard of. (I just made that percentage up, but it doesn't mean it's not totally, absolutely accurate.)

Among the women, who turn out to be visitors with Elder Hostel, is another: She is in her twenties and sporting a two-piece. Nicole, a graduate student working with sea turtles over the summer, would prove to be our interpreter, unofficial guide, and friend for the fortnight to come.

After brief greetings, we are shown to our room. It is a bare concrete shelter with two bunk beds, like a college dorm built to survive the conflagrations of a nuclear holocaust. We'd paid bottom dollar to volunteer with sea turtles for two weeks: $400 each.

An hour or so after the sun descends and our first dinner of beans and rice, we meet up with Nicole and the Elder Hostel ladies. We are all rocking headlamps and hiking boots as we begin what will become a daily routine: walking along the beach, looking for antediluvian behemoths that have crawled up from the abyssal deep. This may sound like an overdramatized description of a sea turtle, but I assure you it is completely accurate. Just wait.

Nicole goes without a light. She says it's easier for her to see by the light of the moon reflecting off the water or, if there's no moon, simply by shapes casting their silhouettes in the darkness. She can catch a leatherback track in complete darkness.

But I'm wholly focused on the beams cast from the red headlamp (turtles cannot see the red spectrum) as I scan the beach in front of me for anything untoward (snakes). Of course, it'd have to be a nutty snake that would hide out on an open beach when the adjacent rainforest provides much better opportunities for hiding and hunting. Most snakes rely on surprise, after all.

Now imagine you're an astronaut landing on some faraway alien planet. Your shuttle descends, your door opens, and as you walk down the metal gangplank, you come face-to-face with a thousand-pound bathtub-sized being. Its face is blue with white mottles, which look like the stars above, and instead of forearms, it has large scythe-shaped limbs. It moves continually with a calm relentlessness, as if the movement were a type of meditation. You can't communicate because you don't speak its language and it doesn't speak human. But it seems to come from a species far older, wiser, and more serene than your own.

Fifteen minutes into the walk, we meet this alien being, not on a faraway rock, but on our very own planet.

A female leatherback turtle rears her head on the night-saturated beach, goo dripping from her eyes as she lays her eggs, around a hundred, and groans. Monstrous, terrible, and beautiful, the leatherback is the oldest and biggest of the world's sea turtles.

Nicole, all business, opens her bag, pen in mouth, and takes out a measuring tape, string, and a scanner for tags. First, we measure the turtle from one end of the carapace (the upper part of the shell) to the other, careful to stay behind the massive, scythe-shaped front flippers because they are strong enough to break a human leg. Next, we scan the leatherback's flippers and head for tags, which other biologists, perhaps half a world away, might have placed just beneath the skin so this female can be identified in a database. Finally, as the leatherback lays her eggs, we leave a string in the nest and tie the other end to a stick placed high in the dunes. The next day Nicole will triangulate the nest's position. If it's too close to the tideline, she'll dig up the nest and move it above the tideline or into her hatchery.

The leatherback turtle is one of our world's most marvelous wonders. It is the last living animal in the Dermochelyidae family, which goes back 110 million years. They swam the Cretaceous seas with long-extinct badasses like Cretoxyrhina and Kronosaurus. It's only very distantly related to anything else on Earth, including our six other marine turtles.

Unlike its distant cousins, the leatherback does not have a normal hard and bony shell; instead, its almost rubbery carapace is covered by skin, leaving no space between shell and body. Feeding almost exclusively on jellyfish, leatherbacks are deep divers. Actually, that is not strong enough: leatherbacks are abyssal divers, having been recorded diving as far down as four thousand two hundred feet, nearly twice the height of the world's tallest building, the Burj Khalifa in Dubai. Migrating across oceans, these great reptiles see more of the world than the vast majority of humans. One leatherback was recorded as having swum twelve thousand miles in a year, from Indonesia to Oregon.

We spend about twenty minutes with the beautiful and awful female before moving on.

When Nicole walks, she *walks*. Exuding assurance as though she's heading up an army, she doesn't watch where she steps. She keeps her eyes ahead, seeking the distinct markings in the sand that signify a nesting turtle.

Walking far more rapidly than I'm comfortable with—as if there was no chance of snakes—we suddenly come upon the unexpected: an aggregation of Dutch. In a moment we are surrounded, the speakers clearly excited about something. Although agitated, they appear to be trying to communicate with us; they are all speaking at once. Nicole pushes past the group like a New Yorker past gawking tourists. And on down the beach we go.

Nicole explains that the Dutch are one-night tourists out to see turtles. They are staying in Galibi village, where we stopped downriver. They come a couple of times a week.

"I don't speak Dutch," she adds as if to punctuate the encounter.

I look back at the group, who had begun walking in the opposite direction, their red-light flashlights crisscrossing and moving rapidly in the night as though somehow signifying their amplified mood.

We press on, moving at Nicole-speed. So I'm thrown when suddenly Nicole pulls up, stops, and takes a few steps back.

A flashlight beam catches our eyes. We follow it to its subject and see a large brownish snake, partially curled up.

"Fer-de-lance," says the flashlight bearer, one of the guys from the lodge. He speaks calmly for the fact that he is standing just a couple yards from it.

My pulse begins ricocheting.

"Venomous," he adds, as though his standing there with flashlight fixed on the yard-long snake requires further explanation.

"Shit," Nicole says. "We could've stepped right on it."

"Strange," he responds. "I've never seen one of these on the beach before."

Sometimes life is like this, even for those of us who are mentally fucked up. You waste untold hours worrying about some occurrence, you tell yourself how ridiculous and fruitless such concerns are, only to have it happen after all. Well, to be fair, it *didn't* actually happen. The snake hasn't sunk its enamel fangs into my flesh, injecting two hundred milligrams of liquid toxin.

The mystery of the excited Dutch now makes sense.

Watching it in the flashlight beam: its sinuous body twist and curl, its yellow stripes glint, its scales like light-reflective chain mail, its well-shaped head and all-too-keen eyes, I can't help but notice how beautiful it is. How independent.

To it, we are an annoyance, an interruption in its hunt. And if we move any closer, it will see us, accurately, as the real threat.

How many more fer-de-lance have died at the hands of humans than vice versa? Shot, bashed, macheted, their long bodies strung up on how many millions of homes over thousands of years?

Since we do turtle transects only in the early morning or just past dusk, we have lots of time to kill. Lots. So we murder it aplenty by playing uncountable rounds of Travel Scrabble and cards as well as reading to our hearts' content. If I had my druthers, I'd pretty much spend every hour of every day reading (such days were my favorite parts of college).

We sit in this ecotone—jungle behind, ocean ahead—and watch the waves forge up the sand, the tide go out, the vultures pick around the debris. We watch the troop of squirrel monkeys feed on the cashew fruit tree, the large beach ants following one another over their sandy mountains, the lizards lying in the sand and soaking in the heat from below and above. We watch the shadows of the rainforest trees slowly grow toward the sea until they are swallowed up by the end of another day.

I sit in the shade of a beach-loving tropical tree while Tiffany pulls her chair into the tropical sun.

Let me be frank: The sun and I have a complicated relationship.

I understand that without the sun, Earth would be just a frigid dead rock, unmoored in space. But on the other hand, the sun…well, let's be honest, is kind of a dick. It shoots cancer rays at us. It's like Apollo (in his immortal beauty), the god of the sun, with his arrows piercing hapless mortals for fun.

But also, the sun makes me happy. During the unbearably long winters in Minnesota, I depend on light therapy to function, i.e., a specially designed light box spewing ten thousand luxes in my face for half an hour at a time. The bulbs are meant to mimic sunlight as much as possible. It's a pretend, tiny sun to replace the bigger one that largely abandons Minnesotans from November through March. I shove my face into those lovely luxes like a starving wolf shoving its maw into the stomach of a newly murdered fawn.

Sunlight makes me happy and not want to spend *all* winter in bed (just most of it). But I also fear sunlight like I fear snakes and cars and stray dogs and mosquitoes because of its cancery powers.

As I said, it's complicated.

I wear long sleeves in the summer. I love hats, the wider the rim the better. I'd wear sombreros for seven months of the year if the fashion police would let me. I stick to the shade in the summer like a spy. I move lounge chairs, picnic blankets, and even kiddie pools beyond the sun's terrible reach. If you ever invite me to a summer party, which you probably won't once you've finished this book, you might find me skirting the sides of your yard, against the house or garage, keeping to the bushes and below the trees. I'm a shade master.

But unlike me, Tiffany likes the sun. Maybe a little more than is good for her. When she was a kid, she says she got "oodles" of sunburns. Tiff has lots of Polish and Irish ancestry, which makes her about as fair as sea foam and as prone to burn as dry kindling that's taken a day spa in lighter fluid.

One morning in Suriname, Tiffany wakes with her skin the color of tomato sauce. Little bumps erupt from her flesh. After consulting various lodgers, we learn that she has sun rash, not a sunburn, meaning her skin has thrown in the towel in the face of all the Surinamese sunshine and heat. It's also called prickly heat, which sounds like a good name for a spicy cocktail. But this is what you get for befriending the sun.

The heat rash means Tiff has to join me in the shade for the rest of the trip. She has to keep her skin as cool as possible, not easy in 90-degree heat with no fans or air conditioning or ice cubes or penguins. I feel bad for her, but in the deep recesses of my brain, I think, *Told ya so.*

After a couple of days, two new American tourists arrive in Warana. The new tourists aren't concrete shelter ones. They'd paid for the upgrade to sleep in the far more comfortable lodge and eat the delicious food prepared daily by the local cook.

Katie is young, around twenty, from Arkansas, who ended up at this far end of the world due to a lifelong obsession with sea turtles.

The other, Simon, is from New York City. I'm not sure how exactly he ended up in Suriname of all places, but this forty-year-old is an animal lover of titanic proportions.

I have a lot of respect for animal activists. The science is wholly on their side. The more we learn about other species' cognition and emotions, the more we realize how unspecial humans are. We aren't the only "conscious" species on the planet (far from it). We aren't the only species that experience suffering or joy. We now know that fish feel pain, elephants mourn, octopi and puffins use tools, dogs learn hundreds of human words (how many of theirs do we know?), bees can count, goldfish can tell the difference between the music of different composers, and animals have personalities.

For centuries (thanks, Descartes), humans in the West largely viewed animals as unthinking automatons, slaves to instinct with no emotional or intellectual capacities. But science is now showing us how ludicrous this view is (ask any dog owner and they will tell you).

But animal-lover Simon . . . well, the first night while we're all hanging out, Simon tells us how he can't watch wildlife documentaries because he can't handle when one animal attacks another. We try to remind him that's nature: Animals eat; animals die. If the deer doesn't die, the wolf cubs will. There is always joy and always suffering. But he persists in his denouncement of animal-on-animal violence. Admittedly, I find this odd, but from one sensitive dude to another, I make an effort to respect it.

Still, Simon's peaceable kingdom ramblings don't extend to his own behavior. He struggles with anger issues, throwing a tantrum whenever he's about to lose at cards or Scrabble. Many a game ends with forty-something Simon storming off to his room to be alone with his mental health problems.

Within a few days on the coast of Suriname, Tiff and I run out of everything that is vaguely interesting or fresh to eat. All our snacks are gone. Our chocolate melted so fast, we devoured every bit of it in twenty-four hours. The fresh fruit is gone in three days. We are hungry all the time but also wholly uninterested in what there is to eat.

Out of necessity, meals become one of three options: beans and rice, pasta with tomato sauce, or peanut butter and jelly sandwiches. We rotate them to keep it diverting.

The alcohol isn't as nice as we'd hoped either. Even when it's stored in the shade, the wine isn't room temperature; rather, it's hot, hot wine. Despite how Europeans drink it, room-temperature beer is gross (when the room is a humid bunker in the tropics). All we want is something cold, like bathing in ice cream. The whiskey at least does the trick with the greatest efficiency.

The ants discover our supplies within a few days, and by the second week, I stop picking them out of our rice bags and peanut butter and jelly jars. We just consider the unfortunate arthropods protein.

When we make rice, tiny ant bodies float to the surface as the water boils. It's like every meal is one ant graveyard or another.

One afternoon, Tiffany, who has eagle eyes, turns to me and says, "A leatherback."

"Where?"

"In the water." She points to a black football-like shape poking just above the waves.

"During the day?" I say skeptically. Leatherbacks are supposed to lay only at night.

But it turns out Tiffany is right, as usual. The black shape is the head of a leatherback who's soon waddling her monstrous body out on the beach. I run to get Nicole, and the three of us watch this expectant mother do her whole business in broad daylight.

Freeing herself from the water and entering the alien world of the land, she uses her massive front flippers to propel herself, stroke by herculean stroke, up the beach. At some point, she decides she's gone far enough. Then she begins the long process of digging out a nest with her smaller hind flippers. When the nest is done, she moves her hind end over the pit and lays her hundred or so eggs. She covers them with sand and then camouflages the nest by moving around in circles while her massive forelimbs toss up sand everywhere, making it so predators, including humans, have little idea where to start digging for the nutrient-rich embryos. The whole process takes over an hour and, by the end, the mother looks ragged.

There's a reason it's called labor.

Finally, she makes her way back out to sea, disappearing beneath the surf.

She will probably resurface a few more times to lay additional clutches—as many as nine—before she quits the beach entirely and heads back to the open ocean to, you know, eat jellyfish in the lightless deep.

She will return every few years to lay again. Her life span has been said to be somewhere between forty and one hundred fifty years. No one knows for sure, and like an anaconda's maximum length, reports vary widely.

I think often of that line from *Hamlet*, "There are more things in heaven and earth, Horatio, than are dreamt of in your philosophy."

We're all Horatio.

Despite our good intentions, Tiff and I are what you might call shitty volunteers.

I don't think this is entirely our fault. Some of it is, but some, too, is a lack of organization on the part of the program. I think we were the first tourists ever to pick this cheap, volunteer, self-serve option. Still, had we been go-getters, we probably could've bugged the staff and asked, "Hey, what can we do to help? Huh? Huh? Huh? Can we fix a roof? Repair a boat? Can we harvest some jungle fruits or hunt some peccaries?" Of course, had we been allowed to do such things, the lodge would've invariably ended up with a leaky roof, a blown-up boat, poisoned employees, and two very lost Americans.

Nothing is wrong with travel volunteering, but I think it's important to realize that it's still a largely selfish and self-involved activity, much like all travel. That's not to paint it with an ugly moral brush, only to say let's not get high and mighty about it. It's still more about *you*. The last thing local organizers need is a bunch of Americans even more puffed up on self-importance than we usually are—we are already some of the puffiest of travelers, and not in the cute jerboa-puffy way. Honestly, probably the best thing we did for Galibi was put a little—very little—money into its coffers.

For one thing, Tiffany and I prove bad at getting up early. I blame it on my sleep disorder, which is pretty much defined by the need to be asleep longer than I'm awake, and to sleep in until at least 10 AM most days. I'll add to that Escitalopram, my psych med, which makes the ordeal of waking up every morning like you're Sleeping Beauty, only you've been asleep for a century because some douche prince never showed up, and now the fairy-tale alarm is ringing! I have to pull myself neuron by neuron into the waking world.

I'm not sure what Tiff can blame it on, probably just the normal human need for sleep. But after a few days of dragging ourselves out of bed at 5 AM to walk the shoreline and see if any turtles are laying eggs, we were like, "Nope."

The thing is, it's not as if *no one* went out on those mornings. Instead, after we abandoned it, the group is just down two Americans, and all the Americans, Nicole excluded, are pretty much expendable.

One morning, Bep, a member of the local tribe and a guide at the lodge, knocks on our door to see if we want to wake up at the ungodly hour of 4:30 to walk with him up and down the beach for several hours. We very much don't.

But Galibi gets its revenge on us. While Bep is at the farthest end of the beach where the mangroves take over and the sandy beach simply vanishes in lush vegetation, he sees something remarkable: A jaguar, the freaking queen of the Amazon, slipping into the line of trees beyond the sand. When he goes to inspect what she'd been up to, he finds a freshly killed, headless corpse of a green sea turtle. The great cat had likely ambushed the shelled leviathan as it came ashore to lay its eggs, crushing its head with its ridiculously powerful jaws, the strongest of any cat relative to its size, and then eating its face.

That afternoon, Bep takes us to see what's left of the body. Not only is the head gone but the great cat has also torn off the front flipper. The turtle's back flippers splay helplessly against the sand, denoting that it had been dragged after being killed. We can see inside the turtle through the gaping hole of its headlessness. And pieces of partially consumed eggs—evidently by some smaller scavenger—lie where they fell out of their mother, who never had the time to cover them before death struck in jaguar form.

The next morning the sea turtle's body disappears altogether. The jaguar had pulled it into the forest, leaving only a lone flipper. Greens are weighty animals, reaching over four hundred pounds. It's incredible to think of this cat, weighing half that (at most), pulling the sea-shelled animal into its realm using nothing but its teeth.

Seeing a jaguar is pretty much the holy grail of wildlife viewing in Central or South America, and to this day I've not had the pleasure (though I'd probably be even more excited to see a giant armadillo or a short-eared dog, both rarer and more elusive).

In the late afternoons, once the sun is in decline, we take long walks over the beach. The thin strip of sand, a barrier between the jungle and the ocean, appears like a snake on the map in the lodge. Walking on it, however, is a different story. The smooth wet sand, constantly shifted by the tides, gives way to a second buffer zone of weedy dunes and tall grasslands that end abruptly against a wall of sixty-foot tall trees. The change is so sharp, it seems almost man-made but, of course, humans have relatively little impact here compared with most of our planet.

Galibi is an ecotone, an area of transition between two ecosystems, or biological arrays if you want to be fancy. The slight beach separates two ecosystems that could hardly be more different: the rainforest and the sea. It's only in places like this where jaguars and sea turtles can meet.

But in a way, we all live in an ecotone, a transition state connecting two worlds. We live in the transition between our past and our present. A transition between who we are and who we wish to be. A transition between our private and public selves. Humans don't so much inhabit places as we inhabit the tension, the transition, between various selves.

Few know the tension of an ecotone better than those with mental illness, where you exist somewhere between "normal" and "fucked in the head" all the time. This is the curse of chronic mental illness. You get so good at hiding parts of your life, you often can pass off as hunky-dory as anyone else. But then you have a bad day, a bad week, a bad month, a bad year, and all of a sudden, you're here again, lost in your personal jungle, unable to see your way out. Your brain is telling you that you're a goner. Now there is only this: stumbling through the undergrowth, stepping on spines, succumbing slowly to hunger and thirst and disease. At the same time, you have to somehow keep plodding on, keep up with responsibilities that feel like vines encircling your body until either you get better or things get worse and worse until... Well, some breakdowns. Some hospitalizations. Some prisons. Some homelessness. And some suicides.

Steve may be my OCD, but my depression is Malachi.[4]

I picture my Malachi as a dark-robed figure who whispers to me about how I'm a failure, how I'm pathetic, how I'd be better off dead, and how the darkness that surrounds me in such moments will never fade. Malachi likes to talk a lot about death and suicide. He likes it when I start hitting myself as hard as I can in the head. That's the kind of guy Malachi is. He is a shabby, bi-horned roadie with a thirst for despair and a penchant for self-violence.

Fortunately, Malachi doesn't tend to show up when I'm traveling. Everything is too new and varied and wonderful for Malachi when I'm in a foreign land. Travel time is Steve time on cocaine. But when I return home, after holding it together for weeks in a foreign culture with a thousand unfamiliar situations to navigate, that's when Malachi turns his pallid face to me and says: "My turn."

Malachi and I met in the fifth grade. A banner year, from my mother's breakdown to my first therapy to my first meds. From fifth grade through my senior year, I was put on (and taken off) pretty much every psychiatric drug on the market. Some are still here, while others have vanished, taking with them their strange names, their byzantine side effects, and whatever good or ill they did to their prescribed.

My mother kept a list of them for years, but it has since vanished, and I have no idea what most of them were, only that I felt like a perverse Goldilocks. *Okay, this medicine makes him hyper, this medicine makes him sleepy, and this medicine does nothing at all.*

Many of these drugs were new. Little was known about what some of them did or why they (sometimes) worked. Less was known about their impact on adolescents, whose brains and bodies are already undergoing remarkable change.

I was a skinny, gawky kid, but one of the meds caused me to bloat and gain weight, making me look like I had a beer gut at eleven. My brothers called me "the beached whale" for months until I got off it. Another put me into mania. On a frigid day in January, I remember running around my house, through ten-inch deep snow, from front door to back, and around again.

One day during my freshman year of high school, I was doing schoolwork at the kitchen table when the next thing I knew I was in the back of an ambulance, the faces of strangers and my mother above me.

I'd had a grand mal seizure caused by Wellbutrin. I'd toppled from the chair like a rag doll—only writhing. I never took another dose of that one.

And then there was Nardil.

Nardil came with some pretty funky regulations. I couldn't eat cheese, processed or cured meats, anything pickled, including pickles. I couldn't have fava or soybeans, some kinds of bread, and caffeinated beverages.

But worse, when my psychiatrist put me on Nardil, she put in another order, too. I was to be committed to the Child and Adolescent Psych Ward for medical management in a more, er, intensive setting.

I think there must have been other reasons for my first *One Flew Over the Cuckoo's Nest* hospitalization. I mean, who ends up in the psych ward because they have to stop eating cheese? But for the life of me, I can't remember. So much I can't remember. So much.

I do know one thing. I was thirteen.

Near the end of our stay at Warana Lodge, the Americans—Tiffany, Nicole, Katie, Simon, and I—are playing another round of interminable Scrabble when we hear a hissing outside.

We toss our tiles onto the table and slink toward the open door. "Snake?" I ask plaintively.

No one responds. When we reach the threshold, we see an opossum on a cactus, hackles raised, spittle jumping from its mouth.

All of us head outside. We pause about two yards from the marsupial, but it seems to care little for us. And then we see why: At that moment *another* opossum shows up on the cactus.

The two opossums square off, draw close, and then their jaws open. The second one joins in the hissing.

It is then that Simon decides to save the day.

"Hey, guys," he says, moving toward the cactus replete with dueling opossums. "No need to fight."

The opossums either don't know English or are unimpressed because battle is swiftly joined. They rear up and launch themselves at each other, making a surprisingly weird sound like squawking birds. Male possums fight over territory—it's what they do.

"Hey, guys, come on, let's calm down now," Simon says to opossums wrestling on the cactus arm.

"Don't touch them," I shout after Simon. "They might have rabies!"

"*Jeremy*," Tiffany says and then turns to Simon. "Leave them alone, Simon. Just let them do their thing!"

"Hey, 'possums," Simon continues, moving closer. He starts to reach his hand out as he pleads.

"Simon!"

At this point, the opossums pause, notice that four *Homo sapiens* are standing within a few feet, including one whose hand is edging toward them, and decide that as much as they dislike each other, they want no part of this bonkers, so they take off in separate directions.

"See?" Simon smiles. "It worked."

That night, with our food supplies nearly gone and our taste buds dying from boredom, Nicole does something daring.

She steals a couple of platefuls of the cook's food from the kitchen—the food that's supposed to go to only the big spenders—and clandestinely delivers them to us, the bunker kids. Lightly fried fish, roasted potatoes, some kind of slaw: it's like eating paradise. It's like this place—this beach, this jungle, this life—only in friggin' food form.

We feel human again.

"What's that?" Tiffany asks in the dark of our night bunker. "Was that you?"

"No."

Some*thing* just made a noise. And it's *inside* our bunker.

"Shhh . . . It stopped."

We wait in the dark. It's only about half an hour after we'd turned off the light for the night. We'd been leaving the door slightly ajar every night because, with no air conditioning, it's the only way we can get a breeze in this stuffy, nuclear-holocaust shelter.

Suddenly, the noise comes again, a clanging as though something is riffling through the contents of our bags tucked under our beds.

"Do you want to go see?" Tiffany asks from her bunk.

We've both taken a bottom bunk and left the tops unused. Bunk beds are another thing I'm scared of but for good reason. Three years before, I'd fallen out of a top bunk and shredded my face as I hit the carpet below.

"Hell, no," I tell Tiffany.

There it is, the noise again. Slap, slap, bang, clank, *roll*—crick, crick, crick.

"One of us has to check."

"It might be a fer-de-lance."

"It's *not* a fer-de-lance," Tiff says with a tinge of exasperation in her voice. Again, crick, crick, crick.

"It sounds *bigger*."

Tiff is right. It sounds like a large animal in our bunker. Plus, snakes are quiet. They are ambush predators not looters. I think of that jaguar that killed and dragged the hundreds of pounds of green turtle into the forest.

"What'll we do?" I ask.

This is pretty much the escalation of every good horror movie. Serial killer? Godless ghost? Surinamese Sasquatch?

"Get a flashlight!" Tiffany suddenly says. Our fear had made us oblivious to the most obvious solution.

I scramble in my bed, arms moving as though swimming, searching for my headlamp. I find it, only to hear it fall off the bed onto the floor. "Dammit!"

I'm not going to put my hand down there with some carnivorous beastie in our room.

A ray of light cuts through the dark. Tiffany has succeeded.

"There, over there," I say, pointing to where the sound has come from, which turns out to be under my wife's bed. She puts her head over the side and shines the light. I expect a scream or at least a good gasp. But all I get is laughter.

"What?" I call out. "What?"

"It's just a turtle. A baby green."

"A turtle?"

She reaches her hand under the bed and gently pulls out a baby green sea turtle on his back, flippers waving uselessly in the air.

"He was rustling against our plastic packing bags."

I'm not sure I'd ever seen anything more helpless than this wee turtle dude.

"I'll let him out." With one step she crosses the bunker and with her bare foot, she toes open our door.

"Oh no, Jeremy, look," she says.

Out of bed by now, I peer out over the light of the ocean and see at least a dozen other hatchlings heading our way. A nest near us must have hatched, and the hatchlings are marching inland instead of heading toward the ocean—as they should be—attracted by the artificial light of the lodge.

"What do we do?"

"Get Nicole," Tiff says. "I'll carry this one down."

I race over to Nicole's bunker and hammer on her door. "Nicole! *Nicole!*" I shout.

Like many field scientists, Nicole is pretty much a superhero. She opens the door with preternatural speed, as if she spends every night waiting behind her door for us to knock with a crisis.

"What's up," she says with her typical Nicoleness.

I don't have to explain the situation as I sweep my arms over the mini-army of hatchlings scurrying our way.

"Get some buckets!" Nicole says. "Over at the lodge."

As I run, Nicole is already scooping up a hatchling in each hand and racing them toward the sea. I meet her on the way back with buckets.

Had they hatched closer to the sea, they wouldn't have needed our help, but the nest's proximity to the lodge meant they mistook its light for the sea's. Newly born sea turtles always head toward the most illuminated area. In a normal world, that's the ocean as it refracts the sunlight bouncing off the moon. But ever since the invention of electric light, baby sea turtles have been getting lost, heading to an illusory ocean that's really the light at the end of an eternal tunnel. By morning, the ants, ghost crabs, opossums, vultures, hawks, or any number of other hungry land animals will have found themselves a shelled treat, and all that will be left of a mother turtle's effort will be a string of tiny corpses littering the beach.

So we grab 'em, dump 'em in the bucket, and drop 'em, not very ceremoniously, into the sea with a "good luck" on our lips. Only to rush back and grab some more. Within half an hour, we'd successfully rescued the hundred or so babies. And I feel for the first, and probably only, time that we'd really done something good, something to help these imperiled reptiles. We gave them a chance to navigate their next round of challenges.

These sea turtles have a journey ahead of them of Lovecraftian perils. From abyssal fish monsters to Roc-sized sea birds to sharks that, let's be honest, are basically Elder Ones. Even if they can avoid these, commercial fishermen can still drown them on longlines with impunity and throw their corpses into the sea. As Lovecraft might write (and a young sea turtle might *feel*), Deep in the stygian sea, unnamable horrors lurk.

As I write this ten years later, I wonder if any of those tiny turtles made it and are swimming the sea. Experts have estimated that only one in a *thousand* sea turtles survives to adulthood. So, mothers have to lay, between them, ten nests to produce just one plucky survivor. But maybe, just maybe, one of those tiny tots bucked the trend, perhaps a female that's returning to the same beach in Suriname where she was born to give life to the next generation.

The next morning, we wave good-bye to Nicole, Katie, and Simon. We climb into the motorboat with our packs and it's all over—we are heading back to Paramaribo, the silence of the unbroken beach and forest replaced by car horns, Dutch, and the droning of conference room presentations.

At least, until we depart Suriname for another little-known country, Guyana.

Chapter Five

Guyana Calling

SUMMER 2008, CONTINUED

Just outside the front windshield of our stopped minibus, two men are arguing. We can't hear what they are shouting, but since we're weighed down by hunger and road lethargy, we don't really care. The argument appears to end when one of the men smolders off. He quickly returns with a two-by-four; he swings it like a bat and smashes the head of the other.

Blood—shockingly red—splatters.

Gasps go up throughout the minibus. People are pointing and shouting.

This surprise attack by lumber leads to a sudden brawl among several men until a few manage to pull the assailant off the victim. Both men are hustled away.

Welcome to the border between Suriname and Guyana, on the picturesque Corentyne River.

I can't tally the number of violent acts I've seen in movies and television, read about in books, and committed in video games, but witnessing sudden violence, real violence, just a few feet from you is altogether different. Even though it's not you who's being attacked, the sight of violence leads to a physical sensation, a cringing, a horror, a sickening pit in the stomach, a memory etched in your mind. The terror of the victim, the rage of the attacker, that thin line between normalcy and horror, it feels like watching a house of cards, which you believed was built of sturdier stuff, fall.

We've been waiting an hour in 95-degree heat, sitting in the bus in a lovely town called South Drain (even though it's in the northern part of the country) for the ferry to take us across the Corentyne River, which acts as the natural border between Dutch Suriname and English Guyana.

When the ferry finally docks and the minibus drives onto it to cross the Corentyne, it feels like a deep sigh. Guyana, here we come; hungry, tired, and grumpy, sure. But our day is better than two-by-four dude's.

Apparently, two weeks on the coast of Suriname followed by a week-long conference on tropical biology in Paramaribo still isn't enough trip for us. So why not travel cross-country from Paramaribo to Georgetown, the capital of Guyana, and then head into the interior of the country to a remote jungle lodge known as Iwokrama? Why not turn this trip into five-plus weeks? I mean Peru went *so* well.

Some people just don't learn (and by some people, I mean Tiffany and myself). So here we are, just a day after the end of the conference, making our way to a new country.

We've been in this minibus for nearly twelve hours by the time it enters Georgetown. Georgetown, named after mad (I hear you, dude) King George III, had much better names prior, including Longchamps (long fields in French, probably named for the slave-plowed fields) and Stabroek. I vote for the latter because when I put it in Google translate (it's Dutch), it comes back with the translation "Stab Pants." And I really want there to be a world where there is a city called Stab Pants. Is it a sexual pun? Is it violent? Is it a Dutch fashion thing? Who knows? It's Stab Pants.

From the perspective of minibus windows and the stagnant depression of a ride that never seems to end, Georgetown doesn't quite live up to its slogan as the "Garden City in the Caribbean" (most Americans probably only think of islands when we talk about the Caribbean, but many in the Guianas view themselves as more Caribbean than Latin American, culturally and histori-cally). Georgetown is a bit "meh" in that run-down, colorful, bustling tropical kind of way, but we're pretty much here only to eat and sleep.

Alas and alack, Georgetown, we barely know you, and given this, we probably judge you too harshly. I blame the minibus.

Finally, despondently, the minibus allows us to escape, and we trudge with our oversized backpacks to our guesthouse, a converted townhouse that seems like it was built during George III's reign.

As we enter, two plump Georgetownean ladies in their fifties greet us speaking English with a thick accent punctuated with words we don't know. (Guyana was South America's only British colony, just as Suriname was its only Dutch.) We understand the basics, though. Our room is ready and they'll have dinner for us in an hour.

We stagger up the long flight of narrow stairs, find our room, toss down our bags, and throw ourselves onto the bed. Tiff gets up ten minutes later and starts vomiting in the bathroom. After purging a few times, she lies back on the bed. The first words out of her mouth are, "I'm fine, Jeremy."

"Really? That doesn't sound fine."

"Just the heat and the day," she says.

In truth, it's not uncommon for Tiff to respond to excessive heat and exhaustion by throwing up. Backpacking together through Europe in 2003 during a historically epic heatwave, considered by the World Metrologic Organization as the continent's worst heatwave since 1540, Tiffany was practically throwing up every other day.

"You're sure it's not...parasite?"

"*Jeremy...*"

To change the subject, I turn on the TV to see what weird shows Guyana airs. An hour later, while she hasn't thrown up again, Tiffany is hardly feeling keen on dinner. So I head down the many old creaking steps—steps that likely had seen a wild, blood-soaked history I had no knowledge of—tentatively, mouse-like, alone.

"Where is your wife?" is the first question I get as I sit at the table set for two.

I explain our day and Tiffany's predicament and suddenly the two old ladies are bustling around me with grandmotherly concern. "Oh, you poor children!" They exclaim. "What can we do? How can we help? Oh, your lovely wife! Such a long trip! How difficult for her."

Their attentiveness is wonderful but also a tad disarming to my modern sensibilities. I'm always surprised by the concern and empathy of strangers I meet abroad. It's a little discomfiting when people with less than you, in a time when America is (once again) an international pariah (the Iraq War), seem to see none of that and just treat you blissfully like another human.

Travel can be punctuated by the best and worst of humanity. You might get robbed one day and taken in by a stranger the next. Throughout most of history, though, the guest, no matter how poor or insignificant, held a sacred status. The host was expected to provide any bed-crashing stranger with food, drink, a roof, protection, and sometimes even entertainment. This ancient philosophy of hospitality and the high status of the guest (called *xenia* in ancient Greece or *hachnasat orchim* in Hebrew) existed across cultures worldwide from China to Native American tribes. And it still survives, at least in part, in some portions of the world to the benefit of humanity, even as these things have largely perished in places like the United States.

I've been hosted by more strangers than I can count. Sometimes the connection is tenuous, a friend of a friend of a friend, sometimes there has been no connection at all, just need.

The two ladies fill me up on food, listen to all our upcoming plans, and then put together a plate for me to take up to Tiffany.

My wife, of course, wants nothing to do with the food, but it's the generosity that counts. Kindness can be a better balm than food or sleep.

Thankfully, night falls with near-perfect stability in the tropics, and soon we put the day to bed.

The alarm goes off in the dark. Tiffany and I pull ourselves out of bed, scrounge around the room for our stuff, and head as quietly as possible down the stairs. Georgetown is still asleep.

Outside the hotel in the quiet of the capital, an SUV idles. Seeing us, Claude gets out, introduces himself in his Guyanaian accent, takes our packs, and tosses them into the back. Just as around 30 percent of the nation, Claude is African Guyanaian, descended from someone who long ago lived bound in chains.

Then we're off, still in the dark, with our destination deep in the interior of Guyana.[1]

By the time the sun begins to make itself known, we're already beyond the outskirts of Georgetown, the city fading into the background like the darkness.

The trip ahead of us will take about seven to eight hours, covering just over two hundred miles or about half the country's length. At first, the drive is relatively smooth. We're on a highway following the Demerara River, which is moving in the opposite direction, bubbling up from the Guiana Shield forests and spilling out into the Atlantic behind us.

After a couple of hours, the river dips beyond our view and the highway continues to Linden. Here the road rises, and suddenly below us, we see a crater in the earth, as far as the horizon, as if some grave kaiju had descended from space and gouged a piece of our planet out with its giant maw. But this isn't the work of a preternatural beast. It's simply that of ant-like humans stripping the land bare for one thing: bauxite.

Bauxite is the primary source of aluminum, and this small country is a major producer. But it all comes with a cost: forests destroyed, massive energy expenditures, and water polluted. Lindenians today recreate in old mining pit lakes, perhaps unaware that they are swimming in a toxic soup.

Aluminum is nearly 100 percent recyclable, meaning that we can recycle it without losing almost any of the stuff in the process (and it can be remade over and over, forever and ever). Moreover, recycling aluminum requires far less energy than digging it out of the earth in the first place. It's odd. People demand austerity from governments, but profligacy and squander are fine when it comes at the expense of the natural resources.

As I watch the destruction mining has wrought pass us by, I feel more like a reporter than ever before.

Only a week before, the night we arrived back in Paramaribo from the sea turtles in Galibi, I met Rhett Butler for the first time, founder of Mongabay. After writing for Rhett as an intern for nine months (over seventy stories), the meeting felt almost momentous and fated, and I had only enough time to shower and dress after arriving at the hotel before Tiffany and I headed down to the lobby.

We waited a few minutes and then there was Rhett Butler, the man himself. Rhett, then thirty, was ruggedly handsome, with a high brow, intense eyes, and tousled hair. When he grinned, there was a crookedness to it that was charming. It didn't hurt that he was also this real-life adventuring environmentalist.

"Hello."

"Hi, Rhett."

"Hi."

Hands were shaken. An awkward pause and then Rhett said, glancing off, "So the Malaysian government is now looking at its forest policies."

It was at this moment Tiff and I realized that Rhett was not one for pleasantries or small talk. Instead, he dove straight into a litany of deforestation data coupled suddenly with "and I had a meeting today with…" he said a name neither of us had ever heard of. ". . . they're here for the conference. They said…" I tried to keep up while Tiff's eyes glazed over, and the three of us, Suriname-misfits, walked to a nearby Indian restaurant.

On the way, we passed a gas station.

"That's where I've been getting all my food," Rhett declared. He'd been here two days—a wholly unique nation—but he'd mostly eaten gas-station food, in part because he'd been holed up in his hotel working almost nonstop (Rhett doesn't sleep much). He continued to talk about how one scientist now disagreed with another over biodiversity strategies, and I felt like he was glad to have someone to unburden all this info onto.

That night's conversation was almost wholly taken up with shop talk, and I found it difficult to keep up with his mind, which was full of data, policy information, and personalities.

At one point, Tiffany tried to steer the conversation to something she could more easily participate in. "What kinds of movies or TV shows do you like, Rhett?"

"Oh, I don't really watch TV or movies, only when I'm on a plane and can't do much offline," he said. "I watched those *Lord of the Rings* movies recently—most boring nine hours of my life. But in Indonesia right now, SBY is…"

Rhett has little appreciation, something he will wholly admit, for things like theater, ballet or Shakespeare, the latter which he finds nail-scrapingly annoying. Instead, Rhett much prefers herps and tropical fish—aquariums and terrariums jostle for space on his desk along with his three computer screens.

Rhett is quite socially deft; you just have to get to know his ways. His sense of humor is as large as his sense of adventure. He has this uncanny ability to size up a person, an organization, or an environmental program with piercing accuracy. To this day, I trust his opinion more than anyone else's when it comes to the effectiveness of an NGO (non-governmental organization) or its programs. Like me, he loves good gossip and intrapersonal drama—just not, apparently, on the stage.

Perhaps, and I'm speculating here, Rhett just doesn't see a tangible stake in whether Frodo gets the ring to Mount Doom or Lear realizes the error of his ways, but falling forests, warming climate, and vanishing species—that's where the real stake is.

In short, while it took me a couple of years to realize it, I'm pretty frigging sure Rhett is a genius—with many of the same idiosyncrasies as geniuses before him.

At the end of our meal, after we'd covered the new photos of uncontacted indigenous people taken from an airplane in Peru, the Bush administration's admittance that global warming was real (eight years late), and the forest policies of Suriname, Rhett goes ahead and says, "I'd like to hire you on full time, Jeremy, once you're finished with graduate school."

"Yes," I breathe.

I am going to be a writer. A real-life writer.

Gulp.

After Linden, the paved highway becomes a wide, muddy track through the jungle, the Linden-Lethem road. Parallel, on both sides of the road, is the forest, dark, thick, foreboding, like a wall of green in the gloaming. It smells like rain and green and heat; it smells like life. Sometimes it shrinks to a thick fringe of foliage or secondary forest, at other times the trees rise above us nearly a hundred feet, culminating in green crowns.

As the sun vanishes for large periods behind the sheltering canopy of the Guiana Shield rainforest, the road turns to shit, a pockmark of puddles, holes, and trenches.

This doesn't deter our driver, Claude, who devises a new strategy. Instead of proceeding slowly and cautiously, Claude hits the gas hard, propelling the SUV forward, and then brakes as soon as a hole approaches, dips into the puddle, and then hits the gas again. Pedal equals metal, dirt flinging, racing toward the next hole. The problem is that the holes are only a few yards apart. At times the road turns into what would be called in New Mexico a lake. Muddy water soaks the vehicle.

To avoid such lakes, we veer onto the far left side of the road, branches scraping the SUV, and then cross to the far right, branches scraping the other side, as if both sides of the car need a scratching.

The passengers inside, Claude and ourselves, are flung about like crash-test dummies. And Claude just keeps on doing his thing. *Gas. Vroom. Brake. Oomphf. Gas. Vroom. Brake. Oomphf.* Just so, we make our herky-jerky way toward Iwokrama.

The hours rush by with the speed of a dead tortoise.

Lunch of chicken stewed in Guyanese sauce at 58 Village provides a welcome respite from the constant whiplashing. A rainforest frontier town, 58 Village's buildings, including one striking church, are built from massive logs carved out of the forest, as if the trees had rearranged themselves.

All too quickly, though, we're back on our whiplash road trip. Only four-plus hours to go.

In some ways, however, the sorry state of the road is a good thing—a very good one. Roads in tropical forests tend to produce one thing: destruction. And the better maintained the road, the more ready the destruction. Roads mean access, and access in modern and capitalistic terms means exploitation. Scientists call this the "fish effect." Looking down from above, one can see the road (the spine) and the destruction branching off on both sides, human incursions into the forest that resemble fossilized fish ribs, its sharp bones the signs of forest death.

Already, we see glimmers of what even this rough road brings. We meet a surprising number of vehicles on the road and nearly all are massive trucks carrying felled rainforest trees out.

Guyana, like Suriname, is one of the greenest countries on the planet and has maintained its environment in a far superior state than almost anywhere else. It has one of the greatest percentages of tree cover on Earth, and the Guiana Shield remains one of the earth's most intact major ecosystems. Yet, like all tropical countries, Guyana still faces, in places, the strip mining of rainforest, the obliteration of biodiversity, and threats to indigenous people.

Claude is driving us to a place that attempts to provide some kind of an alternative to this constant tension between neoliberal capitalism and ecological preservation.

Iwokrama, or more formally Iwokrama International Center for Rainforest Conservation and Development, is an NGO that manages nearly a million acres of rainforest in central Guyana along with indigenous partners. What makes this group unique is that their whole modus operandi is to develop ways to "sustainably" manage the forest.

Most of the time, when one hears the word *sustainable*, it's complete and total bullshit. It's a corporation or government trying to sell a lie. It has come to a point where, alas, the word is mostly meaningless.

My *Oxford English Dictionary* defines *sustainable* as "able to be maintained at a certain rate or level." This means that one could use resources at the same rate or level seemingly indefinitely without drawing down on the ecosystem. Sustainable fishing would then mean catching only so many fish as to not disturb the overall population or other species dependent on the fish, such as birds and whales. Sustainable logging would be felling trees at a rate in which one could cut down trees at that rate forever without doing lasting damage to the forest.[2]

Iwokrama, which is split into an untouched wilderness and a "sustainable" utilization area, is curious about the *real* definition of sustainability, and they do the research and due diligence to back it up. They are trying to earn money from the insane natural riches surrounding them without degrading the treasure they sit on. It's like having a million dollars in a bank account but living off only the interest—nothing else.

Iwokrama does log the forest, but only less than a half percent of the area is open to the program at any one time, with only five to six trees cut in every hectare. The center logs on a sixty-year cycle, meaning it will not return to a logged area until more than half a century goes by. Basically, such logging is meant to mimic natural loss and not deplete the resource on which it depends, again drawing the interest without touching the principal.

In addition to small-scale logging, the center runs a tourism lodge, a research center for scientists, and a butterfly farm that sells the bejeweled beauties abroad. They do all this while partnering with sixteen local indigenous communities, including hiring directly from many of them. Essentially, they are trying to say, "Hey, it's possible. We can gain income from the resources of the forest without destroying the forest itself."

Iwokrama has this going for them: It's mind-boggling stunning. On the banks of the Essequibo River, a two-story building overlooks a lawn often populated by white egrets. This building is the headquarters of Iwokrama, housing the administration and the dining hall. Meals are taken on the second floor overlooking the river and the canopy, high enough to get views of parrots, macaws, woodpeckers, and other good denizens of the treetops. To one side of the headquarters, guest cabins attractively line the river's bank.

Just beyond is the forest. Aside from the center's activities, the forest here stands unbent and untrammeled. Other than the deepest reaches of Manu, it's probably the most intact wilderness I've witnessed—and maybe ever will.

But by the time we reach Iwokrama, I don't care about any of this. It's late afternoon and travel exhaustion has set in like the flu. Shown to our cabins, I throw myself onto the bed and feel something I rarely suffer while traveling: debilitating depression. This is our twenty-fourth day of travel, and I don't want to do it anymore. I don't want to be a traveler. I want to be home on the couch with my dog, reading a book for grad school, preferably one longer than eight hundred pages and written by a long-dead Russian. I want to be awaiting the near-daily evening rainfall of Santa Fe's magic summers.

There is a knock at our door. It's our guide, Louis, a twenty-something Amerindian from the local Macushi tribe. Dinner will be ready in an hour, he tells us. But I don't want dinner, not unless it's a burrito smothered in hatch chile, Christmas-style. Which it won't be! I just want to lay here and whine the rest of the trip away.

Part of traveling is finding the will deep inside oneself to carry on, even when the carrying on seems not only impossible but, worse, ridiculous.

During the last couple of days—from Suriname to Guyana—I felt Malachi stalking my tracks. My anthropomorphized depression seemed just a few steps behind me at all turns as we crossed the border.

But being in the unbroken rainforest again soon forces my blighted comrade back.

At night we go caiman watching, shining our lights for the telltale spots of glimmering red that prove a crocodilian. We see dozens upon dozens. One morning we do a bit of fishing, not something I'm too keen on or adept at. But we manage to catch a few small fish, including a piranha with teeth like a mini-mini-great white's, before throwing them back into their river home. At night in the forest, we hear millions of insects calling out to one another, warning, loving, or just singing with the rapturous joy of existence.

During the hot hours of the afternoon, I interview the Iwokrama staff, trying to, you know, be a real journalist. I attempt to wrap my mind around this unique place's values and how it's making good on them. Meanwhile, our morning coffee is punctuated by the flight of scarlet macaws like daytime comets, our evening beer by the breeze of noiseless bats.

Every night the bats are our dinner guests. They show up, crawling with their hind legs and wing-hands from the thatched roof above. Upside-down, they drop. Then with precision the envy of any engineer, they catch themselves midair and wind along above the tables of Iwokrama, seeking out insects attracted to the electric lights. In the hunt, they fly by us, sometimes the wind from their wings caressing our faces but never actually touching. They are flirting, it seems. It has all the hallmarks of ballet: precision, beauty, grace. All we need is an orchestra.

✧ ✧ ✧

I've loved nature for as long as I can remember. Wildlife and trees are kind of my thing, but it's not just me who finds the natural world a tonic to our increasingly chaotic and discordant post-modern lives. There is now scientific evidence, indeed lots of it, affirming that the natural world is palliative for those suffering from mental illness.

The evidence that nature is good for us has gone quickly from compelling to overwhelming. Hundreds of studies compiled provide a picture of our species, deeply connected—mentally, physically, emotionally, spiritually—to nature. Or more simply trees, lakes, rivers, sky, mountains, birds, and bugs may be as vital to our health and happiness as laughter.

For example, scientists have found that taking a ninety-minute walk in a green space reduces anxiety and stress considerably more than a similar walk in an urban area. Spending time in nature has also been shown to hugely benefit those with ADHD, in some cases as much or better than medication. And it's not just ADHD sufferers. Nature seems to have an uncanny ability to increase one's focus.

Research is also finding direct links for someone like me. A study from Stanford University in 2015 found that a walk in nature reduced obsessive negative thinking (dubbed "rumination" in the study) much more than walking in urban areas. It also shows that people living in urban areas report *more* mental illness than other groups.[3]

Physical health is improved by nature, too. Hospital patients heal faster and need less pain medication when they can see trees through the window of their rooms. Seriously. Having a window view on a natural setting has also been shown to decrease stress, increase academic success, and mitigate things like aggression and impulsivity.

Research from the Japanese Society for Forest Medicine shows that spending time in nature, especially longer bouts, may well increase natural killer (NK) cells in our immune systems, which help protect us from viruses and even cancer. Ruminate on that for a moment. Time in nature may help prevent cancer.

It all adds up. Research from Europe, the UK, and Canada has shown that living near green space increases the chance of a longer life. A study out of Canada found the risk of dying from common ailments, heart disease, or respiratory illness dropped by 8 to 12 percent for those living near green space.

The research is sussing out the reality behind E. O. Wilson's biophilia; we are made to love the natural world, and nature, in its way, loves us back.

Nature is magic.

Personally, when my depression is at its worst, I want to go to a little house on the coast or a cabin in the woods. That sounds much healthier than a psych ward. I can't help but suspect that perhaps, just perhaps, what some have described as a mental illness epidemic in the United States—and around the world—may be partially connected to our alienation from, and destruction of, the natural world.[4]

The days in Guyana continue to drift by like a rowboat unmoored. There is Louis politely laughing at my feeble jokes; there are the evening cane toads lining up from the lodge to our huts; there are the geckos on the wall, the morning toucans in the canopy, and the spiders caught in flashlights. There is the river, the endless green, and the clouds. There is rain sometimes; and lightning brightens the sky one night; for a moment, brilliant day.

Iwokrama has a mascot named Sankar. Sankar is a ten-foot-long black caiman.

When Sankar is in the viewing, Louis heads to the kitchen. He picks up some freshly killed chicken bits or the flesh and bones of recently filleted fish, then he carries the meat in a bucket to the riverside.

"Here Sankar!" he says coupling the call with a clicking sound. "Here Sankar, here Sankar!"

We'd gotten to know Louis, our Macushi guide in Iwokrama, quite well over the past days in the forest and on the river. The Macushi people, whose language sits in the Carib family, inhabit the Guyanese interior, northern Brazil, and eastern Venezuela. Like nearly all Amazonian groups, they have spent the last few centuries in forced migrations to escape the influx of colonizers seeking rubber, logs, minerals—anything that can be exploited.[5]

With a strong sense of humor and deep knowledge of the rainforest, Louis is a delight to be around. Sankar, the black caiman, seems to enjoy Louis's company as well, either that or the raw chicken, because he does indeed come. He glides in without a sound and barely a visible movement—hardly a ripple—to where we await him.

Then Louis removes the meat bits from his bucket and throws them to the patient crocodilian. Sankar opens his seventy-six-toothed maw and grasps the flesh and swallows whole. Sometimes he dips below the surface for a moment after a bite as if shy.

He's a lovely beast.

Caiman are in the alligator family and the black is the largest of them, reaching lengths of sixteen or so feet. They are the biggest predator in the Amazon, eclipsing both the anaconda and the jaguar.

Sankar feeding time is also a good time to pepper Louis with questions. We find out he went to university in Georgetown for biology, the first in his family to attend higher education.

"I've had malaria three times," Louis also says one morning, with the nonchalance of someone announcing they'd once had the flu. He tosses bloody chicken to the caiman.

"Three times!?" we exclaim.

"Oh yes. It nearly killed me when I was seven."

Louis's family did not have access to antimalarial pills or even mosquito nets. They simply lived and died with the world's most dangerous fever, as their ancestors had for hundreds of years before.[6]

Malaria may have actually been brought to the New World from the old. Recent research has found no evidence of malaria prior to Columbus. Some believe it was brought over on slave ships carrying Africans, the mosquitoes riding their shackled victims like Pestilence on his white horse.

You know, when you see a kid acting spazzy and you say, "Oh, they must have ants in their pants," I never really understood that phrase until Guyana.

After a morning hike one day, and as midday grew ridiculously hot, Tiffany and I both de-robe, and Tiff sets our pants on a shelf. We nap. When we get up for lunch, we put on our pants—as one should do when going to lunch.

Everything is fine for about eight seconds, and then a single jot of pain, as if a tiny lighter has brushed my skin. For an instant, I think maybe my muscles have spasmed. But then the pain comes again, only on a different spot. And again, and again. It's like a hundred Lilliputians are shoving fiery brands into the fleshy part of my legs.

"Ouch! Ouch! Ouch," I'm shouting as Tiff is just getting dressed.

"What's wrong?" she says, wiggling into her pants.

"I don't know. Something—agh—hurts!"

Pants on, she comes over to me. But in the time it takes her to reach me, she, too, suddenly feels the angry Lilliputians with their jabby weapons (oh, maybe this is why it was called Stab Pants!).

"Me, too! Me, too!"

"What's happening?" I ask desperately, stupidly.

"I don't know—" and at this point, Tiffany is slipping back out of her pants and scanning them.

"Ants!" she says. "Ants! Literal ants in our pants!"

"Oh, shit." I'm now following suit and pulling off my pants. We spend the next couple minutes pulling ants off our flesh. We probably should've been a little less surprised since we'd seen ants devouring the residue off our toothbrushes and watched as lines of the eusocial insects marched across the cabin's wood floor. But we'd thought they were a peaceable bunch. We were wrong.

In researching this book, I spent more time than was necessary looking up the phrase *ants in the pants* in dictionaries. There's another meaning to this idiom, which goes like this: "Dude, John really has ants in his pants for Nancy," i.e., he's hot for her.

Having now experienced *actual* ants in my pants, I can declare this meaning is quite wrong. There is nothing sexual about having dozens of mandibles slicing through your flesh. Have you ever heard of anyone bringing in biting ants to spice up their sex life? Nope.

It certainly isn't an aphrodisiac for Tiffany and me. You might think that spending a week in the beautiful Amazonian rainforest would prove romantic. But it's less romance and more dirty, sweaty, and exhausting. It's more a relationship tester than a love-filled holiday. Tiffany and I never got a true honeymoon, though, she often points out, glass half full, that we did get to, you know, travel the world together. That's true, but most of those trips have been less *ants in our pants* and more ants in our pants, if you get my drift.

Sometimes, the best romance isn't on the beach but in the comfort of home—when you've both showered sometime during the last fortnight.

My first kiss was in the psych ward of a hospital. I was thirteen, she was fifteen. I was geeky, small, and pretty confused. She was gorgeous, unruly, wild, and really fucked up.

When she told me that I was going to be her boyfriend, I didn't feel there was much I could say beyond, "Okay!," enthusiastically. I mean, what straight adolescent boy would turn down a beautiful girl two years older, even in a medical facility? I wanted to be her boyfriend (I guess?), but more so I just wanted someone to sit me down and explain to me what that meant.

The medication Nardil had landed me here for a month. Plus, probably, behavioral issues. In my anger and despair, I very much liked to break things.

This boyfriend-girlfriend thing had to be done clandestinely because romantic relationships were not allowed in the hospital's adolescent psych ward. When they ran through the rules, the nurses told us this was because we were here to get ourselves in working order (like robots) and not to complicate our lives with romance. Sure, that makes sense. But I also think it was done partly for them because, let's be honest, none of the staff wanted to deal with a bunch of hormonal teenagers anyway, let alone the drama of a bunch of hormonal teenagers pretending to be in love.

In reality, it felt like no one wanted to deal with us. It felt like we were dumped there because it was a way to get us out of our parents' hair. Today, as a parent myself, I realize this is bullshit. There are few things I can imagine being more difficult than committing your own child, but if my child truly ever needed it, I'd do it in a heartbeat.

But there is much we don't understand at thirteen. And when you're a teenager sitting in a psych room, what you think is, *Well, I guess I'm too messed up to be home.*

My roommate, a sixteen-year-old boy with drug and alcohol as well as psych problems, was dating a patient, too. Together, the four of us were supposed to be like a little battalion against this world of adults where a nurse gave you your mood-altering pills in small white paper cups, where resident psychologists made you talk ad nauseam about your childhood and your family (shit you'd already discussed way more than was good for you), where you had to turn in everything from razors to floss, where your bedroom not only lacked any individuality but where someone probably committed suicide at least once, where every hour was scheduled on a big board: group therapy, lunch, personal therapy, visiting hour, art time, bed, even ironically, "free time."

When the four of us were watching a movie one night, my ward girlfriend decided to kiss me. I don't remember what the movie was, but the TV room was in a small enclosed area, were the nurses and officials could see only if they craned their necks. So when they weren't looking, she went at me hard. It was wet, confusing, and quick because she didn't want to get caught. It was too fast for me to get a chance to learn what to do and too wet to enjoy. I recoiled at the sudden unknown sensation of a tongue in my mouth.

But it was my first kiss.

Our ward girlfriends then talked about how they planned to sneak into our rooms at night and do stuff to us, which my roommate informed me meant sex. I *really* hoped they wouldn't do that. If kissing was a bridge too far, sex would've been like trying to land on Mars using a kiddie wagon and a loaf of bread.

It didn't take my ward girlfriend long to notice I was becoming a bit lukewarm about this whole relationship thing. And I didn't have the communication skills to tell her it wasn't that I didn't like her—I was entirely entranced and mesmerized—it's just that I didn't know what I was doing. *It's not you, it's me.* Really.

Looking back, I realize this wild, beautiful girl was just desperately wanting someone to want her, to love her. She was making up for something, and whatever it was, I couldn't imagine it'd been pretty.

Within three days, my fifteen-year-old psych ward girlfriend dumped me and started dating the resident twelve-year-old who looked as baffled about it as I did.

Early one morning after breakfasting with the rising sun and the early birds of the rainforest, we get into a large four-by-four vehicle and drive half an hour to the Atta Rainforest Lodge run by a local Macushi village. Here, they have a trail that culminates in a canopy walkway, a hundred-foot-tall tower with bridges, allowing you to be eye to eye with one of the true wonders of the world: the rainforest canopy.

At the entrance to the trail, Louis hands us off to a local guide, a Macushi man in his fifties. He smiles at us with a toothy grin and motions for us to follow. Then hopping impishly, but not exactly steadily, he proceeds into the forest.

Tiffany and I exchange a glance. Then getting our stuff together, we follow behind. He's standing a few feet down the trail and gives us that same toothy grin. Then he says, "Will-am."

"Will-am," I parrot, though confused.

He points to himself. "Will-am."

"Ah, you're William."

He laughs, nods, grins, and scampers away.

"That can't be his real name," Tiffany says to me.

"No, probably just the name he uses for tourists. Like I doubt Louis's real name is Louis. It's probably much more interesting than that."

We quickly follow as Will-am disappears down the trail, and for a moment he's nowhere to be seen, until suddenly there he is, right beside us, standing off the trail laughing.

"This plant good for fevers," he says, pointing to a plant.

"Oh, okay. Good to know, thank you."

Indigenous people have spent thousands of years case testing every plant in the rainforest against the various ailments of existence. They have developed a rich and deep pharmacology in the forests of the world, one only recently taken seriously by some in the Western world. In his way, Will-am is trying to educate us.

"And this good for—" he points to Tiffany.

"Ahhh . . ." I say.

"Menstruation?" Tiffany offers.

Will-am claps his hand, grins, and nods.

We carry on, a motley trio. "This good for fever." "Yes, yes." "This good for—" and he holds out his stomach. "Okay." "This good for headache." "Uh-huh." "This good for fever."

It's after Will-am shows us the plant that is good for fevers the *fifth* time that I realize that our guide isn't just a little tipsy, but four-sheets-to-the-wind wasted.

The path from the village to the canopy walkway isn't long, but we move at a disorienting pace as Will-am keeps disappearing into the forest and then reappearing like some manic sprite.

"Should we just go back?" Tiff asks after Will-am has disappeared again.

"I think we're almost there."

And at that moment, Will-am, skinny and lithe but strong, shows up behind us. I wish I knew the Macushi word for "Boo!"

We reach the ladders leading to the walkway. Will-am urges us up, and not knowing what else to do but follow his gesticulations, we oblige. He follows behind us most of the way up, but when we reach the top, he motions for us to stay with one arm and then he scampers back down.

Confused, we watch him descend. But we spend a few minutes enjoying the view as we wait. I hand Tiffany the camera and take out our water bottle.

"He's coming back up, isn't he?" I ask as I peer down the tower.

"I'm sure he is," Tiffany says. "He probably just forgot something."

"Maybe he needed to piss."

"Maybe."

"I don't see him."

Tiffany looks. "Neither do I."

We cross the bridges from tree to tree, with the view of a high-flying sloth. I take out my binoculars and scan for birds, but there isn't much to see. Plus, we're preoccupied with the fact that it appears Will-am has run away.

A few minutes go by.

I look through the binoculars, not where birds might be but at the ground. "I still don't see him."

"He'll be up," Tiffany says with an encouragement I don't think she feels.

We wait. I pretend to scan the trees.

"He's not coming up," I say.

"Yup." Tiffany agrees.

We wait. Ten minutes.

"Well, if nothing else, once the others realize we've gone missing, they'll come and find us," Tiffany says.

It's not like we couldn't just climb down the towers and hike back to the car. It wasn't far, and it was pretty much a straight shot. Even two gringos like us with about as much wilderness experience as a DVD player could probably make it back without getting lost or dying.

"Well, I don't want him to get in trouble," I say aloud.

"He's drunk," Tiffany says.

"Yeah, but... you know."

She nods.

In that is the knowledge of the hundreds of years in which alcohol has been used as a weapon to destroy indigenous communities. Europeans often paid indigenous tribes in alcohol for work and, in some cases, for sex. While some pre-Columbian people certainly consumed alcohol, it's believed the alcohol was weaker and likely taken more for ritual purposes or specific ailments, not as a recreational drug as it was in European culture for thousands of years. There remains some debate over whether or not indigenous communities are genetically more prone to alcoholism than Europeans, though the best evidence to date is a likely nope. Still, myths persist. Alcohol issues in indigenous communities today may be more about an exploited past, present socio-economic hardship, and racism. But there is little question about the impact of alcoholism in some indigenous communities (though statistically speaking, many indigenous communities tend to drink less alcohol overall than European ones). Like most things, it's freaking complicated. Tiffany and I at least know that.

We wait. Fifteen minutes. Twenty minutes.

"How long is this whole canopy walkway thingy supposed to last?"

"You got me," Tiffany says. I can tell her anger is rising.

Thirty minutes pass... and then we hear, "Huuuu-loooooo."

And there is Will-am, nearly a hundred feet below us, the size of a doll, shouting up at us.

"Hey!" Tiff yells. "Where have you been!?"

Tiffany and I both grew up in Minnesota, where confrontations are almost always avoided, no matter the cost. But that lesson never fully enveloped Tiffany. Her anger is slow to boil, but once it's bubbling, it requires acknowledgment. I, on the other hand, like a good Minnesotan, will take any number of offenses while humming. As Shakespeare says, if a gentleman bites his thumb at me, instead of drawing my sword, I'd inquire after the state of the bitten thumb and offer a Band-Aid.

Will-am doesn't respond to Tiffany's question but just looks wounded.

"Come down," he shouts meekly. "Come down. Time to go."

On the way back, Will-am tries to show us which plants are good for stomachaches, fevers, and menstruation. But we're both clearly sour faced and done with this tour.

When we reach the vehicle, Louis can tell by our faces that something is amiss. As we enter the vehicle, Tiffany just says, "He's drunk, and he left us up there."

We leave it at that, and we leave it with Louis, knowing—hoping really—he may just let the whole thing slide.

I lift my camera bag, shoulder it, and step into the motorized canoe. Breakfast sits heavy in my stomach. It's our last day in Iwokrama, and we're headed to a place called Turtle Mountain.

Truthfully, I just want this day done so we can head home tomorrow. Malachi has sneaked up again, that shadowy, seductive bastard. Perhaps it's because I know we're leaving the forest and am dreading the long trip home, or perhaps the travel weariness has finally overtaken the forest's wonder.

Whatever it is, I'm done with Guyana. I'm done with traveling.

"When you travel, you learn it's possible to be miserable anywhere," my friend's mother likes to say. It's true this morning, at least. Usually, the novelty and adventure keep my depression away, but there are limits even to my enthusiasm.

This morning the motorized canoe passes over the surface of the Esse-quibo River, almost humming like a bird. The blue sky, running from not quite turquoise to ceramic, and white clouds above are doubled in the wide, slow-moving river below.

Our driver turns the motorized canoe toward a smaller riverine branch just off the Essequibo, and we soon hum into trees standing out of the water, a flooded forest. The boat makes its way through the branches, as if we'd climbed halfway up the trees, gliding slowly till we reach land.

The driver drops us off, and the three of us, Tiff, Louis, and myself, hop out onto the dry ground and head up the path leading to Turtle Mountain. The hike isn't particularly long, a couple of hours, but it's steep and momentarily grueling in the tropical humidity.

At one point, we have to crawl under a spider web the size of a floor rug, thousands of strands between the understory. Whether this is the work of one particularly industrious, hobbit-sized spider or a multitude of arachnids, I don't know. The latter seems more likely.

A little later, Louis stops and crouches. We follow behind quietly. He puts a finger to his lips, and I can see a few yards out the outline of a large bird paused mid-step and looking through the gloom, but not at us.

"A tinamou," Louis whispers.

The tinamou resembles a grouse, only with a longer neck and a more svelte body. Thick feathers and fat are less needed here. While it can fly, poorly, it far prefers the ground.

The bird looks regal in the ever-present dusk of the forest floor, like a prince surveying his domain, however small. The tinamou stays awhile, then makes its way deeper into the forest, living a life wholly unknown to us, mysterious in every way.

Drenched in sweat, we finally reach the top. The mountain is only 538 feet above sea level. In the United States we'd call this a hill, but we started at sea level. Just beyond the trees, at the summit, are massive rock slabs overlooking the great forest of Iwokrama. We set down our bags and sit in the sun on the pinnacle of Turtle Mountain.

For a few minutes, we watch a troop of spider monkeys below us making their way along the branches—their limbs long, hairy, and coal black—with an adroitness that requires marveling. These large monkeys spend nearly their entire lives among the canopy, rarely ever setting a prehensile foot on the ground.

The Essequibo River winds below like a silvery road to the gods, and on all sides lie forest, unbroken, unblemished, alive with the brightness of photosynthesizing green. The sun, no longer behind the clouds, sends flickers of transient gold along the river's surface and the green-reflecting leaves. From our rock slab in the sky, the world looks young once again.

And I recall why we came, why I travel, and why I would continue to do so, despite Steve and Malachi. It's to behold places like this. I want to know as many worlds within this one as possible—and there are so many. But also, as the youthful burgeoning journalist that I am at that time, it's to do my utmost, with whatever talents God has granted, to safeguard places like this. I feel that afternoon, not only the sublime beauty of our little planet, but a purpose rising in my soul.

During our last dinner, as we tuck in, the bats come again from above us, like dark angels, one by one until a dozen or more are circling the dining area's atmosphere. Tiffany is about to dig into her chicken and rice when guano strikes her plate, a smattering of black pellets filled with desiccated insect bits.

A final goodbye from our nightly hosts.

PART THREE

Nature
Disturbed

Chapter Six

Of Diplomats and Palm Oil

FALL 2009

The train pulls away, and I wrap my fingers around the small plastic tiger in my pocket. I am going on a trip. I am going to Asia for the *first time*. And, most notably, I'm doing this without Tiffany.

I've only just left her at the train station a few minutes ago, but already I feel a rising mix of panic, excitement, and resignation. I haven't traveled solo since being diagnosed with OCD. And the last time (six years before), I nearly lost it during a particularly Kafkaesque trip to Bucharest. I clutch the little plastic tiger—the only one we could find last minute was all white with black stripes—but don't remove it from my pocket.

I can do this, I tell myself. *I want to do this.*

We've been living in Santa Fe now for two years, and my therapist there encapsulated everything about the city's reputation. Liberal, radical, and mystical—in a good way.

After learning my personal history, she began guided therapeutic imagery sessions with me, a sort of blend of meditation, hypnotism, and psychotherapy.

I was skeptical at first, thinking, *Well, we've entered kooky land now*. But then I think I entered kooky land when I started digging through my feces.

It went something like this. I laid on the couch. Literally. She told me to breathe. She said when to breathe in and when to breathe out. She asked me to imagine my ten-year-old self, just after my mother had crashed and burned.

"How do you feel?"

"Lost."

"Where are you?"

"In the woods."

"There is an animal," she said. "It's your spirit animal. What is it?"

"A giant cat." My answer surprised me. I would've figured a wolf since I'd always loved wolves.

"What kind of cat?"

"I don't know. Just a really big cat, like a tiger, but not a tiger."

"What do you say to this cat?"

"What do I say?"

"Yes, talk to it. It can hear you and understand."

"I guess I am...um...I ask for its protection?"

"That's good. Protection from what?"

"I don't know. Everything?"

"It says yes."

And then things got really weird, as if my bubbling cauldron of a subconscious (double, double, toil, and trouble) wasn't weird enough. I found myself getting on the cat, like it's a horse, and riding it bareback out of the forest.

Forget Freud, though. It's not sexual. The sensation was one of freedom, maybe even healing.

When I left the appointment that afternoon, I was surprised at how light I felt. The desert sun turned everything aglow and hot as I got into my car and headed home.

To prepare for my trip, my therapist said that I should buy a totem. Her word, not mine. "Just buy a little something that reminds you of that cat, that big cat you rode out of the forest."

"Isn't that kind of pagan, Harry Potter magic?" I asked.

"You don't have to believe that a totem is magic," she said. "You don't have to believe it will protect you or perform miracles or anything like that. But it's often helpful for people to have something physical, something tangible that they can touch that represents an important image or symbol to them. It could be a cross or a moon or a Star of David. But I think yours right now is a cat."

So, on the day before I am to leave, I run one last errand and find a small plastic white-and-black-striped cat made by the toy company Safari Ltd. This plastic cat accompanied me on the train from Santa Fe to Albuquerque, the flights from Albuquerque to Los Angeles to Taipei to Kota Kinabalu. It came with me to the Coral Triangle to the Kinabatangan River and the forests of Tabin. And whenever I felt homesick or scared or anxious, I stuck my hand into my pocket and stroked my cat.

Okay, maybe it *was* sexual.

I awake my first morning in Kota Kinabalu at 6 AM to the *adhan*, or Muslim call to prayer, as it rolls softly through my dark room—shades drawn against the rising sun—like a slow-churning river, a cry of beauty. The whole little hotel room is filled with song and then silence and sleep.

Hours later, I wake again. After dressing and brushing my teeth, I hop the elevator and take it down to the lobby for a hotel breakfast of hearty noodles and toast with jam.

Kota Kinabalu, which is named after the stunning nearby mountain of Kinabalu (Kota means "city" in Malay), is the capital of Sabah, the state that makes up northern Borneo, the world's third-largest island. Borneo is politically split between three countries: Indonesia owns just under three-fourths of the country in a territory called Kalimantan. At the other extreme, the tiny country of Brunei (smaller than Yellowstone National Park) makes up just 1 percent of Borneo. Finally, Malaysia owns a smidge over a quarter of the island, split between two provinces: Sarawak and Sabah.

I'm in the capital of the latter for a two-day colloquium on Orangutans vs. Palm Oil (not the official name), followed by a week visiting various sites across the province.

The whole trip happened quite suddenly. On August 14, 2009, Rhett got an email inviting him to this emergency colloquium. But he would be in Madagascar during that time because that's how Rhett does. So within a couple of days, I was booked. Then on September 29, just over a month later, my plane touched down halfway across the world. The short timeline was psychologically helpful. The less time I have to freak out about an upcoming trip, the better.

What would be really great is if I could just wake up one morning and be told over breakfast, "You're leaving in an hour for two weeks in Mozambique. Here's your ticket, here's your itinerary, here's your Malarone, and here are your packed bags. We've been giving you vaccines while you sleep. Don't forget to kiss your wife goodbye!"

After breakfast, I head back to my room to spend way too much time staring at my room. Just like Nairobi seven years prior, I'm attempting to raise the courage required to leave the confines of the hotel, to see a little of the city and not spend all day hiding away, which is what I most want.

I give myself a pep talk.

"You came all this way, Jeremy. You can do this."

"Really?"

"It's a new continent."

"Yes, but—"

"Come on, dude, what's the worst that could happen?"

"Uhhh . . . I have a list. It's 573 items long."

"My bad."

"There's an addendum, too."

"Yeah, okay. But you didn't come here to sit in a hotel room. Look at your cat, dude."

I pull the cat out of my pocket, still shiny with its newness. "Well, shit," I say, stick it back into my pocket, and head to the elevator again.

At the lobby, I nod confidently to the hotel clerk and then force my legs, *step one, step two*, toward the front doors, which slide open, revealing the world beyond: a parking lot. But a parking lot in fucking *Borneo*.

The island of Borneo, a name that, at least in the West, conjures images of exoticism and jungle, has been inhabited by humans for a very long time, far longer than the Americas. In 2018, archeologists announced the discovery of what's been called "the oldest figurative art" in the world. It's not in Africa or Europe but a cave in Indonesian Borneo.

Forty thousand years ago, a group of humans made a difficult climb up a forested limestone peak to reach remote caves. There they painted the animal that sustained them: the banteng. A species of wild cattle, banteng still roam parts of Borneo today, though in much-depleted numbers. One of the bantengs on the cave wall, ochre in color, looks engorged like a tick—perhaps it's pregnant? Another appears to have a spear in its belly.

Was this a kind of religious ritual or simply a desire to leave something of their thoughts and lives behind, as so many humans have done since? For whatever reason, they made the climb and the message of their existence has reached us two thousand generations in the future.

What would they make of Borneo today?[1]

I breathe and wander the streets with no real destination, just to see this place. I stroll past market stalls selling unrecognizable fruits and vegetables, shops selling bubble tea, electronic stores advertising new cell phones and minutes. Everything is modern, colorful, and bustling.

I'm surprised by something missing from Kota Kinabalu: the obvious markers of urban poverty. The streets are clean, I encounter no beggars, and shops sell goods that look as modern as any back home. There are no signs of slums, no homeless children wandering the back alleys, and no old people whiling away their last days on street corners. Instead, shops and restaurants inhabit endless pastel-colored strip malls or the ground floor of apartment buildings. After South America and Africa (and, let's be honest, New York City), I expected a similar experience here, signs of a so-called developing country.

Kota Kinabalu immediately feels more like a European city than a Latin American or African one. Not European in terms of culture (the culture here is wildly unfamiliar) but in terms of affluence. Indeed, comparing international poverty rates as defined by the World Bank—the number of people living on less than $1.90 a day—the United States has a *higher* poverty rate (1.2 percent) than Malaysia (zero percent). Of course, 1.2 percent may not sound like much, but that still means about 4 million people in the United States survive (or die) on less than $700 a year.

Despite the lack of visible urban poverty, everything else feels exotic, unknown, and different: the food, the flowers beautifying the city, the faces. I remember stopping outside a mosque, wondering what it looked like inside but uncertain whether this was a place I, a foreigner and non-Muslim, could, or should, enter. I don't, not because I'm incurious, but because I want to be respectful. Over 60 percent of Sabah is Muslim, although allegations continue that some of the population, including indigenous people, have been forced to convert.

I head back to the hotel after my little sojourn, feeling I've done my bit. I got out. I walked some of the city. Now I can lie in bed in my closet-sized room, put my feet up, and read *Our Mutual Friend* (apparently, I really like to read Dickens in the tropics). I feel like this trip might go even smoother than I'd anticipated.

Lucky tiger.

I've always wanted to see a giant clam. I'm not sure a lot of young boys in the 1980s shared my ambition, but then I was never one to run with the crowd.

This means on my second full day in Borneo, I find myself sucking on a snorkel and spitting out seawater in the Coral Triangle, the most wildlife-rich region of the world's vast singular ocean.

I can trace my desire to witness a giant clam to when I was five, my first visit to Disneyland. I remember an explosion of bubbles and then sudden clarity at the bottom of the tropical sea before the giant maws of clams appeared, bubbles shooting out of them and up to the surface like carbonated soda. For some reason—and it's difficult to know why in childhood—these monster clams dominate my memory of the park's *Submarine Voyage* ride, while more fantastic things like the sea serpent, mermaids, and even the Lost City of Atlantis have fallen away. Perhaps it's because the clams are based on something real, something no less wondrous, that exists beneath the waves of our world.

Admittedly, I'm not exactly adept in the water. Growing up in Minnesota, I was at least a thousand miles from the ocean on all sides. Minnesota has plenty of lakes, though, around twelve thousand by the last count, and for a time my parents had a cheap pool, so I should probably be a better swimmer than I am. But I was never much of an athletic kid (shocking, I know!), and when I did swim, I mostly focused on splashing. I never took the time to develop a technique, so it's pretty much moving my arms a lot, kicking my legs, and hoping for the best.

Luckily, we are in shallow water with scenery that looks like it's been pulled from the cover of *Travel + Leisure* magazine: resplendent beaches, rainforest islands practically bursting with green, and water so clear it could be glass.

With snorkel on, I break through. On the seafloor, only a few yards deep, my giant clams are just filter feeding their day away, not animatronic falsities but real living creatures. They are breathtakingly beautiful. Their ribbed shells like plumped lips open to reveal a rainbow mantle beneath, which appears to sparkle and ripple in the sunlight. Such giant clams are key to healthy tropical ecosystems, for they recycle nutrients, take in carbon dioxide, and produce oxygen, as well as provide a home and food for several hanger-on species. Indeed, these real-life clams prove far more stunning than those built for Disney, though significantly smaller.

The largest of the giant clams I see is about eighteen inches across. A far cry from what I've long dreamed of. It's not that truly giant clams don't, or didn't, exist, but they are super rare now after hundreds of years of plundering. Their meat is a delicacy in a number of cultures, and, of course, their massive shells are often sought as decorations. The biggest in the species *Tridacna gigas* have vanished from most of the world, plundered by diving *Homo sapiens*.

The Disneyland ride was discontinued in 1994, after twenty-three years, and replaced with a *Finding Nemo* ride, little more than a commercial for the film and lacking the adventurous wonder and awe of the original. Yes, I have devolved into a grumpy Disney critic now. Also, kids these days.

My next few days in Sabah are taken up with the colloquium. Palm oil industry figures make speeches about their environmental stewardship, conservationists make dueling presentations using actual data, something lacking from the palm oil side, showing how plantations have trapped hundreds of orangutans in shrinking habitats due to vast deforestation.

The once abundant great ape, the only one left in Asia, is vanishing.

And everyone grumbles about the other. Then we all eat luxurious meals and sleep on comfy beds in the five-star Shangri-La Rasa Ria Resort, all paid for by the Malaysian Palm Oil Council (MPOC).

The MPOC is a notoriously dissembling industry group, but like most such industry groups, flush as hell. Think of the oil companies in America. The whole colloquium was kicked off by Mongabay reporting three months earlier that then head of the MPOC, Dr. Yusof Basiron, claimed orangutans "benefit" from living next to oil palm plantations. They don't. Unless by benefit he meant slowly starve or get shot. Basiron added that orangs have year-round access to a buffet of oil palm fruit, giving them a "healthy shining coat." He seriously said that.

The reality is orangutans eat four hundred types of plants in the wild, and when they lose the forest, they not only lose their homes but their grocery stores, too. They tend to slowly die when trapped in small forest remnants by oil palm plantations, or they are shot since they are considered nuisance animals to the industry—as are elephants.

So when sparring between the industry and conservationists hit an eleven, the industry did what it does best: It threw a two-day luxury meeting. I'm here only because MPOC allowed local NGOs to pick some journalists to attend.

Oil palm is a fruit that when compressed creates a thick edible oil. Technically, oil palm refers to the plant and the fruit, while palm oil refers to the oil created after refining, but increasingly people just use "palm oil" for everything. At the time of the colloquium, the oil was in wide use across much of Asia and was beginning to storm the United States and Europe. But it came with a cost: endless miles of rainforests and peatlands razed for plantations, leading to the mass obliteration of wildlife and equally insane emissions of carbon, further heating up our melting, desiccating, burning world.

Not that long ago, Borneo was pretty much forest from one end to the other. Of course, there were villages, cities, roads, and trails, but most settlements would have stuck to the coasts or the larger rivers, and the vast majority of the landscape would be rainforest, some of it over 140 million years old and inhabited by hundreds of thousands of creatures.

That Borneo no longer exists.

Beginning in the 1960s, Borneo suffered a frenzy of industrial logging unmatched anywhere in human history. Sabah and Sarawak, the island's Malaysian states, first began mass logging to feed the insatiable appetites of Americans, Europeans, and Japanese for things like outdoor furniture, paper packaging, and throwaway chopsticks. In Kalimantan, Indonesian dictator Suharto handed out swaths of forests as gifts to top military cronies. In total, Borneo has lost around *half* of its forest cover, an area nearly the size of California. And only a quarter has never been logged. All that destruction in less than one human's life span.[2]

At the resort, the palm oil executives are desperate to make themselves and their industry look like golden boys. Meanwhile, the conservationists are simply desperate to get the industry to make some changes that would give orangutans and other species a better chance at long-term survival, namely connect rainforest areas via forest corridors so animals could move through and around plantations.

It's as if David and Goliath spend two days being polite to each other while sniping behind backs. And then eventually Goliath walks away and does what he will anyway, and David would never be the David of myth, but instead takes a couple orangutans in hand, puts them in an orphanage, and walks off into the long dark night called the modern world.

Where is the government in all this? They are there, in some cases hob-nobbing with the palm oil executives and in others courageously pleading with the industry to change some of its ways: to stop polluting rivers, to build forest corridors, and to act as a steward of the remaining forests. But it becomes quickly clear who holds the real power, and it's not the Sabah government democratically elected by the people. It's the industry. Welcome to neoliberal economics, where corporations, like vampires, slowly suck out the power that had once been entrusted by the people to their elected governments.

At this point, I am still very new to this whole journalism thing. I've only graduated from St. John's that spring and been working full time as a journalist for four months. And the whole thing—the posturing, the politics, and the lies combined with cultural norms that I don't understand—makes my head spin.

But for all the colloquium's focus on orangutans, I feel this is missing the ocean for the boat. Palm oil isn't just about orangutans; it's about hundreds of thousands of rainforest-loving species, many of them undiscovered, unnamed, unstudied. The cure for cancer could be bulldozed for the next oil palm plantation, just as it could be for the next cattle pasture in Brazil or the next rubber plantation in Cambodia.

And beyond the myriad life forms, the rainforests of Borneo cool the climate, both locally and globally, providing a service that's needed more than ever now. Destroying forests releases tremendous amounts of carbon dioxide into the atmosphere, while preserving them is probably our most efficient and cheapest way to fight global warming. It's also the best way to stave off mass extinction and maybe, just maybe, to give our kids a world that isn't on its knees.

Yet, we can't seem to do it.

Despite all the posturing, the colloquium results in something significant. The palm oil industry makes a bunch of surprising pledges, including wildlife corridors between forest patches and a little over one-half-mile buffer zones along all major rivers.

Still, one conservationist tells me that they think the whole thing is just "another publicity stunt" for the palm oil industry. "I just really doubt that there's an ounce of sincerity in the organization," they say over breakfast one morning.

It's a moment when all the BS seems to fade away, like dew attacked by the morning sun. (Ten years later, the industry has still not made good on its pledges from that meeting.)

The day after the colloquium's dust settles, I head out into the bush to get a firsthand look at what this whole thing is really about.

I can see the orangutan's face flanked by leaves, peering at me like some wild, hairy red woman. She has an expression of stoic resignation, a kind of long, drawn-out sigh. I feel as if I've time-traveled back into some distant age and met an unnamed ancestor. Then the red ape retires, the foliage closing behind her.

This isn't a wild animal. Well, she's more like half-wild, half-captive. The young adult female is in a rehabilitation program at the Sepilok Orangutan Center. The world's first orphanage for orangutans (opened in 1964), Sepilok takes in orangutans that have lost their mothers due to the illegal pet trade, logging, or plantations.

The first part of the center feels a bit like an overcrowded zoo, with dozens of young orangutans hanging out and feeding in a small forest area. They are all juveniles living communally and learning from older mentors that act as the mothers they've lost to bulldozers and bullets. In the wild, orangutans spend their first eight years wholly in the care of their mothers, who will nurse their infants for six months.

Once the apes have graduated from this stage, they are allowed to roam freely in an adjacent forest to help strengthen their survival skills. On a walkway near the top of the rainforest canopy is where I have a fleeting meeting with the female.

Sepilok is no longer an anomaly. There are now numerous orphanages for orangutans. Many are overrun with the gentle apes as oil palm as well as pulp and paper plantations continue to raze their homes. Some are trying to rehabilitate the orangutans to a point where they could be released into the wild, but *where* remains an open question. Every year we destroy more of their forest home.

To get to Sepilok, I and a couple of orangutan researchers have flown in from Kota Kinabalu on the western end to Sandakan on the eastern, almost two hundred miles.

Sabah is shaped like the profile of a bi-horned dragon facing east. And Sandakan is its eye.[3] The horns are the Kudat and Bengkoka Peninsulas. The Dent Peninsula forms the upper jaw and the Semporna Peninsula, along with Bum Bum Island (yes, it's really called that), is the lower jaw. The capital, Kota Kinabalu, rests on the nape of the dragon's neck, overlooking the South China Sea.

From Sandakan and the orangutan orphanage of Sepilok, we head nearly two hours to the village of Sukau lying on the Kinabatangan River. The entire drive punctuates the colloquium: oil palm plantations as far as the eye can see. I put my camera out the window and just *snap, snap, snap* then switch to video. Two hours through an ocean of palm fronds.

A plantation has a certain beauty to it. Euclidean lines of palm trees paired by paths vanishing into the distance. Each tree is a single trunk crowned by massive fan-like fronds that create a pergola-like structure down a straight path. Everything is the same height, the same width, the same age. There is a certainty not found in the messy complexity of a real forest.

"Trace lines across the slope and put in your pegs in straight lines; leave 7.8 meters between rows and 9 meters between pegs," reads a manual in the Food and Agriculture Organization's Better Farming Series from 1967. At the time, the manual was written only in French and printed for the African grower. This species, now planted across much of Southeast Asia, is actually from another continent, the African oil palm or *Elaeis guineensis*.

"In this way you can plant 143 oil palms per hectare; this is the best density."

As we drive, I think about something one of the MPOC figures said during the colloquium in a rare moment of candor. "Wildlife protection has been one issue where the oil palm industry finds itself in unfamiliar territory," he stated. "After all, we are planters who do what we do best."

A few decades ago, the area around Sukau and Sandakan was home to rainforest recovering from extensive logging and small-scale farming by local people. Today, it belongs to the planters.

There was a hill I loved in my hometown. Driving toward home, you could see it rising along to the right, like the great hump of some grassy whale. Often the sunlight would shower the grass, making it seem as though the little hill wore a golden halo.

Today, the hill has been taken over by housing developments.

So many places have been lost in my hometown, it's hard to keep track. None of them, of course, were what one would call forest or wilderness. All that was destroyed by white settlers, my ancestors, over a century ago. But small groves of trees or grassy areas of untilled lands once abounded. To a child, these places all seemed large and wonderful and brimming with magic and wonder.

Now, most of them have been turned into McMansion developments, houses so big a family of five has a hard time locating one another after the doors are shut.

When I was born, Buffalo was a small farming town of fewer than five thousand people. Today, it's more than three times that size. It lies in the exurbs of the Twin Cities of Minneapolis and St. Paul, a part of the state that has been consistently swallowed by poorly planned sprawl.

I have always viewed the loss of nature as a wound, something that feels physically painful to my being. As a child, the destruction of nature just hurt; as a teenager, I funneled that pain into rage; and as an adult, it's like a well of sadness. I'm now armed with a decade of writing about the destruction of the natural world. I know all the reasons why we've taken this course: the rising human population, the embrace of unfettered capitalism, the stain of materialism, the all-too-human addiction to money and power. I get it.

But I also see more and more that the world could be different. That this wasn't the course we had to take, and it's not the course we *have* to take.

And that makes me sad. Not resigned, not hopeless, not enraged, just a sorrow that ripples beneath the more tumultuous nature of my daily emotions, like the deep ocean under a mighty storm.

Despite all I heard at the colloquium, I'm honestly surprised at the extent of the oil palm, the unbridled success of the planters against everything else.

Finally, we arrive in the town of Sukau and see the winding jungle river that is known as the Kinabatangan. Likely bestowed by Chinese traders centuries ago, the word *Kinabatangan* stems from Chinese, meaning "long river." Indeed, the Kinabatangan runs 350 miles from the interior mountains to the eastern coastline.

Once a small village, Sukau has become a tourist mecca for those interested in seeing the splendid wildlife of the Long River. Its once small-scale farmers and fishers now turned into tour guides and guesthouse managers. They didn't have much choice after the oil palm plantations took over the forest where they had planted and hunted. And, arguably worse, the plantations then decimated the great Kinabatangan and its rich fish life with the unmanaged runoff of fertilizers, herbicides, and pesticides (nearly 40 percent of freshwater fish in Borneo are found nowhere else).

We pull into a local guesthouse, and it is here we finally meet Diplomat and Diplomat's Assistant. While the pair are stationed in another country in Southeast Asia, they are tagging along with our motley crew of orangutan researchers, journalists, and NGO employees for the next two days.

Diplomat looks like a middle-aged high school football coach with his full face, short hair, small nose, and white-man khaki dress. He likes to wear sunglasses against the tropical light, and you can just picture him running around the field yelling, "Goaaaaaalllllllll!" Or whatever it is that football coaches say. I don't know.

Meanwhile, Diplomat's Assistant is thin and lanky. He's in his mid-twenties with a wife and baby back in whatever tropical country they're stationed. He has a constantly harried look about him because, we soon realize, he's constantly fetching things, making calls, and coming up with excuses for Diplomat. At times, an expression of resentment flashes in his eyes, but it's quickly gone. He's nice enough, but it appears his entire existence is wrapped around moving up the ladder of government hierarchy, like the Russian officials that populate the novels of Tolstoy and Dostoevsky.

Diplomat's Assistant also wears sunglasses against the tropical light.

It's not that I'm coy about revealing the country where US Diplomat serves, but Diplomat and Diplomat's Assistant are very careful about not saying where they serve, as if doing so would betray some state secret.

We all have a tropical siesta. It's wonderful to lie in the afternoon humidity of my very much non-five-star room in a guesthouse overlooking the Kinabatangan's waters and do nothing. I place my plastic kitty on the side table along with my sweat-soaked money bag, which holds my passport, credit cards, and cash and goes with me pretty much everywhere. I take some deep breaths.

I tend to be quite adept socially when I need to, but it's friggin' exhausting. I realized only in my late thirties that I'm more introverted than extroverted —like so many things, it's a spectrum—something that left me a bit shocked.

While I love socializing, I'm deeply sensitive to the emotions of others. Too much makes me feel like a straw-inserted milkshake that's been sucked dry. And to recover I need to be alone, preferably with a book.

I listen to the sounds of the river and read *Our Mutual Friend* and feel glorious in the silence. For a couple of hours, at least, there's nothing but me and my prudish pal, Victorian England.

Dinner arrives as dusk falls over the river, the water turning from a milky dark blue to purplish black and then dark gray. The guesthouse serves us a splendid repast of fish, rice, noodles, and various Bornean sauces. We sit together and eat. Soon, my head gets lighter due to the beer in my hand, and I start asking questions of Diplomat.

"What's it like since Obama took over?" "What are the biggest challenges in the region?" "And what's the best thing to eat in Southeast Asia?"

"Okay, okay," I say, sufficiently tipsy. "I've never understood this. Can you explain diplomatic immunity to me?"

Diplomat sits back, twines his fingers, smiles. He takes a deep breath. "Well, let's say I get caught raping a young girl..."

For a moment I wonder if I heard him right. The whole table goes silent. Everyone stops eating for a moment and eyes focus on Diplomat. Well, I guess I did. Oblivious, Diplomat blithely continues his explanation of what would happen, which is basically that he couldn't be charged for it.

But all our heads tilt in a way that expresses our collective disbelief. Meanwhile, Diplomat's Assistant has lowered his eyes in consternation.

"Oh, I'd probably be kicked out of the country, but I'd never have to worry about a trial or jail time because I'm immune. And so that's basically what diplomatic immunity is."

Thanks, Diplomat man. That was probably the least diplomatic (and most god-awful creepy) response to that question possible.

But out loud, I respond with something to the effect of, "Oh...okay."

And Diplomat leans back in his chair and smiles as if he'd settled that like a fucking ambassadorial pro.

✧ ✧ ✧

The next morning, we boat out onto the Kinabatangan. The wild things are abundant. Proboscis monkeys, whose males sport one of the most splendid schnozzes in the animal kingdom, hang out on massive trees bending over the river. A pair of Asian small-clawed river otters, small as Chihuahuas and much cuter, pop out onto one of the banks, look at us, and then disappear into the forest. Violet kingfishers dip along the river as the boat passes, creating an arc of color from bank to bank. Large monitor lizards slouch in the gloom, and at the water's edge I remember the bloating carcass of a dead pig, the water still tickling its hairs.

An orangutan, this one wild and free as anything can be in this world, hangs nearly upside down from a fruit tree on the adjacent bank. Our boat driver pulls the vessel aside, and we watch our kin for a good ten minutes. At one point the ape looks back at us, as if to say, "Come on, haven't you had your fill? I'm just trying to do my thing here. Can I please do it in peace?" And at that moment, the driver starts the boat again and off we go.

But with all the Kinabatangan's abundance comes a harsher truth: Just beyond the banks of the Kinabatangan stand trees perfectly spaced 7.8 meters apart. Some of the palm oil companies illegally plant straight up to the river, the messy jungle making way for human order. The plantations in the Kinabatangan floodplains have forced the animals into small pockets and corridors, making them easy for tourists to see but imperiling any future their descendants might have.

Ironically, the one animal we don't see on our boat trips is the largest in all of Borneo: the pygmy elephant. Although it's lovingly called pygmy, it's still friggin' huge, just a little shorter than mainland Asian elephants. No one knows how these elephants made it to Borneo, but there are two competing theories. One is that they crossed into Borneo via land bridges hundreds of thousands of years ago, but to date, no one has discovered any fossil evidence of elephants on the island. The other is that this population are descendants of a gift of elephants to the Sultan of Sulu by the East Indian Company in 1750. Reports say these elephants were eventually let loose in the forests of northern Borneo. Genetic evidence so far supports the first theory that the elephants are, in fact, native to Borneo, having migrated across land bridges from Sumatra. But scientific consensus still awaits.

Like so many species in Borneo, the elephants are vanishing. Oil palm plantations don't like elephants because they tend to destroy young palms, so plantations routinely shoot and poison elephants. Meanwhile, the loss of habitat has pushed elephants and humans ever closer, leading to conflict with casualties on both sides. The latest survey estimated anywhere from a thousand to three thousand, six hundred Bornean pygmy elephants left.

Despite the beauty of the Kinabatangan, the whole experience leaves me struggling against sadness. A wildlife sanctuary has been set up on the lower Kinabatangan River, but the sanctuary covers only haphazard and often disconnected forest fragments, leaving the rest to oil palm. Species are having to migrate farther to find food or attempt repeated perilous transects through plantations. Behaviors are changing in a bid to survive. For example, orangutans here have been caught on camera moving across the ground, an abnormal and vulnerable behavior for the red ape; elephants have been photographed ducking impossibly under barbed wire into plantations in a bid to migrate for food. Still, the palm oil industry has foiled any attempts to turn the Kinabatangan Wildlife Sanctuary into a full national park or further restrict destruction.

Unless measures are taken, the wildlife abundance we see today will almost certainly dwindle over time—until most of these animals of the Long River will vanish altogether, with a few smaller species hanging on, but bleakly. And if that happens, no one will visit Sukau anymore.

The next morning, we all pile into a couple of cars to visit a set of nearby caves.

Diplomat seems to constantly forget that we, i.e., the other travelers in this group, are not his help. No, Diplomat, I'm not going to carry your luggage for you (your assistant will, though!). I'm not going to fetch your shoes or find your sunglasses or massage your sore shoulders.

As we drive, we pass, again, a seemingly unending expanse of oil palm.

"Oooh," Diplomat exclaims. "What's that out there?"

"Oil palm plantations," one of the researchers tells him.

"Huh. Interesting. They must be very climate friendly with all those trees sucking up carbon."

No one says a thing, but we all roll our eyes.

I wonder how someone working in Southeast Asia could remain so blithely uninformed. But if Diplomat is characteristic of those representing the most powerful country in the world, perhaps it's little wonder the world is the way it is.

When we part, Diplomat gives me his card, I think as a means of getting me out of trouble in case I should happen to get into it. I keep it for years in my wallet because it makes me smile whenever I see his name gilded in gold. Now I regret tossing it into the recycling one day. I mean, whom will I call the next time I end up in an Asian jail?

At the last possible moment before my trip kicked off, I tacked on four extra days for a stop at Tabin Wildlife Reserve. I did this for one reason: a rhino named Tam.

A little over a year before, a Bornean rhino walked into an oil palm plantation. He'd recently been caught in a snare trap, probably set by oil palm workers for pigs or deer, and has a white scar around one of his forelegs to prove it. A couple of workers found him wandering below the shadows of the endless fronds, and instead of butchering him—as had been done to a female rhino seven years earlier—they called the authorities.

To understand how insane a Bornean rhino walking into an oil palm plantation in 2008 was, you have to understand that at the time, scientists believed only forty survived across the island (they were wrong—it was far fewer). It was such a rare animal even then that few locals had ever seen one, or even knew they existed. When I asked a forest ranger and guide if he'd ever seen a rhino, he told me had once, when he was a boy. He was now in his fifties and had spent his whole life in Sabah's forests.

Tam was rescued and brought to a hastily built enclosure in Tabin Wildlife Reserve, a park established in 1984, in part because conservationists still believed rhinos lived there.

The Bornean rhino is a subspecies of the Sumatran rhino. A subspecies is a lower class of species, i.e., the animals are more closely related but still distinct.

For example, a coyote and wolf are different species, but a timber wolf and an Indian wolf are different subspecies. Bornean rhinos tend to be a little smaller than other Sumatran subspecies, making them the smallest rhinos on the earth.

When I visit Borneo in 2009, there are an estimated 250 Sumatran rhinos in the world—*total*—including the supposed 40 in Borneo.

This critically endangered species is considered one of the most threatened mammals on Earth. It's also unlike any other rhino on the planet. It's the last survivor of the genus *Dicerorhinus* and the closest living relative of the woolly rhino, which went extinct during the Pleistocene's human blitzkrieg. It's also the oldest rhino on Earth. One might even call it a living fossil of otherwise vanished megafauna.

Like the woolly rhino, the Sumatran rhino is weirdly hairy and sports two horns (in Greek, *Dicerorhinus* means "two-horned nose"). While it is smaller than all other living rhinos, it's still a hefty beastie weighing around two tons.

When I read about Tam, I couldn't pass up the opportunity to meet him.

Back in Kota Kinabalu, the morning after the colloquium, I meet with John Payne and Cynthia Ong. John runs the Bornean Rhino Alliance, BORA, which is charged with Tam's care. At the time, John hoped to breed him, if only they could find a fertile female. I can't visit Tam without his permission. Cynthia, meanwhile, runs a local NGO called LEAP and has become paramount in supporting the state's last rhinos.

Cynthia is a Sabahan and previous expat, having worked in juvenile justice in California. She's one of those rare people who exude a kind of soulful positive energy. John is quite different, at least on the outside. He's prickly and opinionated but whip smart, and when he gets to know you, he is warm and very funny in that wry British way. Although he's lived in Sabah for years, he has little patience for the time it takes to get things done in Asia, which makes it all the crazier when he tells me that in the face of endless bureaucracy and stakeholder meetings, he's devoting the rest of his life to trying to save the species.

I like them both immediately.

John runs through the almost impossible challenges ahead of the program: catching more rhinos, the propensity of females to have uterine tumors, the near impossibility of breeding. The list goes on and on.

When I ask him if he thinks the species is doomed, he shrugs. "Probably. Yet maybe not."

Cynthia, however, focuses on Tam's personality. She tells me how Tam has gotten very *manja* since his capture, a Malay word meaning "lovingly spoiled." She compares him with a housecat. I have a hard time imagining this because, let's be honest, rhinos have a reputation for being grumpy, ornery, and dumb. Charge first, ask questions later. Until this moment, the only rhinos I'd ever seen were in Kenya—charging vans (in their defense, they had cause).

But my date with Tam, who's guarded twenty-four seven by rangers, will have to wait until I can secure permission.

On my first evening in Tabin Wildlife Reserve, we go on a night safari using a spotlight. It's a rowdy bunch: wild pigs leaping in front of the car, owls hunting from the branches, leopard cats—eyeshine like tiny sun-yellow jewels—sitting on their haunches in the brush on the roadside.

As entertaining as it all is, the presence of all these species is due to one reason. Yeah, you guessed it: oil palm. Tabin Wildlife Reserve is enclosed on nearly all sides by vast oil palm plantations. Plantations harbor a ton of rats, hence the abundance of rat-loving leopard cats, owls, and snakes, including venomous cobra. (We saw a juvenile cobra, all black and lithe, as we drove into the park.) Plantations are also havens for animals like wild boar and macaques, species that are willing to eat pretty much anything and can survive, thrive really, alongside humans.

While most species in this part of the world are vanishing due to oil palm, that same palm oil is boosting the numbers of pigs, rats, snakes, and crab-eating macaques, a common monkey in the region.

The next afternoon, after a morning hike and drive, I'm sitting out on my room's porch reading *Our Mutual Friend* when I feel the need to use the bathroom come on me. I head inside, leaving the book for when I return in a few minutes. After using the toilet, I open the door to the porch and—

"Holy fucking shit Jesus Christ—"

A child-sized monkey sits on the porch railing, just above the book. It looks at me with the audacity of one who will not be moved.

"Okay," I say. "Just stay there, little dude. I'm backing up. See, I'm moving away." And I backtrack the few feet to the door, slip through it, close it behind me, and lock it.

The macaque continues to stare at me keenly, but its expression is disturbingly blank, like it's a sociopathic monkey trying to decide what to do next about this other, bigger primate.

Can monkeys have rabies? I wonder. *Of course, they can, stupid; they're mammals!* (Not only can monkeys get rabies, but in tropical countries, they are one of the largest transmitters after dogs.)

Suddenly, another macaque drops down onto the porch. I look up and see the branches of the tree under which I was sitting just a couple minutes ago are now full of monkeys. Full. Like a horror movie.

A few more come down. One sniffs at the book and nudges it, then leaves it alone. Apparently, more of a Thackeray fan. The monkeys are not noisy or riotous, but they just hang out on my porch as if they expect something to happen. They stare at me, waiting. Am I supposed to go outside and feed them? Pet them? Maybe give them each a bath and foot massage?

Fat chance, monkey dudes.

It's a waiting game. They wait for me to do something while I wait for them to leave so I can get my book back and go to supper. There's no way I'm leaving for supper now with a whole troop of macaques staring at me with dead eyes.

Macaques have a terrible reputation in Asia. They steal, plunder, and run wild, generally making a nuisance of themselves, like wicked sprites. But really, I think it's just that they remind us a little bit too much of ourselves. It's disconcerting to see another primate look at you like they know what you did last summer. They are more mirror than monster.

The monkeys stay on my porch—well, really *their* porch since I am, after all, in their rainforest—for a half hour before they grow bored with staring at me with cool menace and head back into the forest.

I don't use my porch again.

But almost every time I look outside now, I see them. Hanging out on neighbors' porches, filling in the wood stairs, taking over the paths. The jungle, it turns out, has eyes.

It's safe to say that Tam changes my life.

To visit him, a flatbed truck picks me up at the lodge in the early morning with several rhino rangers. We drive over rough jungle roads just a few minutes to the lone male rhino.

I can see a man there holding on to a branch while a massive grayish animal, horns blunted, grips the other side. It looks like they are playing tug-of-war for a moment until I see that the rhino is just methodically pulling the branch into its mouth and chewing.

I stand back and watch in awe. He's bigger than I anticipated and hungrier.

One of the men smiles at me and motions me forward. I move toward the pen. It has bars on three sides, but beyond it is a much larger enclosure of rainforest. Tam's little rainforest.

When the last of the foliage is devoured, Tam turns his attention to the foreigner. He presses his massive snout through the bars of the pen and I can hear him. Puffs of air erupt from his flaring nostrils. He's smelling me. He's not afraid. Just curious.

Then Tam calls out to me. It's a sound between a whistle and a squeak, like something coming out of a dolphin, only it's produced by a fourteen-hundred-pound rhino.

"He says, 'I'm still hungry,'" one of the rangers tells me.

Sumatran rhinos are the most vocal rhinos on Earth, making all sorts of noises that are surprising, to say the least, coming from a rhino. They chatter almost constantly. They *sing*.

Without really knowing when I pulled out my camera, I realize I'm taking pictures. I'm taking pictures of his eye, the scar on his snared foot, the long black hair that sparsely covers his grayish skin.

Tam wants to smell the camera. Maybe eat it? He keeps trying to touch it with his snout, just as I feel the desire to touch him. He pushes his snout, his once long front horn blunted from rubbing it against the bars over the last year, toward me. Perhaps it's the sound of *click-click-click* that's attracting him? "What's this? A new sort of insect?"

He rubs his great hefty body against the bars as if in need of a scratch. And a ranger nods to me, clearly seeing that I, too, have a need to touch Tam.

I let myself. I run my hand over his thick hide and the long hairs that curl off. There is something truly surreal about meeting an individual that is one of the last of its kind. Here you are, here the animal is, yet you know the species rests on a ticking clock. I know, even at this moment, that I could very easily live to see this species go extinct. We all could.

When Tam has smelled me to his satisfaction and realizes I don't have food for him, he trudges back to the rangers, who have been busy gathering more foliage, and continues his repast, eating massive rainforest leaves, whole branches, and intestine-looking vines in a crisp, business-like manner.

I spend about an hour with Tam before he heads back into the forest. Satiated after breaking his fast, it's now time for hours soaking in the warm mud of his wallow.

Sumatran rhinos are not necessarily social creatures in the wild. Babies spend two years with their mothers. And males and females will meet up for what can only be described as raucous mating (Sumatran rhinos are pretty S&M—they have to beat each other up a bit before actual mating occurs). But Tam appears, to my nonexpert self, quite taken with being cared for by humans. He seems not only *manja*, lovingly spoiled, but loving it. It's certainly a better life than he had before, stuck in shrinking forest patches, none of his kind anywhere within miles, always smelling man and never knowing if or when man would kill him.

What madness compelled him to walk placidly into an oil palm plantation in broad daylight is beyond me. Desperation is probably the only word that aptly describes Tam's decision. But what luck he survived.

After I leave Borneo, Tam haunts me. And the story of the Sumatran rhino, so close to extinction, yet men and women devoting their lives to its survival, haunts me.

The idea of extinction has always haunted me. As a child, I had a book that depicted endangered species fleeing the shadow of a giant man, covering them like suffocating smoke. It's a terrifying but wholly apt image. Extinction, like death, is forever. Only unlike death, there are no children with extinction, no community, no continuation, nothing. Just oblivion.

After meeting Tam, I'm determined to do what I can, in my small way, to tell the story of this species. Because of him, I think it's safe to say I've written more words today about the Sumatran rhino than any other animal.

On my last day in Asia, I fly from Tabin back to Kota Kinabalu. Rhett asked me to get as many photos as possible of oil palm plantations, and the view from the window is clear and sunny. I take out my camera and shoot quickly as the plane rises.

Alas, Rhett's hopes are dashed. I'm a really shitty photographer. About 95 percent of my shots on the Borneo trip are out of focus. Tiffany is far more adept with a camera, and had she been here, the photos would have, at least, been in focus.

Still, from the plane's eye view, the takeover of oil palm is even clearer than from the ground. The plantations march across the undulating land like conquerors, which, let's be honest, they are. An African tree has successfully conquered Borneo, Sumatra, and is now marching on New Guinea, Latin America, and returning to Africa. Today the price of palm oil has dropped because the industry has sufficiently filled demand. However, instead of saying enough is enough, they are trying to push palm oil as a major biodiesel.

In many ways, the oil palm is a miracle plant. The species produces more edible oil per hectare than any other oil crop, including soy, corn, and rapeseed. This means far more palm oil can be produced on a hectare of land than any of its competitors. If only this point is considered, then palm oil is far better ecologically than any other edible oil.

But the problem is not oil palm itself. The problem has always been where and how companies choose to grow it. They cut rainforests to sell the timber to pay for the first planting; they drain carbon-rich peatlands, thus warming the planet, for a quick buck; they steal land from local communities and indigenous tribes; they wipe out millions of tropical animals and turn complex, multilayered forests into a singularity; they clear land by burning peatlands and forests, creating seasonal hazes that have resulted in the deaths of thousands of people from air pollution.

The big companies have operated with impunity in an industry that began entirely unregulated and today is only marginally so. Some companies have made ambitious pledges but struggle to keep them, while the governments of both Malaysia and Indonesia continue to hand over the reins of regulation to the palm oil producers themselves.

The most infuriating and common argument made by the industry goes something like this: "Well, you Westerners cut down all your forests, so why can't we do the same?"

On the face of it, of course, this statement is absolutely true. Why shouldn't we cut down all the world's rainforest, like Britain cut down the bulk of its forests three thousand years ago, or American settlers destroyed the prairie over the last two hundred years?

The logic of this argument quickly falls apart, though, because it hinges entirely on the assumption that we should always do what we have done, no matter how blindly stupid and immoral. One could make the same silly argument in favor of human sacrifice, genocide, or burning heretics on a raft of flame. Remember slavery?

History need not be a spiral of repeating mistakes.

We also inhabit a different world than that of most of our ancestors. In 1800 we had one billion people on the planet—today we are a population of 7.7 billion and are facing the twin tsunami of mass extinction and climate change, whose impacts on human society will likely be catastrophic. The oil palm industry and the governments involved, whether they like it or not, will have to wrestle with this reality—and the sooner, the better for everyone. The same is true of cattle ranching and soy crops in Brazil, rubber and pulp and paper in Southeast Asia, oil and coal everywhere, and any other number of commodities that are running rampant over the world's last wildernesses.

Conservation is always messy, complicated, and rarely as black and white as either side likes to admit. And I fully understand the need for nations to develop economically; I understand the benefits of better education, health care, and steady eradication of poverty. However, having covered issues across over a hundred countries, I wonder why our approach to development is so blind, stupid, and reckless. Why does GDP always come before the public good? Why do we still think so little about the planet we will leave to our children and grandchildren?

Tam died in 2019. He never fathered a child.

It turns out there weren't forty rhinos left in Borneo. In fact, Tam may well have been the last male Bornean rhino on the planet. Today, a single Bornean female survives in captivity. The subspecies is just a few years away from total obliteration.

So much of writing about nature in the twenty-first century is writing about loss. I've made a career of writing about the most depressing subjects imaginable: extinction, climate change, ocean acidification, deforestation, the plight of indigenous people.

I believe, though, growing up with mental illness in some ways helped prepare me to write on such subjects. I already intimately knew loss and despair. And conversely knew healing and hope.

I experienced firsthand that with time, support, and love, I could heal and have good days again. And I knew that nature, with its inborn resilience, a kind of love, could also heal one day. Maybe I won't be here to see it, but the possibility is always there, like a seed germinating.

These experiences built a kind of armor around me as a journalist. This is not to say I haven't at times felt fear and despair for our collective future. I feel that a lot. But I still hope—it always gleams beneath whatever transient emotions afflict me in the moment. I hope that our descendants will be wiser than us and that they can heal and repair at least some of what we've discarded and desecrated.

I think the kitty in my pocket works, either that or it's the Escitalopram and the countless hours of therapy. But Sabah proves one of my least ludicrous trips yet. Anxiety, of course, but no major panic attacks, no wholly ridiculous mishaps. Ever since then, I don't leave home without a totem. Sometimes it's a tiger again; sometimes, though, it's an otter or maybe a pangolin. Sometimes I forget to stuff it into my pocket and have to buy something small at the airport. It's still nice, after all these years, to have something to physically clutch.

Maybe, I think when I get home from Borneo, exhausted beyond belief, *maybe I'm a kickass traveler after all. Maybe I'm the Meryl Streep of traveling. Maybe Tiff and I should spend a year abroad doing that whole encircle the world thing. Maybe…* and then I fall asleep and spend the next few days in bed, debilitated and recovering.

Two years after I leave Tabin Wildlife Reserve, a woman dies there, gored to death by a male pygmy elephant. Her name is Jenna O'Grady Donley. She is just twenty-six and a veterinarian in her native Australia. According to press reports, she was photographing a lone male elephant when it charged her, a friend, and a guide. The latter two managed to escape, but Jenna didn't.

Incidents such as this are incredibly rare, almost freakishly so. However, the story has stuck with me for years. As a traveler like her, I stayed in the same lodge and walked the same trails, and if I'd seen a male elephant, I'm certain, like her, I would have tried to photograph it. Elephants can move fast—running at fifteen miles per hour. When frightened or spooked, they can be mortally aggressive.

Jenna was likely a better traveler than I, less prone to panicking and sobbing, but that didn't help her against the randomness of tragedy.

One of the undercurrents of OCD is a desire to achieve control over the uncontrollable, which is pretty much all of life. It's a belief that, if I just obsess enough about horror, I can stop horror from happening. If I turn off all these lights in a specific order, then the house won't burn down. If I wash my hands ten times before bed, I won't catch pneumonia. If I circle my neighborhood twice before getting onto the freeway, I won't have an accident.

But none of us live in a world we can control. Elephants are perilous. Travel is perilous. Staying at home is perilous. Life is perilous. And it always ends one way, sooner or later.

I try to tell myself this daily. I try to convince myself of it. But still, Steve rears his Stevey head. "Hey, Jeremy, if you spend forty-seven hours thinking about plane crashes, that will cut your chances of being in a plane crash by at least forty-seven percent."

Thanks. Helpful as always, Steve.

Chapter Seven

The World According to Yasuni

SUMMER 2010

I open the door and get into the cab of the stranger's truck.

I don't speak Spanish. He doesn't speak English. The only thing we have connecting us is that, when my plane landed at Francisco de Orellana Airport an hour ago, he was outside holding a piece of paper with my name on it.

Even if he could speak English, I'm not sure he would. He has a strong build, a scruffy mustache, and a cowboy hat. He looks like a cutout of the taciturn machismo type, a common archetype of these frontier Amazon towns.

El Coca is a rough, tumbling, chaotic oil town, resting at the pivot between the Amazon rainforest to the east and the Andes to the west. It feels as if the whole city just sprouted up overnight and thousands of people were bused in, dropped off, and given one instruction: Survive.

It has none of the charm of older Latin American cities, with their large squares, ornate churches, and oppressive colonial buildings. But El Coca does have one thing the world very much wants: oil. Just outside the city, gas stacks rise from above the Amazonian canopy, the flames atop ever alight with combustion, giving the town a post-apocalyptic flair.

Amid El Coca's apartment buildings, stacked like beehives, I smile wryly when I see the image of Che Guevara beautifully graffitied on one of the walls. That Marxist revolutionary who has become (rightly or wrongly) a pictorial symbol of countercultural rebellion, presiding over a town given existence by big oil and unchained capitalism.

Suddenly, my machismo driver pulls off onto the side of the road next to a group of people waiting for a lift. I know we're not where I need to be yet because we're not even a mile out of town. But are we really picking up hitchhikers? When a lad with two chickens hops onto the flatbed and two others push into the cab, pressing me closer than ever to the monosyllabic driver, I realize we are. Or maybe this is part of the plan? Who knows? I know I don't.

Is this just something you do in Coca? An informal public transit service?

At this point I'm thinking, *Okay, I'll probably die now. I'll get robbed, and my body will be left on the side of the road, never meeting my unborn child.*

I'd left Tiffany behind in St. Paul, Minnesota, six months pregnant. After three years of living in Santa Fe, we moved back to our home state to be closer to family. And after two years of trying in Santa Fe, Tiffany got pregnant on our first full day in Minnesota (that's what we call "Minnesota Nice!"). Our whole lives were about to change in ways we could then only barely imagine.

The person next to me, a girl of about twelve, stares. When I catch her looking, she smiles shyly, gap-toothed. She has dark charcoal eyes and a face puckered by the beginnings of acne.

Some words are exchanged in Spanish in the truck, which I assume mean, "Let's kill the gringo at the next stop." "Si. Si."

The girl's probably the one who does the murdering. Has a machete in her Disney Princess backpack.

This El Coca welcome is all the more discombobulating because just a few hours ago I was having a delightful breakfast in Quito, the 9,350-foot-high capital of Ecuador (if you have sex in Quito, you're automatically a member of the mile-high club), in an indoor garden among bright flowers and happy geckos. I slumbered like a Quechan king the night before in a room where my bed was strewn with rose petals and the wardrobe sported lovingly painted avifauna. It was all far fancier than I expected.

Then, fanciness thrown overboard, came a hair-raising thirty-minute flight in a plane the size of a trash can, which I only got through without a full-blown panic attack because I spent the whole time with my camera pressed to the window taking pictures to distract my brain from the fact that I was about to die, trash-can-plane-style, photos of the unbroken Amazon and the very broken Amazon split by new settlements. Houses like tiny toys, recently felled trees like matchsticks, cars and logging trucks like trinkets, roads and routes splitting the forest, and as we drew nearer, that familiar site from Borneo: oil palm plantations.

Then El Coca came fully into view, colorful and makeshift and manic with all the sudden chaos of the modern world.

And now this. I feel like I have to keep pressing into the truck driver just to avoid the murderous smiles of the twelve-year-old until it's pretty much like he and I are on a date in a drive-in theater. Listening to the chickens clucking with gossip behind us, I wait patiently, breathlessly for that killing blow to come.

It doesn't.

After two hours of highway roads along newly felled rainforest, the truck pulls into a smattering of buildings and a dock on the Napo River. Called the Pompeya Market, it's an open-air market that sells bushmeat killed in the interior,[1] though today it's quiet. I find a bathroom and a bottle of Coke and await my fate. Machismo man heads off. And for the first time, I wonder about him. *Does he have kids? A wife? Maybe he's gay. Is he in love? Is he happy?*

The others remain behind with me. What would become of us all? Only God could tell.

The Coke tastes like saccharine ash, but at least I know it's not tainted with cholera.

I'm here in Ecuador for Mongabay to get a firsthand look at Yasuni National Park and the world's decision to despoil it by oil drilling. This park has become a rival for the title of the "most biodiverse place on the planet," which also means, just so you know, definitely the solar system and maybe the universe.

At the time I visit, an international plan is in place, notable not only for its novelty but also for its ambition. It's called the Yasuni-ITT Initiative. In 2007, then Ecuadorean president Rafael Correa offered to keep three oil blocs of Yasuni, a national park of which large sections were already overrun by oil companies, from being drilled if the international community donated $3.6 billion, or half of what Ecuador expected to reap from the petroleum buried under the forest's rock, really just the bodies of trillions of long-dead zooplankton and algae, maybe a few dinos.

The plan would not only spare the remotest part of Yasuni from rapacious oil companies but also secure untold wealth of biodiversity (much of it never explored) and keep numerous communities of uncontacted indigenous people secure from the modern world. Moreover, it would keep 410 million metric tons of carbon dioxide under the ground at a time when we were already near overtaking the carbon budget to keep us under 1.5 degrees Celsius (it's worse now).

The money raised would not go to the Ecuadorean government. Instead, it would go into two massive trust funds run by the United Nations Development Program, one of which would finance renewable energy projects and the other reforestation, conservation, and social programs. In other words, it would be billions of dollars directly employed to move Ecuador from a state almost wholly dependent on its oil revenue onto a new and better path.

Tragically, Ecuador had become addicted to oil money. Around half of Ecuador's export money came from oil, and, even worse, the entire government budget was one-third oil money. No country should depend on the oil market for basic social services—it will bring only disaster.

There was nothing like the Yasuni-ITT Fund on the planet, and for all the criticism lodged at it (and I'd read it all), it was an exciting new path for crossing the threshold between a fossil fuel economy to one driven by a wider, more diverse, more ecologically and climate-sane strategy.

There were three components to my trip. First, I would spend a few days at a science station called Yasuni Research Station. Next, I would join a band of rowdy undergrads at another science station, Tiputini Biodiversity Station.

Finally, I'd spend my last days of the ten-day trip nestled on Anangu Lake in the Napo Wildlife Lodge. I was hoping to get a sense of not only the wildlife here but also the indigenous tribes who'd already been impacted by fifty years of oil exploitation on their lands and pollution in their waters.

A number of those groups, like the Huaorani and the Kichwa, were battling through legal and political means to create a space for themselves on their land, free of oil madness.

Eventually, a boat, the large motorized canoe so ubiquitous in the Amazon, glides up to the dock and we all trundle on, heading down the Napo River to the national park and my first stop, Yasuni Research Station in Orellana province.[2]

The Napo feels larger and more industrial than the other Amazonia rivers I'd been on (maybe it's just all the oil company boats?), and it takes us a long time to cross from one side to the other, where we depart at a building that resembles an airline hanger. But it's really oil-company security. Military men stand around with automatic guns slung over their shoulders, and we wait to go through what feels like immigration at an airport. My passport is checked, I'm asked questions, I have to show documentation of where I'm staying inside the oil blocs that govern this forest. Then finally I'm let through.

It'd be grand if all this was for keeping indigenous communities secure and keeping out illegal loggers, miners, and settlers, but it's not. It's for protecting the oil, not human beings.

After leaving security, I find another man with another truck who has my name written on a sheet. It's enough for me to trust my fate with him. After all, what choice do I have? I get in and almost immediately the security station and the river vanish behind the dense understory of the Amazon. The sun, beating down on me all day, also vanishes beneath a ceiling of green.

By late afternoon we arrive at Yasuni Research Station. With its white walls, teal roofs, and red railing, the site is functional but hardly inviting (*where are the rose petals?!*). It's like staying at a Motel 6 in the United States but housing an odd riffraff of scientists, students, and photographers on the edge of one of the world's greatest national parks that in terms of species makes Yellowstone look like a potted plant next to the friggin' Hanging Gardens of Babylon.

Night falls quickly, and I head to the mess hall where dinner is served like a high school cafeteria, complete with trays and schlops of food. Afterward, I return to my Spartan room and read, stopping in the glow of electric lights several times to takes photos of moths, cane toads, and large alien-looking insects that I couldn't even place.

Suddenly, I hear people talking loudly and excitedly outside. I set down *Middlemarch* and emerge to a sight that's about as expected as Albert Einstein standing there with a pink umbrella.

Under the stark lights of the station, a tapir, a five-hundred-pound prehistoric-looking, gangly-nosed mammal, stands unperturbed at the entrance to the cafeteria. One of the station's staff members, a local from Quito, is feeding the tapir by hand.

"Her name is Umi," he says. I approach slowly, worried I'll spook her, even as a small crowd has gathered.

"She has a name?"

"Si, Huaorani hunt mother years ago, but after killed her, they discovered this orphaned calf. Huaorani hand-raised her. She's mostly wild now, lives in the forest, but sometimes she'll head back this way because she knows she can get a snack. You want feed her banana?"

Who could say no to such a wonderful proposition, feeding a *Tapirus terrestris* a banana? She takes it greedily from my hand, pulling with force and then *chomp, chomp, chomp*. She appears to have no fear of me although I'm a stranger from a strange land.

"Can I touch her?" I ask, noticing he's running his hand on her back.

"Of course."

I put my hand on her mane. Her hair is coarse, bristly like broom wisps. It bends against the force of my hand and then springs back into place.

"Oh, give her a good pat," he says and displays this for me by banging his open palm against her massive neck like you might a horse. I try the same and can feel the muscles and strength just beneath.

Umi hangs out for an hour as darkness falls over the Amazon, eating bananas and posing for flash pictures until it seems she's had enough humanity for one night. She then ambles back into the nighttime forest, where she'll bed down. But she'll be back again tomorrow night.

The next morning, I get up early, plow down breakfast, and meet my guide for the day, a Huaorani man named Nemote. He looks to be in his forties with an unflinching gaze, hair cropped almost like a monk's, and a big laugh, which isn't heard often. He wears a red-and-white shirt with *Skaen Jeans Italy* emblazoned across.

The Huaorani tribe, also written as Waorani or Waodani, is comprised of a few thousand people living in Amazonian Ecuador, speaking a language unrelated to any other on Earth. Traditional hunter-gatherers who lived nomadic lives, the Huaorani have a reputation for violence, and according to outsiders, feuds were often solved via the spear. The Kichwa gave them the name *Auca*, which means "savages." But, like everything, it's more complicated.

The Huaorani, long-ignored by the rest of the world, exploded on the scene suddenly in 1956 when a group of missionaries planned a daring expedition (one could describe it as foolhardy) to interact with the then-uncontacted tribe and bring them the word of God—and potentially Western diseases.

Operation Auca, as it was called, went terribly. After initial contact and an exchange of gifts, the Huaorani ended up attacking the missionaries, spearing and killing all five men. One of the missionaries may have shot and wounded a Huaorani, who eventually died—but accounts remain hazy, even now.

Despite the death of the five missionaries, other evangelicals eventually succeeded in many of their aims. Today, many of the Huaorani live in settled communities, no longer nomadic, with increasing connection to the modern world. Some converted to Christianity. Many have been taught that going about nude, as they used to do, is shameful. Even dance has been banned among some groups.

While the Huaorani have secured rights to a portion of their land, the government of Ecuador still has the rights to the oil beneath, essentially undercutting the Huaorani's self-determination. Today, they are in a new fight for their lives, one against big oil and government ambivalence.

Nemote and I spend the day together, speaking in the nonverbal signals that serve as humanity's only universal language: lots of pointing, smiles, laughing, head shaking, sometimes speaking in one's language in some desperate hope that even if they don't understand your words, at least they might the intonation.

Maybe it's because I'm with a Huaorani guide who moves like a ghost along the path, but I see more wildlife during this morning hike than any other. Nemote picks tiny poison-arrow frogs out of the leaf litter; he finds little bugs that seem only to appear when he points at them. Even birds are wholly unperturbed by our presence. It's as if he's supernatural.

No one knows how many species are in Yasuni, but it's a strong contender for the most biodiverse place in the world, perhaps toppling Manu.[3] In 2010, a study found that Yasuni sits in a small part of the world that includes the richest areas on the planet for at least four groups: mammals, birds, amphibians, and vascular plants. And Yasuni is the *only* national park within this western Amazonian explosion.

Nemote takes me first to a small lake where wildlife is abundant. A pair of great kiskadees greet us noisily. More monogamous than most humans, these birds defend and hunt their territory with the fierceness of two-ounce winged tigers. Meanwhile, large, fat, unknown fish peek their heads out of the surface while an elegant, giraffe-like anhinga sits atop a long branch.

We watch as a hoatzin appears from the nearby vegetation and takes off gliding over the lake. There should really be a requirement by law to have hoatzins appear in every book ever written. When Andrei rides into the Battle of Austerlitz, he should've done so with a hoatzin on his shoulder. When Heathcliff is brought to Wuthering Heights, he should have a hoatzin chick—complete with dino claws—in his pocket. When Odysseus reaches Ithaca after twenty years, he should be greeted not by his dog but by a hoatzin.

Hoatzin heads look like the heads of the Celtic warriors that faced off with the Roman Empire: blue face, spiked orange hair, red eyes (maybe from all the drinking the night before a battle). Their feathers go from ruddy-brown to black streaked with white, while the base of their necks and their chests are near yellow. When they lift their wings, a sudden shot of rufescence catches the eye.

Researchers have tried to lump hoatzins with tinamous (remember them from Guyana?), cuckoos, crane-like birds, pheasants, plovers, doves, and something known as mousebirds among other bird families. Nothing sticks. Research in *Nature* in 2015 argued that the hoatzin is, in fact, its own thing. Looking at its genetics, the scientists said it was the last survivor of a family of dino-birds that evolved shortly after the comet blast 64 million years ago. In other words, you want to see a real dinosaur? Go see a hoatzin. Why this isn't bigger news, I don't know. It's incredible how many amazing discoveries biologists make and how few of them ever trickle to public consciousness.

When I showed my daughter, now eight, a photo of a hoatzin, she said, "Oh, a phoenix."

That's good enough for me. Maybe Fawkes of Harry Potter fame was really a hoatzin with a different name, and my dream of hoatzins in every book is slowly coming true.

Nemote stops at a tree the size of a medieval tower, and perhaps as old, and motions to me. He points to the camera and then stands over by the tree. I get it. He wants me to take his picture. So I take one of him with his intense eyes and cool expression, his machete shoved into the ground next to him hilt up. He looks particularly badass.

The one language Nemote and I do share is photographs. He takes a keen interest in my camera, and whenever I snap pictures, he wants to see them. So I pick the better ones and hold the camera out to him. He responds with a thumbs-up.

There are so many questions I'd like to ask him, but even if we could speak to each other, it would be beyond impolite to pepper the poor man with queries about his peoples' past and their uncertain future.

Still, the one question I would like to ask, and perhaps the least likely to offend, is how he feels about the oil companies. Resistance against oil exploitation is not universal among the Huaorani, and some have even been employed by the corporations. But even a query that simple eludes our illiteracy of each other's tongues.

At a hundred-foot observation tower, mostly to see birds, we climb to the top and get a vision of the Amazonian canopy. About halfway back down,

Nemote suddenly points to my camera and him again. Then he hangs off the side of the tower while I'm taking photos. For a moment I think, *Oh shit, he's going to jump.* This man may be Spiderman-like, but a fifty-foot drop onto earth is likely fatal no matter who you are. Instead, he just leans, one arm still around the steel of the tower, and grabs on to an adjacent tree. He moves his other hand there, so he's got two hands grasping the tree and his bare feet on the tower (oh, yeah, he's been running around the Amazon barefoot this whole time), then one foot at a time, he swings them over to the tree until he's holding it, hugging it really, like the tamarin monkeys I'll see in a couple of days.

And then Nemote shimmies down the tree. He gives me a big thumbs up when I show him the photos.

It's about lunchtime now, but as we trudge back, me covered in sweat, Nemote suddenly looks up and then runs off into the forest. If there's one thing you're told never to do in Amazon, it's leave the path. Leaving the path is like doing group bungee jumping with some twine you found in your garage. But, of course, that's only if you're a gringo. If this is your home, then leaving a path in a forest is little more than stepping off a sidewalk.

I'm paralyzed for a moment. Nemote, seemingly noticing I'm not on his heels, pops his head back out and motions with some urgency. My mind is thinking of all the snakes, the mosquitoes, and the venomous spiders. But if I can trust anyone to walk me around the Amazon without incident, it's this dude. I follow.

We run under the canopy, over the forest floor, which is open, almost park-like, due to the little light that reaches us. I can tell Nemote has seen something high in the trees, but I can't see what. Instead, I keep my eyes on my feet to keep from tripping on the roots and vines. He's tracking something, and I imagine that if I weren't here, he'd maybe have his blowgun out ready for a shot.

He stops me and points up. You know when a person points at something small and faraway and expects you to see it? It's like that all the time in the Amazon. There's a bird in that tree, fourth to the right, see the bend in the branch, follow that up, then over, then down, then follow the trunk to the sixteenth branch, then keep your eye along the vine, and then track the leafcutter ants going up one by one, and at the head of the leader is the lesser wagtail tyrant (a real bird).

I don't see shit. Nemote points more emphatically, but unfortunately, or fortunately, we can't communicate in words, so I don't have to listen to arcane directions on how to see what his super eyes see far away. Finally, something moves, and there it is. It comes into sudden focus. It's a mound of dirty black-and-white sheep wool on the branch. Why is he pointing to *that*?

Oh, it's a freaking monkey!

I can see the fat little arms and legs, probably only fat because they are covered in the same shaggy hair. It's a monk saki monkey, who for some unknown reason has evolved a coat of fur that looks like it's made for Siberia, not the Amazon. The creature, which seems more at home in a 1980s alien movie than here, moves silently through the trees. We track it, rushing underneath. At one point, it looks down at us with an expression of unutterable melancholy, and I wonder if monkeys have existential crises, too.

Why not? A number of monkeys can make and use tools; they are born, love, and die; they have big brains and even bigger metaphorical hearts. If they do have existential crises, then I think this poor lad is wondering, *Why, in this land of heat and humidity, won't God allow me to take off my coat?*

Just a few yards from the station, Nemote stops me suddenly and points again. A collared puffbird sits on a branch above the trail as if posing for us, but really it's waiting still-as-a-stone for an insect to pass by, then it will burst into sudden action and slaughter its lunch. The bird has a massive black pupil, haloed by a bright orange iris, and a black stripe beneath its cinnamon-colored head. It doesn't move as I take around fifty photos—Tiffany always says I take too many photos—and stays chill even as we pass underneath.

Ecuador is my first trip as a father...well, father-to-be. And it starts to hit me for the first time that my life matters in ways it never did before. It matters to an unborn human to whom I am supposed to be a father. If I'd perished on a trip before Tiffany's pregnancy, it would've sucked for her, but I knew Tiff was strong and would very likely fall in love again and remarry. Of course, I would want her to. I knew as hard as it would be, she'd be okay.

But a child is different. A child losing a parent leaves scars that may never heal. All of a sudden, things begin to take on a greater meaning. I didn't fully reckon with this in Ecuador because Aurelia was not yet as real and tangible as she would be in just three months. But it was like a hint of the weight of responsibility and vulnerability that happens when one becomes a parent.

We had been trying for a child for two years, but when Tiffany told me she was pregnant, she didn't get the response she wanted. I was working on editing an interview with Jane Goodall—a hard thing to forget—when she handed me the pregnancy test.

"How much work do you have to do today?" she asked. "Because you're going to be a little distracted."

I stared at Tiff, mouth slightly agape, for a few minutes. "Aren't you excited?" she finally posited. Not the word I'd have used. Panic rose in me. I felt unready, unprepared, overwhelmed. Sure, we'd been trying for two years, but it had also failed to take for two years. Now the vulnerability of parenthood, the open wound of loving someone so much, took hold for the first time.

I'd have to raise a living, breathing, feeling human being. Part of doing so, I'd discover, would be reliving my days of brokenness.

In the autumn of 1994, during the first weeks of my freshman year, I grabbed a lunch tray and disinterestedly picked out what I was to eat over the next half hour. All summer my brothers had filled me with terror. "Just wait till you get to high school. You'll be at the bottom then."

I'd already felt at the bottom, or beneath it really, during junior high. How could I go lower?

Buffalo Senior High School was dizzyingly large. My class had over three hundred students, and the high school itself, from ninth to twelfth grade, had well over a thousand. This meant that all of the students couldn't eat lunch together, so it was split into shifts. I'd drawn the short straw. My lunch shift happened to include zero real friends. It did have one acquaintance. He and I shared a largely silent lunch, eating as quickly as possible before dispersing. But, today, he was out sick.

My social strategy in school was invisibility. Keep low, keep to corners, and don't make eye contact. I had a few really good friends by this time but no real group to speak of. Most groups I had no chance of gaining entry to and wouldn't have wanted to anyway. Others I desperately avoided because I didn't want to be labeled a nerd. I knew what happened to nerds in 1990s Buffalo. But this meant I had only a few, select people I could count on by the time I turned fourteen.

I emerged from my shell only when I did theater, when I could be someone else. I'd just been cast in *West Side Story* as old man Doc, one of the few roles available to a guy who can neither sing nor dance. It was small but dramatically meaty. One scene I was already rehearsing in my head: when Doc informs young Tony of his beloved Maria's death. Doc gets to slap him!

Looking grimly at the gray slab of what was supposed to be ribs on my tray, I had two options given that my buddy was out. First, I could find a table or corner by myself and eat and read a book. This sounded great, but I felt doing so would pretty much label me a social pariah in the first month of high school. The second was to find a group of kids who were adjacent to me on the social hierarchy.

So that's what I did. Tray in hand, I scoured the tables, found a few faces I kind of knew, and made my move to sit down.

But one of the boys used my sudden, uninvited arrival as a chance to prove his dominion.

"What are you doing sitting here?" he asked. "No one said you could sit here."

I mumbled something indistinct.

He grandstanded. "Do you all know why Jeremy is so weird? It's because his parents are brother and sister! Did you know that? They had sex. And they produced him." He pointed at me, as if to extenuate his point.

The other boys around the table chuckled, not so much out of the hilarity of the bully's joke, but more because they felt like they had to. They didn't want the bully's attention turned on them. I laughed as well, chokingly, full of fakery, but I felt it was the only way to counter the joke. Today, the fact that I laughed sits hardest with me.

I stayed there long enough to eat, my head mostly down, shoving food into my mouth. I left after about seven minutes and dumped the rest of my lunch.

And that was it. That was all it took for me to make a decision. *Screw this* (only not in those exact words). *I'm not coming back to this school.*

I'm ashamed now to say it took so little for me to turn and run when I'd seen others endure much worse bullying. I recall the image of one kid licking the bus floor. But there it was. On the one hand, I've always been deeply sensitive. On the other, I have a surprising characteristic of my personality. While I am usually timid and malleable, I have a line, once crossed, where I will act.

I'd made the decision, and it was ironclad. I wasn't going to endure another lunch without friends, another opportunity to be bullied. I simply wasn't going to put myself in their power.

Conversely, I couldn't tell anyone about this. The whole thing—attacking my parents, their laughter, my stupid laughter—stank too much of shame.

So when I started skipping school again, literally running out into our farm in the morning to escape my parents, threatening never to return, I ended up, hardly surprisingly, at an emergency appointment with my therapist.

"Jeremy," he said, "tell me what's going on."

"If you make me go back to school, I'll kill myself."

To me, it was simple and rational. I knew the only way to keep adults from physically forcing me back into the Buffalo Senior High School lunchroom was to threaten suicide.

I'd hoped the therapist would come up with some magical solution, some way in which I'd never have to go to school again but, instead, stay home and read books (isn't that what we all want? Just a stack of books?) *and* still do the play. Solve it, magic adult! But instead, he said, "Are you serious about suicide?"

"Yes. If you make me go back to school."

I don't know today how serious I was about the suicide part. In one sense, it was the best I could do as a fourteen-year-old to protect myself. But in another, desperation breeds desperate measures. I wouldn't have put a suicide attempt, probably shabbily done, past myself.

"Okay, then I'm sorry to have to do this, but for your own safety, I'm committing you to the hospital."

That night I was back in Minneapolis, in a locked-down psych ward. Only this time there were no girls who wanted to date me.

I'm being canoed by two men down Anangu Creek, a tributary of the Napo, but as its title implies, a thinner, shallower wisp of a thing from its parent mother. The forest canopy above covers the creek so easily that on Google Earth, it's impossible to follow the waterway's every bend.

In all the time I've spent in the Amazon Basin, from Peru to Suriname, this is the first time I've ever been powered by humans through the forest's watery courses. On the one hand, it's lovely. Rather than kicking up a rapid wake that causes turtles to drop off logs and pushes birds into flight, we're moving at a speed in which animals stay put. The rufescent tiger heron in the brush; the squirrel monkeys all in a row, using branches to cross the creek above us; the hoatzins barely batting a red eye.

On the other hand, it feels more than a little weird to be canoed downstream by two full-grown men for two hours. One can't escape that unsettling sense of privilege—one of travel's most constant companions. Part of me wishes they had another paddle so I could lend a hand. But most of me is glad they *don't* have another paddle because I know myself well enough that, if I start paddling, I'll make a fool of myself.

So I do what I always try to do in these awkward situations. I attempt to be as kind and appreciative as I can, given the language barrier, while also just telling myself, *Shut up. Just try to enjoy it. Look at this: You're in the Amazon rainforest being canoed up a creek. This moment is amazing, so just shut up, brain.*

I'd just come that morning from my second residence, Tiputini. There one can catch a glimpse of the spines of Amazonian dolphins as they curl up through the Tiputini river. We visited an oxbow lake replete with piranhas, stingrays, electric eels, and caimans while hoatzins lined the banks. On one trail, a guide found a dead banana spider, or Brazilian walking spider, in the family of one of the world's most potentially deadly arachnids. Another morning, a giant land snail, bigger than my fist, had taken over the guardrail.

I'd spent three days with a bunch of undergraduates visiting the Amazon for the first time, adding a wonder, rowdiness, and drama to the stay. During one of their classes, their professor allowed me to give a full-throated defense of the Yasuni-ITT Initiative.

The impact of the oil industry becomes increasingly clear every time I make my way from one stop to another. The paved roads, the barred gates, the gun-toting guards. It's quite clear where the power lies in Yasuni, and it's not with the indigenous people rowing me deeper into their lands.

Once I finally settle into the rowing up the Anangu, I enjoy the quiet. No undergrads, no scientists or photographers, just the pull of paddles, the swish of water, the call of some far-off bird, the lulling chatter of insects.

The creek widens as we near our destination, the bank turning into a marsh. And it's here, amid the swampy reeds, that one of the men notices a juvenile anaconda sleeping among the lily pads. A young green anaconda is still large, about two-and-a-half feet at birth. Unlike most reptiles, anaconda mommies don't lay eggs. The young are born wiggling, hungry, and ready to hunt.

It's difficult, if not impossible, to estimate how long a snake is when it's curled up in a spiral, but I'd hazard this was probably around three-plus feet, so not very old. Still young enough to be eaten by a caiman or another anaconda, which is probably why it's in hiding.

The green anaconda has one of the silliest Latin names ever: *Eunectes murinus*. The first name, the genus, is fine. It's a Latinization of Greek meaning something like "awesome, kickass swimmer," but the species name *murinus* literally means "of mice." Apparently, when Carl Linnaeus named the species in 1758, he was under the impression that anacondas liked to eat mice. But a mouse would be like a single potato chip to an anaconda, hardly worth the effort.

What it should be called is *Eunectes irrumabo*, which means "good swimmer, *oh, fuck!*" Because that's pretty much how you feel when you meet an anaconda in the wild. Either "Fuck, that's insanely awesome," or "Fuck, I gotta get the hell out of here," depending on your disposition and the situation.

As we float through this swampy, reedy area, a number of black-capped donacobiuses, another bird whose taxonomy is hotly debated, chirrup to us in a haunting "Wha! Wha! Wha!" The widening creek eventually spills into Lake Anangu, and I spot my third homestead.

The Napo Wildlife Lodge is like a vision of heaven. Seriously, if this is what you see after you die, I think your first thought will be, "Well, everything is going to be okay now." Lake Anangu glimmers unruffled in the sunlight. At the far end, flanked by the forest, red buildings with thatch roofs seem less to contrast with their surroundings than accent them. Their shape, not rectangular but pyramidal, suggests one of humanity's oldest forms of building, from the Egyptians to the Assyrians to the Aztecs. The main lodge sports a tower that rises above the canopy, perfect for viewing birds and other wildlife.

From the flat calm of the lake, everything rises upward, the trees, the buildings, the tower, eventually to the sun. And that sun, our sun, mirrored in Lake Anangu, appears as if it may hold together another solar system.

The canoers paddle me to the dock, at the end of which stands a young man (Saint Peter?) holding a tray. On this tray is a cold glass of freshly pressed juice.

Even amid this felicity, I do think for a moment as I drink the delicious tropical cold something-or-other about the water and the ice. Is this okay? But, nah, they house tourists here nonstop. It must be fine. And it tastes like the place looks, Elysium.

It's almost unsettling after a week of scientific centers, which were fine but hardly luxurious, to be a tourist again in what I can only describe as the most impressive Amazonian hotel I've ever seen. It's like Shangri-La with malaria.

After the cold fruity drink, someone takes my bags, and I'm escorted into the main lodge where I meet my guide, a Kichwa named John. He's quite young, early twenties, eager, and dimpling.

Napo Wildlife Lodge is run by local communities of Kichwa people, who are the largest ethnic group in the Ecuadorian Amazon and speak a language that is closely related to Quechua, which may have arrived here deep in the rainforest with the advent of the Incan Empire.

I paid extra for a personal guide. One sees and learns so much more if you're not shackled to other tourists, many of whom have completely different ambitions and expectations and a few who seem to constantly forget they're in the freaking Amazon rainforest. People will complain about the food, the warm beer, the cold showers, even the bugs. Yes, people will go to the Amazon rainforest—have I said it's the most startling diverse ecosystem on the planet and most of that, the vast majority, is insects?—and whine about the bugs.

After dinner that night, I stand on my deck and watch the stars appear in the sky behind the canopy. The cross, or crux, probably the easiest constellation to find in the Southern Hemisphere, burns outward toward me. Four suns, four alien systems.

And I wonder if any of those solar systems could even hope to house a world as marvelous as ours.

Sitting in my bath at my family's old farmstead, I stared at the moon out the window and cried silently. I was fourteen, and it felt like my only success to date was getting myself committed to psych wards twice.

It's a strange thing to have no memories of what must have been seminal moments in one's life, but there it is. I remember next to nothing of my second hospital stay. It's a clean slate, a window into nothing. It's almost as if it never happened.

But it did, and whatever events occurred there are hidden somewhere deep in my subconscious, perhaps consciously forgotten. Not that I think anything nefarious or awful occurred, but a stay in the mental hospital is an extreme enough experience that forgetting may have been my brain's best coping mechanism.

The same is true of much of my childhood and teenage years, whole periods wiped clean, I assume, by depression and desperation. Maybe all the meds, too. It's almost as if a guardian spirit visited me one day with a flask of forgetfulness, where I could vanish some of the most painful moments but still hold on to some of the good stuff: the plays in the summer, the sleepovers with friends, the books, the hikes, the sunny days roaming the farm.

The one thing I do remember from my ninth-grade hospitalization is lying in the bathtub back at home, weeping. For some mad reason, the psychologists and psychiatrists allowed me to go home for one night on the condition I returned to lockdown the next morning. I have no idea why they did this. Perhaps a novel experiment? Perhaps active torture?

Being home again but not able to stay, I couldn't help but note all the things I loved about this near-centurion farmhouse: the creaky stairs, the rust-tinted water, the dogs barking at my feet, my parents, and brothers. Outside the bathroom window, the barn was shadowy gray, the trees dark silhouettes, the moon whole, and stars aflame with different constellations than those I would see sixteen years later in Yasuni.

I went back to the hospital the next morning without a fuss, but it broke my heart to do so. I'd won so far in my game to stay out of high school, but the price was high. And the fee would only increase.

The beauty of Napo lasts three days, but all those blissful feelings disappear on the night of the third when I head to bed after another full day of wonders. My tummy feels *iffy*.

Earlier in the day, stomach gurgles and discomfort tempted me to cancel my afternoon hike, but I went ahead anyway and was awarded with a pair of capped herons, a splendid beauty found only in the Amazon, standing white and blue against a darkening sky as afternoon rain drizzled on our upturned faces.

I awaken at 4 AM rushing to the toilet. I vomit once. I look for blood but find none. Then I lie shaking on the floor.

Steve says one word. "Gotcha."

Before this, Napo has been as delightful as I could have expected. One morning we headed to a clay lick and watched a multitude of parrots and parakeets aggregate like people in Saint Peter's Square. Another afternoon I spent hours watching a party of golden-mantled tamarins raiding the lodge's maize garden, something they do with great regularity. They are the size of squirrels, with black heads, white-and-gray faces, orange torsos, black tails, and a black-gray-white stripe saddle. I'd wanted to see tamarins in the wild for years. Another day we hiked to a nearby Kichwa settlement where I had the (awkward) pleasure of watching Kichwa women dancing. I learned about the tribe's various trapping methods and received a blessing from an indigenous elder, which involved a ritual tobacco smoke and chant. (John asked me, "Would you like a blessing?" I said, "Sure, I'll take any blessing I can get." He asked if I wanted photos of the elder performing the blessing ceremony. Nope, that felt weird and sacrilegious.) Another day we spent hours in a 108-foot canopy tower watching many-banded aracari, a type of toucan, forage amid the sky trees.

But I'm thinking of none of this now. Instead, I'm crawling back into bed, where I spend a few miserable hours between sleep and awake, assumed fever and panic. I remember straining against the white sheets, sweat pouring down my face. Alone. At that moment, I'm unable to clearly distinguish between the tropical death illness I've clearly imbibed and the symptomatic panic it's induced.

Past trips flash through my mind, all the marvelous places I've visited: Kenya, Peru, Malaysia, Botswana, South Africa, Suriname, and Guyana. And how lucky I'd been each time to get out alive. But this, here, is my payback. And I'm alone. No Tiffany to massage my back and put cold washcloths on my head. No Tiffany to read me my last rites and bury me in some unmarked spot in the forest.

More melodramatic thoughts burst from my neurons like fireworks. *My unborn daughter will never know her father, only that he perished in the Amazon while trying to write courageously about oil and the world.* (If Steve likes an addled mind, Malachi likes a melodramatic one. When they work together, I'm a monster.)

The dawn chorus finally comes, and light creeps across my room as if it is the tide coming in.

When the clock strikes seven, I peel my perishing flesh off the bed and head over to the lodge. Today, John and I are supposed to hike to a nearby clay lick often visited by mammals like tapirs and peccaries. The visit has been at the top of my list.

"Hey, John."

"Hello! Good morning. Are you ready to see if we can find some mammals?"

"Look," I start in. "I'm sick. Really sick, I think. I can't go today. I'm sorry."

He looks a bit taken aback. Maybe the flesh is not melting off my face as I expect? But he says, "Okay, okay, I understand. I'm sorry to hear. Maybe you should just rest today then—and hopefully you will feel much better tomorrow?"

Guides always do this, talk like everything's going to be great if you rest, and tomorrow will be as pretty as daisies.

"No, no, no," I say. "I'm really sick. Is there a doctor or nurse at the lodge? Do you have a thermometer? I really need to see how high my fever is."

I can tell I've caught him off guard. "No. No doctor here. But"—I hang on that "but"—"we can go ask the lodge manager."

Yes, the lodge manager! He'll know if I'm dying or not.

I very much approve of this idea and march, body somewhat bent, after John to the office. A small scholarly looking man, also Kichwa, in his forties introduces himself to me after chatting with John. He takes off his glasses and rubs them on his shirt.

"You feel ill, sir?"

"Really, really sick. Do you have a thermometer?"

"Sorry, we do not have a thermometer."

My panic rises. "What!" I erupt. I can feel the blood pumping in my temple. *Boom-boom-boom.* "Really!? How can you not have a thermometer!?" (It's almost as if this lodge is in the middle of a giant rainforest, two hours by canoe away from anything and everything, as if I'm in the heart of the Amazon, staying with indigenous people. Almost.) There is an unhidden twinge of desperation in my voice.

"Sorry, sir, do you mind?" He asks as he lifts his hand toward my head.

"Nope," I say, knowing that when he touches me and feels the heat of my skin, he'll call El Coca for a helicopter.

He places his hand on my forehead. "Hmm...You don't feel feverish."

In my head, I explode. *What do you know!* and *You'll be sorry when I'm dead!* But out of my mouth comes, "Oh...But I feel so sick."

"Perhaps, if you just rest today and sleep, tomorrow you will feel better? I can bring you some medicine for travelers' diarrhea if you need some."

I shake my head. I took my first ciprofloxacin last night, an antibiotic I bring on every trip, just in case. I return to my room, deflated. *Okay, this would be a good time, Tiffany, for you to parachute in. If you've been hiding in my suitcase for the last week, now would the moment to jump out and say, "Surprise!" and save me from anything stupid.*

She doesn't.

As the next hour progresses, and the disease (or panic) worsens, I finally summon all my courage—or my fear? I stumble out of the cabin and march to the manager's office. I knock. When he appears, I say, "I *really* need to go to the doctor. How do we do that?"

And this, folks, is how I end up having two indigenous Kichwa men canoe me upstream for two hours while I sit glumly hunched over in the back, barely noticing the biodiverse bliss all around me. I imagine some capuchin monkeys see me and say to each other, "Damn, what's wrong with that dude?"

After two hours, we finally reach the Napo where I transfer onto a motorized boat, heading another hour or so upriver until we reach a dock that leads to a path taking me to a line of people waiting to see the only doctor for miles whose office is a white building the size of a motorhome.

Sheepishness overcomes me the moment I step in line, seeing mothers holding their sick infants to their chests, and young listless children perhaps stricken with malaria. It hits me suddenly, *finally*, that I'm not as sick as any of them. That I'm consuming people's precious time and energy, that I've become, once again, an OCD-hole.

I give you, ladies and gentlemen, the American douche in paradise.

But now that I'm here, I have to go through with it. So I wait in line, often sitting on the grass, for an hour until I get to the beleaguered doctor, a haggard man in his fifties with a salt-and-pepper beard. He asks me a few questions. He feels my stomach. Then he gets out a thermometer—they have those here! — and sticks it into my mouth. After a few minutes, he takes it out and looks at it.

There is a moment. (*Here it is! Buckle up! It's gonna be a doozy of a diagnosis,* Steve sings out. *Woo-hoo!*)

"Thirty-seven degrees," the doctor says.

"Uh . . ."

"No fever. You said you're taking ciprofloxacin?"

"Yes."

"Well. No severe abdominal pain. Vomited once. No blood. Keeping water down. Si, just travelers' diarrhea. Probably *el poco* bacteria that your body wasn't used to. Very common. Keep on cipro and you'll be A-OK in a couple days."

"Okay . . . thanks."

"Si." And his attention has already shifted to the woman behind me, pregnant and scratching at red splotches that have spread up all along her arms.

It's back into the motorboat for an hour, then to the canoe-launch and then two hours back in a human-powered canoe to reach Napo Wildlife Lodge by dinnertime. And by then my body, at least, is feeling good enough to eat a little something.

And this is how I spend my last night in heaven on Earth.

The next morning, it's all done in reverse. Row upstream back to the Napo, motorized canoe upriver to the dock in El Coca, driver to the Francisco de Orellana Airport, and prop plane westward over the Amazonian basin, up the shoulder of the Andes, over the great mountain chain's pinnacles, and down to the mountain capital, Quito.

The following day I am in Quito, but instead of eating an empanada de viento in the Old Town, or spending hours in Museo Casa del Alabado exploring all things pre-Columbian, or visiting the Compañía de Jesús, a Jesuit church with a nave that is nearly entirely covered in gold, I wake up with panic in my breast.

"That doctor in the Amazon barely looked at you," Steve says. "This isn't just travelers' diarrhea."

"Shut up, Steve."

"Okay."

"Thanks."

"My bet is cholera."

After breakfast, I head to reception.

"Excuse me, is there, like, a doctor you recommend for travelers?"

"A doctor? Are you okay?"

"Fine, fine. Just feeling a little . . . just looking for a doctor who works with tourists."

She gives me the name of a clinic and tells me how to get there. I get a cab and spend my last day getting blood tests done in the old colonial city. In the end, the doctor, a pleasant fellow with a big smile, sits me down in the chair across from him.

"Well, Mr. Hance, I can guarantee you that you'll be bringing no unwanted passengers back home with you. All the tests look good. It was probably just some bad indigestion. Happens all the time."

I nod and say, "Gracias." I take a cab back to my hotel, eat some dinner, and go to sleep. But as I head to the airport the next morning, I begin to think maybe the doctor in Quito missed something. Maybe whatever bacteria got in my body is good at hiding, maybe it's stealthy as hell.

I board my plane feeling fine, but I'll definitely need to see a doctor when I get home.

The Yasuni-ITT Initiative crashed and burned in 2013. In its six years, the fund staggered along, raising pledges of only some $336 million, about 10 percent of the asking price, and only received around $13 million of that. So, President Correa decided to kill it. He accurately said, "The world has failed us. It was not charity that we sought. It was shared responsibility in the fight against climate change." He then opened up those final blocs of the park, home to the voluntarily isolated Tagaeri and Taromenane tribes, who have managed not to be meddled with for millennia, to industrial-scale oil exploitation.

Ecuadorean civil society tried to stop its government from opening up Yasuni —polls showed a large majority of Ecuadoreans opposed it—but Correa time and again defied them.

The oil blocs were granted to Petroamazonas, one of Ecuador's national oil companies. In 2016, the company began drilling. Somewhere now, a car burns gasoline punched out of one of the most remote and biodiverse places on the planet.

And for what? Because we lack imagination.

When I left Ecuador, I wouldn't say I was optimistic about the Yasuni-ITT initiative. I'd heard all the criticisms, I knew the challenges, but I would say there was a sliver of hope that the world could, at least, pull this one off. But, once again, we didn't collectively come through.

Every year our inaction mounts up. The world is on fire, underwater, and feverish, yet we continue with business as usual in a world where such business is the definition of madness. According to World Wildlife Fund (WWF), the monitored populations of nearly seventeen thousand species have declined by more than 50 percent since just 1970. Think about that for a second—that's *insane*. Likewise, we've destroyed half of the world's tropical forests (our most biodiverse gems) in just sixty years. Recent studies have found insect populations collapsing in some parts of the world. Meanwhile, 20 percent of the Amazon rainforest is gone, and scientists fear we are now headed toward a tipping point, where the world's greatest wilderness could collapse into savanna.

And here at home, our government is gutting the Endangered Species Act, diluting the Clean Water Act, opening the Arctic National Wildlife Refuge to oil exploitation, and instituting policies that will drastically amplify global warming.

We're lighting a match to our children's future.

I have nights now where climate change keeps me awake. I think about my daughter and what the world will look like when she's my age, not yet middle-aged.

I've learned through my life that I'm *not* good at many things. I'm not a good activist because marches and parades cause my anxiety to skyrocket. I can barely go to Target without having a mini-anxiety attack. I'll never be a leader or a politician, not only because I'd be terrible at it, but I love imagining the attack ads against me. "He's on psychiatric meds!" "He's been committed twice!" "He's diagnosed with OCD, depression, anxiety, and, maybe, depending on which doctor we talk to, bipolar. Do you really want a wackadoodle representing you?" "He needs a nap every other day!" "He sometimes sleeps twelve hours at a time." "In the winter he has to sit in front of a happy light just to kind of function."

I realize these are pretty tame and surprisingly accurate for political ads, so imagine the other sort. "He's been to Malaysia; he must be a secret Muslim!" "He likes rhinos more than he likes you!" "He says climate change is *real*!"

So, what can I do? I can write. It's all I have to give, but I'll fucking give it my all. There are things in the world we've taken advantage of for our ten thousand years of civilization: a stable climate, a rich biodiverse suite of wildlife, healthy oceans, and a deep connection to other forms of life. We're risking all of these now. We're risking not just our survival but any chance of fulfilling the United States' July 4, 1776, declaration of inalienable rights granted by the Creator for all. "Life, liberty, and the pursuit of *friggin'* happiness."

I added the friggin'.

PART FOUR

Survivors

Chapter Eight

Of Lorises and Men

FALL 2017

Tiffany says the reason she knows I'm banana-ripe bonkers is because of my dreams.

Some people might call them nightmares, but I have these dreams so often—several times a week—that to me, they're just slumbering wisps of delight. I won't bore you with the details. (but Steve will: homicides, suicides, a regular appearance by a terrorizing teacher, fecal matter, car crashes, dead people walking about, or I go and see the new *Star Wars* movie and it's just really bad. I have that dream a lot, weirdly.)

Tiffany doesn't dream much. But when she does and attempts to tell me about it, it sounds like, "And then I walk into the room…and…uh…oh…I don't know. I can't remember."

I *always* remember. Tiff sleeps the slumber of the innocent and righteous and psychologically secure. I sleep the slumber of the neurotic, tormented, shamed, and fearful that Jar Jar Binks will make a comeback.

My dreams get so bad that Tiff pushes me to try Eye Movement Desensitization and Reprocessing (EMDR) therapy for post-traumatic stress disorder. The idea of EMDR is that relating horrible things that happened to you while focusing your eyes on either a therapist moving his or her finger or this machine thingy with lights that go back and forth mitigates past trauma. The theory is that moving your eyes in a specific pattern while relating the awful things eventually gets your brain to reprocess past trauma, and you heal. It sounds wackadoodle, I know, but there is solid clinical research behind it. I also have friends who testify to its amazingness.

But I find the whole experience a bit discomfiting. I'm so used to telling therapists my terrible shit face-to-face that I find it odd delving deeply (really deeply it turns out) into childhood memories as I watch this therapist's finger. Instead, I find myself wanting to look at the therapist's face and eyes, like a person would normally do.

"Just sit with it," the therapist says and then does the finger thing. But by the time it takes for her finger to go from right to left, my impish brain comes up with all sorts of deliciously horrible things I could say, things to shock or horrify this perfectly nice therapist. I have no rational desire to say any of these things, but Steve tells me such things must be said. I summon all my will to ignore him, which requires a ridiculous amount of effort. Such impulses, called intrusive thoughts, are a pretty normal (is normal the right word here?) symptom of OCD. I remember as a kid having to bite my tongue, sometimes until it bled, to avoid saying something unspeakably sexual to an adult, and not out of anger or curiosity, but just because my brain dared me.

Still, despite having to fight intrusive thoughts, I did feel over time that EMDR was helping. I could view the specific episodes and my relationships around them with more rational clarity and less—I guess?—terror.

Eventually, though the cost of these appointments began to stack up to ridiculous proportions—thanks, American health care—and I had to bail before we got anywhere near the juicy stuff.

So, the dreams just keep coming. Night after night.

A week before a reporting trip to Indonesia, I wake at 3 AM sweating. I'd just dreamed of motorbikes and death. Awake and under the cover of darkness, I vow fiercely never to set my ass on a motorbike.

Tiff and I had visited Indonesia two years prior, so I knew motorbikes were as ubiquitous there as they are across much of Asia. These are the slimmer underbone version of motorcycles as opposed to the more robust bikes in the United States. They are an affordable transportation option for much of the world, but I find the idea of riding around on an unarmored, open-air thingy at the speed of forty miles per hour absolute madness.

I don't ride bikes or motorcycles or camels at home. Why would I willingly set my haunch on one in Asia?

After nearly thirty hours of traveling, my plane finally lands in Jakarta. I can't believe it's actually happened. Are they really letting me off?

I made it through the lady vomiting, the panic attack at thirty-thousand feet, the temptation to jump ship and move to Tokyo, and then the final leg from Tokyo to Jakarta.

It's nearly midnight as I walk outside the airport. Instantly, I'm double slapped with the sudden humidity and the god-awful air pollution. Jakarta's air quality is notorious. After hours of airplane quiet, my ears buzz with the sounds of honking, vrooming, and shouting in Bahasa. I take a ticket for a cab, but as the wait lengthens, I grow increasingly despondent.

Did I die on the flight? Is Jakarta purgatory?

Finally, deliciously, one of the cabdrivers lets me get into his car and drives me to my hotel ten minutes away. When I get to my room, the first thing I do is call home on Skype. Tiff, after listening to me talk about my last thirty hours, gives me a much-needed pep talk.

Then I sleep. And oh, do I sleep. I sleep one of the deepest slumbers I've ever known.

The next morning, I awake like one reborn. Everything feels different: The noodles for breakfast taste delicious, the shower is a joy, and the whole trip—eleven days in Indonesia—now feels surprisingly doable. It's like, suddenly, I'm a good traveler.

I'm here to report on the progress to save the Sumatran rhino from total extinction. It isn't looking good.

After breakfast, I take a cab through Jakarta to a city in the south called Bogor. Lying within Jakarta's sprawling metropolis, Bogor is known as the metropolis's nicer greener district. Most travelers I know have few good things to say about Jakarta: It's massive, overcrowded, smog choked, congested, and, some say, lacking charms of any kind. The city is home to over 10 million people—larger than London—but the metro area is home to over *30 million*, that's more human beings than in Texas.

I don't see enough of Jakarta proper to form an opinion, but recently the government has announced it is moving the capital from Jakarta on Java to some unbuilt city on Borneo. Aside from the reasons above, Jakarta is literally slipping into the world's rising seas. Situated on swampy marshlands and the confluence of several rivers, the seaside city floods regularly. Nearly half the city is now below sea level. As climate change raises the oceans, portions of the metropolis will become uninhabitable. Fifteen inches of rain fell in Jakarta on New Year's Eve 2020, killing at least sixty-six and displacing nearly two hundred thousand people.

While moving the capital may relieve some of the awfulness of Jakarta, those in the know fear it will unleash even more destruction on Borneo's already burning, dwindling, beleaguered forests.

By late morning, I arrive at Hotel Santika in Bogor, a lovely place recommended by my contact, Rahmadi, at Mongabay-Indonesia. Mongabay-Indonesia is the news site's first international bureau established in 2012. Since then, Mongabay has also set up bureaus in India and Peru. What started as a small news site, for years just me and Rhett, has grown into an organization of over fifty staff around the world and hundreds of freelance contributors.

A lot of this is due to Rhett's decision to switch from a for-profit to a nonprofit. After the 2008 financial crisis, advertising revenue online plummeted, leaving Mongabay stranded. Nonprofit was the best way not only to survive but thrive. Mongabay is doing things today no other site is capable of: hard, in-depth, and contextualized environmental news often produced by local reporters.

In 2015, I left Mongabay as a staff reporter and editor and struck out as a freelancer. To be honest, I'd burned out. I'd been on staff for six years and produced around one to two stories a day. I just couldn't keep up anymore. My lunch breaks had gotten longer, my days off more frequent, and nearly every spring I'd need to take off a week or two for unpaid emergency leave.

Spring, for some inexplicable reason, is when my mental illness hits its extreme. You'd think spring would be a time of joy and renewal after the long doldrums of Minnesota winter (a terrible, horrible thing that should never be inflicted on man or beast), but instead, it's like the sudden uptick in light and heat supercharges my anxiety, OCD, and depression. I usually have a week or two in March or April where I'm basically an inhuman slug, incapable of anything but bed and TV and, sometimes, if I'm lucky, books.

Freelancing gave me the freedom to take better care of myself. I took up meditation, yoga, and swimming with greater frequency, as well as more guilt-free naps...well, more naps (still lots of guilt). But the financial hit was severe. Overnight Tiffany became pretty much the sole breadwinner because I was now making crumbs. Still, I had a blog on the *Guardian*, my relationship with Mongabay, and contacts at several other media outlets to at least keep me busy.

Also, it was a good time to go. Not only had Mongabay grown spectacularly, but also the culture had changed necessarily. There were regular staff meetings now instead of just emails between Rhett and me. There were programs with large budgets and new systems to learn. I quickly felt overwhelmed, and thought, *Well, now's a good time to let some other young writer have a shot.*

This trip to Indonesia is my first big trek since going freelance. And I'm determined to make a success of it.

Shortly after checking in, Rahmadi arrives at the hotel to pick me up. We're getting lunch first and then I'll interview the head of Yabi, Indonesia's rhino organization, and several staff members. Rahamdi, a staff editor at Mongabay-Indonesia, will be accompanying me to see the rhinos.

In his thirties, a father and husband, a huge birder, and, of course, passionate about conservation in his country, Rahmadi and I start this adventure with a lot in common, despite growing up in nations wholly different in terms of language, culture, and history. Rahmadi is smart, pleasant, and generous. From our many emails, I could already tell he is one of those people for whom hospitality and amicability are very important.

After introductions and a little small talk, Rahmadi and I head out into the heat of Bogor and walk to the parking lot across the street. Rahmadi tells me to wait, and he'll pick me up. I set down my bag and watch the traffic, almost entirely motorbikes zip-zooming around. And then Rahmadi pulls up on a motorbike. He hands me a helmet.

"Hop on, Jeremy," he says.

I carefully consider my options.

One: run away.

Two: demand we call a cab.

Three: suck it up, break my middle-of-the-night vow, and get on the god-damn bike.

Steve votes for making a run for it.

I fake a smile, take a deep breath, put on the helmet, fasten the strap under my chin, and climb on behind Rahmadi. I wrap my arms tight around his stomach until we're spooning motorbike style. Then we're off.

I don't remember much of the ride except the thump of my helmet against Rahmadi's. *Thump, thump, thumpity, thump.* At one stoplight, I look over and see dozens of other Indonesians unworriedly and mundanely riding their motorbikes. I see helmetless kids sitting more chill than me. Someone is transporting a cupboard on his bike. A woman holds an infant on her thigh. No other passengers are clinging to their drivers or thumping heads; they're just sitting back as if on a bus.

But I decide that I don't care as the light turns green and Rahmadi takes off. *If everyone jumped off a cliff into a lake of lava filled with lava-proof alligators, would you?* I only squeeze Rahmadi tighter. *Thump, thump, thumpity, thump* go our helmets all the way through Bogor.

It's only about a twenty-minute ride, but as we pull into the headquarters of Yabi (short for Yayasan Badak Indonesia, which translates into the Rhino Foundation) on a leafy street, it feels gloriously quicker than I expected. I'm not splattered on a Bogor roadside! It's a miracle!

At the Yabi office, we pick up two staff members and head to lunch, this time in a car, thank God. The Indonesians pick a *warung*, a small family-owned restaurant; this one is known for its fish, Indonesian-style.

Indonesian food, I'd argue, is on par with some of the world's greatest cuisines: the taste-bending sauces, the blend of surprising flavors, the creativity, and the boggling diversity. But it's largely unrecognized outside the nation. When's the last time you went out for "Indonesian"?

I let Rahmadi order for me. Quickly, the food appears: fish in a dark, rich, perfectly flavored, wholly unknown sauce. Beside each of our plates is a small bowl of water called a *kobokan*. In many parts of Indonesia, it's customary to eat with your fingers—no utensils needed—and then use the *kobokan* to wash your hands. You always eat with your right hand (because, across pretty much all of Asia, you wipe or wash your ass with your left).

It happens near the end of the meal, as I've been convivially grilling the rhino dudes (off the record) about the situation for Sumatran rhinos and listening to their stories. I dip my greasy and reddish hands in the *kobokan*, for like the fifth time, and then pick up some saucy-rice and bring it to my mouth.

The realization sinks, inexorably. The connections jumping from neuron to neuron. I set down the rice, uneaten. None of the other three men have touched their *kokoban* washing bowls. But I had. I'd eaten with my fingers, cleansed my hand, and then eaten again. But the water... where was it from? A Fiji bottle? Oh, Christ. Why would a local joint like this employ bottled water for washing bowls, especially if no one touches them till the end of the meal? (Indonesia is another country where drinking tap water is to be avoided at all costs.)

Of course, you idiot, you use the kokoban *to wash your hands at the end of the meal, not every five seconds!*

At once, the awful picture is rendered. I feel heat spreading through my body, sweat beading on my temples, my mouth goes dry, my heart pumps *boom, boom, boom*, my stomach clenches.

The other three men are talking as if nothing has changed, as if the very air in this place has not grown tighter and uglier. But for me, everything moves more slowly: the men's mouths, their fingers scooping up the fish and sauce, the beating of my pulse.

I find myself staring at the *kokoban* as if by doing so I could glean its origin and, perhaps, the rogue bacteria performing underwater ballet in the bowl.

"I'm sorry," I hear myself stuttering out. "I need to use the toilet."

Three faces turn to me, various expressions of surprise taking each not so much at my words as the stultifying tone in which I clothed them.

They gesture to a room in the back, and I quickly head there, more to escape their inquisitive looks than anything else. Maybe I'll feel better after a few minutes alone.

I open the door that's partially off its hinges and discover the toilet: a hole in the ground with a bucket of water next to it. Floating in the bucket is a plastic scoop. I stare dumbly. What am I supposed to do with this? Shower?

I discover now that I'm shaking and saying, "Shhhhh...shhhhh...shhhhh." It's never a good sign when you start shushing yourself aloud. I feel like I might throw up.

Fearing that if I start this toilet process, I'll somehow screw it up (how am I supposed to flush?), I quickly escape its inexplicable puzzle back into the restaurant proper.

"I'm sick," I say when I return to the table, standing before the trio of Indonesians like a queasy kid before a new teacher. "I need to go back to the hotel." This spoken with the air of utter defeat.

The three men bolt into action. Within the next half hour, I'm taken to a pharmacy where they kindly load me up on medicine ("Oh, yes, you should try this. Very good. Very good. For stomach.") and then to my hotel.

All my afternoon interviews, which I'd traveled only nine thousand miles to conduct, are canceled. Well done, Jeremy.

Alone in my posh room, I dissect my symptoms with the meticulousness of a taxonomist specializing in leafhoppers. My heart is thumping, my stomach tight, my hands clammy, and my frame shaking.

I head downstairs and borrow a thermometer from reception. My temperature is fine.

So, either I've had *another* anxiety attack or the naughty water has injected some tropical disease in me, and it's acting with incredible rapidity. It's been an hour, at best.

I take an Ativan in case it's the former and turn on the TV. One of the best ways to break escalating panic attacks is to distract Steve with something shiny.

Skipping around, I find *Fletch*, that old Chevy Chase comedy. I lie in bed and drift through the romp. By the end, my symptoms have subsided.

I lie in the open-air pool for hours that afternoon, peering at the tropical foliage and various birds that fly overhead. I watch the clouds in the sky and become entranced by a small moth that shelters in one of the potted tropical ferns. I'm drifting back into myself like a lost puppy who found its way home.

As I dry myself off at dusk, I come to the obvious conclusion: The whole thing was just another panic attack. I feel friggin' fine now. So here I am, hours into my tough-as-nails reporting trip, and I've already screwed things up.

I email my editor and lie.

I write, I got food poisoning and couldn't do my interviews today but would reschedule.

In truth, I *had* become sick; it just wasn't food poisoning or bad water. It was my stupid brain. It was my annoying-as-shit mental illness. I vacillate between beating myself up and trying to let it go and focus on tomorrow.

I lie to my editor because, even with some advances in recognizing mental illness in some societies, most people still don't equate mental illness with physical illness. Many still see one as real and the other as not real or simply an excuse (or even worse, a weakness or failing in your character). Physical illness is real, respected. Mental illness is fake, unserious. Anyone who has lived with mental illness knows all too intimately the stigma, the inability to know whom to trust.

And we sure as hell are far from seeing mental illness as something that makes individuals who they are, something that adds to them rather than subtracts, that may indicate their potential for creativity, empathy, kindness, and open-mindedness, all things that I see in many of those I know who have suffered from mental illness.

Going through history, you'll find that pretty much every great artist suffered from some mental affliction or another: melancholy, addiction, bipolar, suicide. When I was seventeen, I read a book called *The Price of Greatness: Resolving the Creativity and Madness Controversy* by psychiatrist Arnold Ludwig. Less a critical analysis than a nonfiction think-fest, the book argues that creative genius (less so other types of genius) and mental illness and addiction

often go hand in hand. Think painters, musicians, poets, novelists, philosophers, mathematicians—you get the idea. It was the first thing I'd ever read
where there was suddenly a sense of potential pride in struggling with demons.
Okay, maybe I'm full of mental fuckery, but perhaps that's a trade-off for the
long, sprawling fantastic novels I wrote in fifth grade, or my empathy for other
species, or my ability to imagine a future very different from the one we are
crashing toward. Maybe rather than being *just* a disability, mental illness is
a part of what made me who I am. Maybe wrestling with Malachi and Steve
strengthened rather than weakened me. Maybe mental illness is the dark coals
from which a flame may come.

More than twenty years later, I'm still not sure how certain of that I am.
It probably depends on the day whether I think mental illness is a total curse
or, at times, potentially a benediction with severe drawbacks. But taking pride
in myself, even in my mental illness, and knowing I am not alone, that some
of the most astounding people who ever lived suffered immeasurably, was
necessary to get to high school graduation.

I go to bed early, for tomorrow we head to southern Sumatra. And I'm
determined not to screw this up any more than I already have.

I was at an old farmhouse on the outskirts of Buffalo where teens from
fourteen to eighteen hung out, downing soda, scarfing chips, and chasing one
another around the rooms. The worst anyone did was smoke a cigarette. I was
at a theater party for a show I wasn't even in.

Somehow I got invited, even though I'd done maybe two rehearsals before
ending up in the psych ward. Someone had probably felt sorry for me; the
word had undoubtedly gone around that Jeremy, "that little freshman," had
ended up in the hospital. No one said anything directly to me about it; no one
asked, "How was the loony bin?," but there was hesitancy by many and a lot of
pitying looks. My secret was out, but we all pretended like it wasn't.

The party ended with wild running in the nearby cornfield, the joyous kind
of thing teens do in Buffalo. For a moment I was a part of this cast again, a part

of something. But the next day they all went to do the show and I went home to uncertainty, a lump of grief like a rock inside me. Alone, again. Still outcast.

During my second hospitalization, the question hung in the air like an upcoming trial: Where would Jeremy go to school?

There weren't a lot of options. I argued for homeschooling, but none of the adults thought it wise to give a so-called "school avoider" the chance to avoid more school. They warned if I didn't go back to a proper school this year, I never would.

And I thought, *So what?*

Instead, I ended up at a school where bomb threats and violent outbursts were a daily thing. It was an alternative junior and senior high school in my county for troubled youth. At least on the surface, none of the kids here seemed to be dealing with what I was: social anxiety, sensitivity, depression, and undiagnosed OCD. Many had come here after drug use or violent incidents.

On the one hand, it was terrifying. On the other, few people paid much attention to me, including the kids and the teachers, because they had enough of their own shit going on. I sat in the back and spent most of the time with my face stuck in a book while whatever daily drama swirled around me.

The teachers had little idea what to do with a student who did his work diligently and quietly and then seemed to withdraw into the walls like a ghost. "Look over there, the twelve-year-old is mouthing off!" is what I willed whenever attention was thrown my way. It was easy to be invisible.

I didn't make any connections at the school, no friendships. I remember watching the 1984 version of *A Christmas Carol* and reading the nuclear-holocaust book *Z for Zachariah* during my stint better than I remember any of my struggling peers. It's difficult when one is drowning to have anything left for anyone else, especially if they, too, are in deep. And goddamn, these poor kids were in so deep.

Really, I just wanted peace. Peace from my peers, from my mental illness, from the drama on the outside and the inside. Peace from the scrutiny.

All my childhood, adults advised me that I could solve all my problems if I just toughened up. "Pull yourself up by your bootstraps!" was the most common phrase I heard—or overheard spoken about me. This is a tad ironic given the origin of that phrase is to attempt to do something impossible and inane. One's bootstraps can't physically lift you. Try it.

Whenever someone would advise me to toughen up, the logical question would be, "Okay, how? Tell me *how* do I toughen up?"

And the answer? Crickets. Well, that's not exactly fair. One therapist told my father that the problem with his youngest son was that he didn't force me to go hunting when I was little. Apparently, shooting animals dead would've done the trick. Some had in mind, I know, physical punishment. A belt would do it. Others proposed sports. They'd clearly never seen me play soccer.

But really, how does one just toughen up? What was the path to get from here to there? No one could tell me.

I have a deeply sensitive and empathetic character. I take in and feel others' emotions potently. What I feel, I feel deeply. It is not something I fashioned to annoy the adults in my world, but something I believe is deeply ingrained in my double helix, much like my OCD, depression, and anxiety, and probably all muddled together like soup.

When people in my circle told me to toughen up, what they really meant was that I should be something I am not. I should become more insensible. I should feel my feelings *less*. I should express them less freely and eloquently. I should, in a word, be more of a man.

I never adhered closely enough to my small conservative town's definition of American masculinity, circa the 1980s. It was a definition steeped in evangelical Christianity and Catholicism, American mythos of the West, and our community's farming heritage: Men were meant to be active, physical, and dominating in all social interactions. They were meant to wrestle, punch, be loud, and pull girls' hair. They should voice their thoughts and opinions loudly and vehemently. If a man was the quiet sort in Buffalo, then he needed to be the strong and silent type, rarely displaying or pronouncing emotion, the kind that liked mechanics and woodworking. A man's intellectual pursuits should be limited to the physical world, like fixing cars or hunting animals or pursuing engineering. They could like math and biology, but loving British novels and film noir whiffed of intellectualism. Being intellectual was not good for '80s Buffalo boys.

The cure for all my oddness: Toughen up.

Be a fucking man.

If I'd had different parents, I could've been forced down that road. Driven to hide my emotions, to ignore my instincts, and to inflict mental (or physical) pain on myself whenever I felt any emotion too keenly, I could've become tough, I suppose—or really insensate.

The ramifications of such a change are hard for me to imagine, but I think, had I done it, I'd likely be dead today. Malachi never fails to remind me that there is always a way out.

It was my parents, who day in and day out saved me, allowing me to be myself, even as they wrestled with how to raise a kid who one day wrote and illustrated an overly fantastic novel and the next broke all of the potted plants in the house.

My stint at the alternative school came to a head after the New Year. One morning, I awoke with barely enough energy to move. When my parents called the school to say I'd be out sick, they got an earful from the head of the school about my "school avoidance." If they let me stay home today, I'd never come back, he'd said.

In a way they were right.

Turns out I had pneumonia and had been walking around with it for a while, perhaps exasperated by the stress and depression of my situation. As I recuperated, my parents took stock and made a new decision: They were pulling me from the alternative high school and moving me into homeschooling.

It was the best news I'd had in months. Maybe years.

It might be controversial, but here it is: I believe Indonesia is the most distinct nation on the planet. To put it mildly, there is just no place even remotely similar. First, Indonesia is made up of some seventeen thousand islands. Yes, you read that right. Seventeen thousand.

This means it has a ludicrous mix of cultures, religions, language, foods, and histories. While Islam dominates 90 percent of Indonesia, religion here can also be viewed as vast and multipronged as it is in the world, with Muslims in Sumatra and Java, Catholics in Flores, Protestants in Papua, Hindus in Bali, and animist religions among many indigenous groups.

Indonesia is also a megadiverse country, a term used only to describe seventeen countries on Earth. To make the list, a nation must have at least five thousand endemic plants, meaning species found nowhere else in the world.

Indonesia covers about only 1.3 percent of the world's land but contains 12 percent of the world's known mammals and 16 percent of the world's bird species. That's more mammals and birds than in the entire United States, in a nation five times smaller in landmass! Indonesia has more than *double* the number of America's plant and vertebrate species.[1]

According to another study by Mongabay itself, Indonesia is the third most biodiverse nation in the world based on percentages of vertebrates and plants, after Brazil and Colombia, respectively.

Indonesia is so special it's almost impossible to overstate it.

The next morning I'm picked up by Rahmadi; Buana, an old rhino soldier with a slight frame, quiet voice, and gravitas mixed with humor; and Buana's nephew, whose name I never discover or, more likely, quickly forget, but who is a god among men.

We are heading almost two hundred miles from Bogor to Way Kambas National Park on the island of Sumatra. The trip requires three hours or so to the western tip of Java, a ferry over the Sunda Strait to the island of Sumatra, and then another three or four hours on a heavily trafficked one-lane highway to Way Kambas, where the Sumatran rhino sanctuary houses seven of the world's captive rhinos. A single female is kept in Kalimantan.

The road through Java is mostly freeway. A couple of hours in, we stop at a roadside gas station. Rahmadi says (as he will do so several more times on the trip), "I'll be ten minutes. Okay?"

"Of course," I say. I don't know at the time that he's referring to his need to fulfill the Second Pillar of Islam, which is *salat*, the obligation to pray five times a day.

Traveling in Muslim countries as an American is problematic. Not because you are treated poorly—I've never been treated ill in a Muslim country; all I've ever gotten is hospitality and friendliness—but because some things remain unspoken on both sides. I'm an American, after all, coming from a country that has become famous the world over for its anti-Muslim rhetoric since 9/11.

While Rahmadi has gone to the prayer room on the far side of the gas station, I head to the restroom. Outside, I see shoes and sandals of all sorts. Am I supposed to take off my shoes before I enter? It's common practice in much of Asia to remove your shoes before you enter one's household...but a public restroom? A man exits, barefoot. I watch him put on his shoes. He smiles at me as if in hello.

Okay, here goes.

I take off my shoes and walk immediately into about half an inch of water flooding the restroom. With every step, Steve screams, "Toilet water! Toilet water! Toilet water!" And each time it's like a jolt of electricity going off in my brain.

Making it to the toilet and back, I feel like what Hercules must have felt after cleaning King Augeas's notoriously shitty stables: I'm never doing that again.

I put my shoes back on under the bright Javan sun and breathe through my anxiety in the car.

Having spent two weeks before in Indonesia with Tiffany in 2015, I really should have known more than I did, but Tiffany and I stayed largely within a kind of tourist-nexus where Western-style toilets are common. I won't go into the gritty details, but, needless to say, if you ever go to Indonesia (or anywhere in Asia), do your research on toilet culture. Traditionally, many Eastern countries do their business much differently than Westerners. And that's cool and probably beneficial (squatting is good for you) and cleansing with water (think bidets) feels way nicer, more hygienic, and more environmentally friendly than wiping with murdered trees. But traipsing barefoot through water was perhaps a bridge too far for this OCD Westerner. And staring at the hole and the water bucket and the scoop (*gayung*) left me feeling like I was looking at a math problem I'd never solve.

We stop for lunch and then head onto a ferry, crossing the Sunda Strait from Merak on Java to Bakauheni in Sumatra. (I love writing Indonesian place names; they bring such pleasure.) About halfway through the two-hour ferry ride, I go onto the foredeck to try to see the remains of Krakatoa, not knowing that it's a good thirty miles from where I stand, well beyond viewing.

Indonesia sits in the Ring of Fire, a massive area encircling the Pacific Ocean where volcanoes and earthquakes rule. While the United States has the most volcanoes of any nation, Indonesia has the most active volcanoes. That's right, I said *active*. That is legitimately terrifying in a fiery, ashen death kind of way.

In two days of August 1883, Krakatoa blew in what was one of the most powerful eruptions ever recorded in history and several times bigger than any nuclear device unleashed by *Homo sapiens*. The four explosions were so large, they shot six cubic miles of the island into the air. They could be heard thousands of miles away, and the pressure waves caused by the angry volcano touched every barograph on Earth.

When the decimated island fragments fell back into the ocean, they caused several tsunamis, some around one hundred feet high. Whole villages were wiped off the face of the Earth.

According to Dutch colonizers, the tsunamis killed 36,417 people, but the real toll may well have been over 100,000. Settlements on the westernmost peninsula of Indonesia were completely wiped off the map and never repopulated. Today it's Ujong Kulon National Park, the last place on Earth to find Javan rhinos, a different species from the Sumatran. In fact, the Javan rhino would probably be extinct today were it not for the devastation wrought by Krakatoa 137 years ago.[2]

We dock in Sumatra and get back into the car. I put on my headphones and listen to podcasts, one after the other, to keep my brain from focusing on the road ahead and the batshit crazy activity in Indonesia known as driving.

The East Shore Trans Sumatera Highway is a packed two-lane road with trucks, motorbikes, and cars. And instead of driving single file in one's correct lane, everyone passes everyone else constantly. Every time Buana's nephew, name unknown, swerves, my heart leaps, as I know without peeking through my fingers that we've veered into oncoming traffic and the race is on. Will we get past whatever truck is going too slowly or collide with some car/

motorbike/truck? Will this be the time when this insane game of chicken ends in a dead bird?

Somehow, by some display of the nephew's incredible focus and reflexes or simply by God's sweet grace, we pass safely every miraculous time. I keep my head down for hours, a hundred panic attacks kept at bay by the podcast *My Brother, My Brother and Me*.

Finally, we reach the gates to the park. Buana greets the guards and the gate is lifted. It's a final half-an-hour drive through the rainforest to the rhino sanctuary.

Established in 1989, Way Kambas is largely secondary forest due to a frenzy of logging in the 1960s and '70s but remains a rare piece of gorgeous lowland rainforest, rivers, and mangroves, still home to Sumatran tigers, elephants, siamangs, and even a few wild rhinos, in addition to the captive ones.

Travel exhausted, we get out of the vehicle and are greeted in the dark and shown to our rooms. I dump my stuff next to my bed and lay down, look at the white plaster walls, and watch a moth, perhaps unknown to science, attracted to the light.

Lights are turned off and Sumatra disappears like a magic land that once seen can never be. Just a few hundred yards from us sleep seven Sumatran rhinos, representing perhaps the last hope for a species 20 million years in the making.

The name Sumatra comes from Sanskrit, meaning something like "the gathering of the oceans."

When I was a kid, my idea of Sumatra, much like Borneo, had the allure of a splendid wild, massive, rainforest-blanketed island sporting villages and towns of diverse cultures coupled with wildlife like tigers and elephants, tarsiers and orangutans. The reality today is very different, and the story here is tragically similar to that of Borneo, only the destruction started later and moved even faster. Corporate greed and mass consumerism are decimating the island with oil palm and pulp and paper plantations overrunning Sumatra in a frenzy whose only rival may be in Borneo.

Today, like so much of the planet, you must travel far to find pockets of wilderness, even on a splendid island like Sumatra.

To get to Way Kambas National Park where the rhino sanctuary is, we drive past towns, villages, agricultural fields, and small plantations. Two years ago, when Tiff and I did this same trip, it was burning season. People were simply stacking vegetation from clearing fields and lighting it afire or burning downed trees. Such fires would often spread to native forests and vegetation. The sky was ashen, and the whole thing had a post-apocalyptic feel.

But this is nothing compared to the plantation areas of Sumatra, where you can drive hours through pulp and paper or oil palm plantations, replacing what had been, not long ago, old-growth rainforests and deep peatlands. It's as if the pallid horse of the Apocalypse recently rode roughshod over all the entities who once inhabited these forests.

Traveling to Sumatra, or Indonesia in general, is always emotionally difficult for me. In the Amazon, where you can at least pretend the destruction is far away, you can lull yourself into naivety far more rewarding. The parks of Africa, where you can spend days viewing megafauna, are equally splendid, but also in an-ignorance-is-bliss sort of way. Southeast Asia can feel like traveling through a graveyard of nature.

This is not to say there isn't splendid wildernesses left—there is—or that there isn't a need to engage in the debate between development and nature—of course—but is this really *development* or, as some might argue, *progress*? The vast destruction of some of the most beautiful, biodiverse places on Earth? The bludgeoning of wildlife? The catastrophic warming of our Earth? The deaf ears given to local and indigenous people urging corporations and governments to stop? Just fucking pause and let us catch our goddamn breath?

Our global approach to development (which could also increasingly be argued as wholesale destruction to feed the wealthy) is beginning to bite back. Annually, due to burning forests and peatlands, Indonesia is now covered in a toxic haze so bad it's likely leading to thousands of early deaths.[3] A study on the record haze in 2015 put the mortality number at one hundred thousand people in Indonesia, Singapore, and Malaysia. The annual haze is grounding flights, decimating the economy, and spreading to other countries like Singapore and Malaysia.

Meanwhile, as the Earth speedily warms, we're still intent on destroying the forests and peatlands that maintain vast carbon stores and splendid wild things. For what? For paper packaging to feed endless consumerism? For oil palm for snack and processed food? For cheap beef? For fossil fuels when our children can't take anymore?

Are we really killing the future for this?[3]

During the next two days, I conduct long interviews with numerous scientists and staff before collapsing into bed in exhaustion. I get to meet a number of the rhinos. Recently arrived Harapan seems well adjusted to his new home; young Andatu loves his foot baths; Ratu shadows two-year-old Delilah (now almost her size!); and Andalas, who promptly devours his ultimate birthday gift basket of pineapples, watermelon, apples, pears, and two dozen bananas. But most of my time is spent trying to wrap my head around the larger conservation predicament and what's to be done.

My reporting uncovers that there are probably between thirty and eighty Sumatran rhinos left in the wild, not a hundred as the official number claims. There are just eight in captivity and only one female is a proven breeder. The window to save the species is closing, and closing fast.

A new partnership, called the Sumatran Rhino Rescue, is working to catch rhinos from the wild for captive breeding in what really may be the last chance to ensure the species' survival. If we lose it, we not only lose a single species—and all the individuals that comprise it—but a lineage of distinct, once diverse animals that split off from all other rhinos an insane 16 to 23 *million years ago*. Do you know what humans were doing then? We weren't even a glimmer in the universe's eye yet.

In many ways, it's shocking that a single Sumatran rhino is left on our planet. It's incredible that the species survived the Pleistocene extinction, the thousands of years of trade with China (which so desired its horns), the modern world, what with our guns, our wire snares, our bulldozers, and our fire. And it's still *here*. All the more reason to do everything we can to keep it around.

After Way Kambas, we drive around seven hours to the other side of the southern tip of Sumatra to Bukit Barisan Selatan National Park.

I'm here to spend time with the men and women in the Rhino Protection Units (RPUs) who are devoting their lives to protecting the last remaining Sumatran rhinos on the ground. Alas, there may be no rhinos left to protect in Bukit Barisan. But even if the rhinos are gone, Bukit Barisan could hardly be more important. It houses some of the last significant populations of Sumatran elephants, Sumatran tigers, and the drop-dead gorgeous Sumatran striped rabbit (look it up!).

We arrive in the late afternoon to a site that looks like a jungle camp straight out of a 1980s action movie. Several green cabins with metal roofs and a camo style sit amid the foothills of the Bukit Barisan Mountains, which stretch from this southern tip of Sumatra to the northern, more than a thousand miles of mountains, volcanoes, and surviving forests.

Most of the RPUs are men, and most are young, in their late teens or twenties. I interview, via a translator, the older managers, but the young men also appear curious about me, just as I am about them. Even though we are unable to speak directly, I find the rangers welcoming, funny, gregarious, and kind. They know the forest intimately and take deep pride in their work.

That night the young men of the RPUs take me and Rahmadi on a hike through a nearby forest just off the main road, looking for tarsiers, a nocturnal ancient primate with the biggest eyes of any mammal in the world relative to their size. Let me repeat that: The head is basically half eyeballs. They also have bat ears and gremlin fingers. Did I mention they can rotate their head 180 degrees? Take that, Linda Blair!

So, of course, I want to see a tarsier. In fact, I think the whole world would be a lot better if instead of power and excessive wealth, we all just dreamed of tarsiers.

With headlamps firmly fastened, we walk into the woods. And by woods, I mean thick, dark, steaming jungle. Our lamps illuminate large iguana lizards clinging to trees, massive roaches, skittering snake-sized millipedes, and a recently bloomed but now diminished *rafflesia*, a giant decay-scented flower. My little group finds no tarsiers, but Rahmadi, with different trackers, spots the goblin hand of one before it disappears.

At one point, my RPU guide has me stop. He bends down and gingerly pulls one leech after another off my ankles. Blood flows into my socks. Sumatra is one of the few places on Earth home to land leeches, which rest in the leaf litter, waiting for some unsuspecting animal to give it a ride and a long drink. They can bite easily through socks.

Ten minutes later, the same young man has me turn around so he can flick a leech off my neck. These babies can also drop on you from above, like leech rain.

There is something sweet and almost tender about these acts. This young man, a total stranger, helps out this visiting foreign American dude. We can't communicate, he and I, but when he sees leeches on me, he helps a brother out.

There is something to this, I think later, something about the commonality among all of us. So many of us see only the differences between ourselves and others, especially those from other nations who live according to different cultural values. But in reality, we're all just human. And every day we can choose kindness or cruelty. We can choose to be brave or ambivalent. We can help others remove their leeches or leave the leeches to feed.

The way back, from Sumatra to Java, is largely twelve hours of silence. We're all too tired to talk. On the ferry, I go out onto the deck, but the journey back is the same there and the remains of Krakatoa are still out of sight.

Forty-four years after Krakatoa blew, a new volcano emerged from the caldera from where the old had blown, like Athena from the head of Zeus. Locals called it Anak Krakatoa, or the son of Krakatoa, and over the next ninety-one years, this little volcano grew to over a thousand feet high.

A year and a half after I visit, Anak Krakatoa blows in the Sunda Strait. A massive section of the volcano plunges into the sea, leading to a tsunami with walls of water up to sixteen feet high. The tsunami kills 437 people and injures over 14,000, the deadliest volcanic explosion of the new millennium. Anak

Krakatoa shrinks from 1,109 feet to just 360. The forest that had grown on its rim for nearly a century, and the animals that happened to find their way there, including birds and bats, all vanish. Now it's nothing but rock, rubble, sand, and bubbling heat.

The journey across the strait and then back to Java seems to take days, even though it's just one super long one. Finally, we reach my hotel, and I'm alone for the first time in nearly a week. I do what anyone would: I buy two cold beers from the downstairs restaurant—alcohol is hard to come by in much of Indonesia and impolite to imbibe if you're traveling with locals—and bring them up to my room. I almost finish one before falling asleep.

"Do you mind if we drop in on a wedding?" the woman I met twenty seconds before asks me. She's an American in Java, with red hair, deep eyes, and a welcoming smile. There's a hint of mischief at the end of her lips.

"A wedding?" I repeat.

"One of our former staff just got married," she says. "We'd like to stop in and say hello."

"Sure," I say. "But I feel a little weird, not being invited and all."

"Oh, it's fine." She dismisses my concerns. It's not so much her words but the glimmer in her eyes that convinces me. "There'll be so many people there. No one will mind an extra American."

"Okay…"

"Plus, there's free food."

"Yeah, okay. I'm in," I say with more certainty than I feel.

Meet Sharon McCabe, the very capable coordinator of the Little Fireface Project, a conservation and research project devoted to studying and protecting Javan slow lorises. With her is Michael, a blond, tall British man in his twenties, who's at the project doing research as part of his master's degree. While he's been in Indonesia only a month, Michael already seems more acclimated than I'll ever be.

I'd hired a driver to take me from Jakarta to the village of Cipaganti, where the program is located. Three hours into the journey, we stopped in Bandung to pick up Sharon and Michael. That's when this whole wedding business started.

Now, I find myself plunk in the middle of a Javanese wedding celebration.

There's a buffet of delicious food, a menagerie of dresses and tuxes, and more strangers than I can count. I keep trying to introduce myself with food in my mouth.

"Journalist...Sumatran rhinos...slow lorises...Mongabay...I've never met the groom or bride. What are their names?"

I don't know how weddings usually go in Indonesia (that's an understatement; I have absolutely *no* idea). And like everything in this megadiverse country, there are as many ways as there are islands. I don't know if we missed a ceremony of sorts, but this is clearly the celebratory part. Like most people in Bandung, the couple is a part of the Sundanese ethnic and linguistic group, which means the bride is dressed in an ornate costume that makes her look like a human deity; the groom is in a suit.

Under most conditions, such a situation would be unbearably awkward. But Sharon, who seems to have a talent for finding the amusing in weird social situations, makes it feel like a bit of a game of pretend.

That is until it's time for us to get into the greeting line. Sharon goes first, hugging the bride—they actually know each other—and shaking the hands of the groom. Michael is next, all easy, even though he's never met either of these people. Then it's me.

"Hi, I'm Jeremy," I shake her hand. "Journalist. With Sharon. Here to cover Javan slow loris."

Why am I telling her this?

I can see by the bride's expression that she's had to say so many hellos in the last couple hours that my words don't register. And it doesn't matter.

"Congratulations. You, uh, look very nice." I add out of sheer awkwardness. But she smiles and takes it pleasantly.

Then I'm shaking hands with the stranger groom and tell him congratulations, too.

But when it comes to getting a group picture with the bride, groom, and those here with the Little Fireface Project, that's where I draw the line. Though

Sharon motions me up, I shake my head. I don't want this lovely couple to be looking through their photo album one day and then stop and say, "Who is that?"

"American wedding crasher."

The Little Fireface Project, the brainchild of slow loris expert Anna Nekaris, is one of those small conservation groups that is having a real impact. I've been hoping to visit for years. It's the only group doing long-term research on slow lorises anywhere in the world and, at the same time, protecting this population of critically endangered animals by working closely with the community.

If tarsiers are real-life gremlins, slow lorises are Southeast Asian goblins. They move like clockwork automatons, have massive shining eyes, and lick toxins from their upper arms, which become dangerously venomous when mixed with their saliva. The eight known species are being wiped out due to, yeah, you guessed it, rampant deforestation as well as slaughter for soup, black magic, and body parts used in traditional medicine.

Slow lorises have also become quite popular pets due to cute videos on YouTube, like the infamous tickling one, but don't put down this book and watch them. Please! Viewing them only gives YouTube algorithms another fix, propelling the illegal trade and the pets' unimaginable suffering.

To catch slow lorises for the pet trade, poachers slaughter the mother and steal the baby. The baby is then often kept in filthy conditions and has its sharp fangs removed with pliers. Many animals don't survive this brutal procedure. Captive lorises usually die quickly. They are often kept awake when they should be asleep, fed the wrong diet, left covered in their feces, and stressed into an early grave.

The slow lorises' big eyes are not an adaption to make it look cute to humans but to grant it night vision for hunting insects and even birds. They move slowly and jerkily, not because they like to be captured and held, but because this is a strategy to avoid getting eaten themselves. Predators can't kill what they can't see moving. Slow lorises are wild animals. They are nocturnal, venomous, and smell god-awful.

They are not pets.

I can barely catch my breath as I follow Michael up, literally, the main street out of Cipaganti village and into the agricultural fields lying on the side of Mount Papandayan. Actually, *mount* is wrong. The village is actually on the side of a volcano. Fortunately, no one told me that before I got there. I might have called in sick. It's amazing to me that human beings, around three thousand in Cipaganti alone, can live on the side of a volcano and go about their daily lives nonplussed.

Remember when Pompeii blew? Thousands fried by heat over 400 degrees Fahrenheit? Their ash bodies still left to see? As I climb, I wonder why people don't think about Pompeii as often as I do.

Like so many volcanoes in Indonesia, Papandayam is an *active* volcano, with the latest explosion in 2002. That was only fifteen years ago, people!

As the sun begins to decline in front of Michael and me, it sheds light with a golden sheen that, while sitting in the shadow of a volcanic peak, is undeniably beautiful. Past the town, the road inclines into green fields of tea, coffee, and chayote squash (here called *labu siam*), all flanked by tall rainforest trees.

As we walk, Michael keeps an eye out for slow lorises among the canopy. I let Michael do the looking because he knows what he's doing. Instead, whenever I get a moment to catch my breath, I take in the view: the sunlit green valley spreading below, the last rays falling behind the volcano's summit above us. It's a dusk of breathtaking beauty. And though we don't catch sight of any slow-moving, big-eyed primates, I find myself blanketed in awe.

That night after the Isha prayer sounds through the village on various loudspeakers, I'm sitting in the common room with Sharon, Michael, Hélène Birot, a French primatologist, and a couple of other expat researchers over a game of poker. After spending a week solely among Indonesians and trying to unravel the cultural differences, the silences, and the inability to communicate, I feel unexpected relief flood my body.

All the Indonesians I met were kind, gracious, and wonderful, but it took work on both sides to understand one another, to communicate in the most basic ways, and even after that was achieved, there stood between us cultural differences that are challenging to eclipse in just a week. Here I was with a bunch of twenty- and thirty-somethings all sharing not only a kind of cultural familiarity but also a passion for wildlife and nature.

Still, the culture shock continues when I head to the bathroom. I take off my shoes, as expected, and step onto the slick floor with as little foot surface as possible, arching my heels until on tiptoes. With every step, Steve screams, "Toilet water! Toilet water! Toilet water!" With every step my glands spit out a little more adrenaline until by the time I reach the toilet, I'm practically panting and hold my feet up over the slick surface.

"Breathe, Jeremy. Just breathe." I do all those meditation exercises I've learned, breathe in for four, hold for seven, out for eight, until my anxiety evens out. *Home soon, home soon*, I remind myself. Sometimes the best way to survive a trip is to remind yourself that you won't always be walking barefoot in wet bathrooms.

And then I have to make it back to the door. Deep breath—and go.

"Toilet water! Toilet water! Toilet water!"

The morning calls to prayer, Fajr, duel from personal speakers set up about town wake me, but only briefly. I've become accustomed to them.

Cipaganti is a conservative Muslim village, and the Fireface project does all it can to respect and build a relationship with the community. The project has banned alcohol and sex on their premises and smoking in public, and all the women dress conservatively. The project has also built a school, started a nature program, and hired several local men as trackers, who, in turn, become ambassadors for the project to the village.

Conservation has gotten better at working with local people in recent years, but some groups continue to act like little colonizers. This isn't the case for Little Fireface.

I spend the day doing interviews with staff, students, and local trackers, but after the sun descends and night falls, it's time for the real fun to begin. I don all my gear and follow Hélène and three trackers along the main street.

We're after slow lorises tonight.

One never knows what to expect when following field conservationists into the wild because they are insane. They do crazy things every day. If you aim to live a life of adventure à la Indiana Jones, don't become an archeologist. That's an inaccurate depiction. Become a field conservationist: exotic locales, fascinating cultures, and crazy adventures in the wild. Of course, you'll also get to enjoy zero money, little job security, and numbing depression as you watch the Anthropocene unfold.

I could never do it but hugely admire those who do.

We begin by heading up the village's main street and then into the fields just above, much like Michael and I did yesterday. But we're on a different mission. One of the local trackers carries an antenna for keeping tabs on a slow loris with a radio collar. We're looking to catch and take samples from a particular male tonight, named Toyib. Lorises are territorial, so the team knows generally where to find him. The device will give us a more exact location.

Once past the outskirts of the village and into farmers' fields, the real fun begins. We bob and weave through various fields, keeping our heads low so we don't hit a squash, all the while climbing higher up the volcano. My breath is like a bellows.

And then the fields fall behind, and we start climbing, really climbing. I have to grip shrubbery and find places for my feet in vertical banks to get up to the next trail. Then we take a switchback for twenty minutes until it's time to climb again. It's not like the vertical climb is very long, but for a thirty-seven-year-old writer who spends most of the day at the computer, this is heavy work.

At one point, Hélène turns to me and with her French accent says, "Be careful here. Lots of wasps' nests on the ground."

All I can do is reply with heavy breathing. But I follow her more closely and step much more gingerly than before as Steve screams in one high-pitched monosyllabic note, "Waaaaaaasps!!!!"

But we pass through unstung and pause on the volcano's side. Hélène lights up one of her ever-present cigarettes as I glug greedily from my water bottle.

"You want one?" she asks, offering me a cigarette.

"No," I manage, "merci," delivering the one bit of French I remember from my five years of study. She smiles in the glow of the cigarette with that wonderful French quixotism that could mean either she's laughing internally at me (most likely) or she's enjoying watching me flounder (also likely).

The trackers sit just a few yards from us, taking in their smoke and chatting in Bahasa. We stay for about five minutes. Below us, the lights of villages and towns spread like a giant Lite-Bright far below and far away. Looking up as the chill of the volcano settles between my beads of sweat, I see the stars, so clear, so close, so full.

Just another jaw-dropping night on planet Earth.

The trackers head out, but Hélène and I hang out a little longer. I think she can tell I need to still catch my breath or, just as likely, because I'm making too much noise bumbling up a mountain and would scare away the lorises.

Then: "Come on," Hélène bids. "We need to catch up."

Catch up? Really? Instead, why don't we just wait here till they come back, and they can carry us back down? The last couple of minutes were the first time in the last thirty that my brain was able to produce words other than "fuck-fuck-fuck-waaaaaaasps-fuck-fuck-fuck," and I'm enjoying the sudden expansiveness of my internal vocabulary.

But this—the long grass touching me, the electric lights emblazoned beneath us, the stars on fire above—was never meant to last. It's my job as a journalist to shadow these crazy conservationists, and it's time to find that goddamn tree goblin.

Ten minutes later we catch up to the trackers. They've already managed to find Toyib in a stand of ten-foot-tall bamboo. Only there's a hiccup. He's not alone. It turns out Toyib has a new girlfriend, a slow loris the team has never encountered before. All I can see are pairs of round massive eyes flashing for a moment in the light of headlamps between the shadows of bamboo.

One of the trackers says something in Bahasa to Hélène.

"Shit, they were having sex. We interrupted them," she translates for me.

"They were…?"

"Yeah," she says. "That's a first. Well, we just need to do what we came here to do and hope they can get back to it."

The decision is made to try to catch them both. Hélène and I hang back as the trackers go to work, young local men for whom this kind of travail is probably much more exciting than farming. They work deftly and quickly, tying a rope to the bamboo and then pulling it down so they can grab the slow lorises. They pull down but miss the first go, and I see Toyib for the first time in full, clinging to the bamboo like he's pole vaulting as it swings back up. His expression, caught for a second in my headlamp, can only be described as "Ooooohhh…shiiiiiiiiiittttt."

But he manages, with his perfectly adapted hands and feet, to hold on to the swinging bamboo. The trackers' second attempt is more successful. They grab both Toyib and the female and put them into cloth bags.

This is when Hélène blazes into action. We do Toyib first while the new female scrambles in the bag. Hélène quickly takes saliva samples and a swab on his upper arm for a study on the venom. Toyib appears momentarily terrified. His eyes are wide (can slow loris eyes go wide when they're always wide?), and his little hand clutches Hélène's thumb. But his ordeal is over quickly. The female is a different beast. When it's her turn, she gnashes her teeth as spittle drips from her mouth. She wiggles like some impossibly dexterous circus performer against the grasp of the trackers, trying to escape, trying to bite.

It takes them only a few minutes to get all the samples they need and to affix a radio collar around the female's neck. Now they will discover where she's from and who besides Toyib she may be interacting with. Slow lorises are much like people—some are faithful; others are prone to lots of cheating. Then the trackers bring the bagged animals back to the bamboo and release them, hoping they can recapture the romantic mood.

This all may seem quite invasive, and it is. But it's also the only way to quickly and safely catch these animals. Moreover, while the catching and sampling are certainly stressful, the researchers say they've observed the animals going back to normal shortly after being released. The reality is that the team can't track the lorises if they can't catch them and install radio collars or replace burned-out ones. Catching and tracking them provides vital scientific information about the animals' biology, health, and range. Their findings will teach us what slow lorises need in terms of habitat so rescue groups have the best information on how to rerelease the animals with success. Toyib and the female's momentary discomfort could lead to better, longer lives for rereleased, former pet lorises.

For a species on the very precipice of extinction, much like the Sumatran rhino, every little bit can help.

The way back down the volcano's side proves much easier than the way up, and my adrenaline is rushing as we get back to the office and share with Sharon details of our night's adventure in all its glory.

Sharon and Hélène give me the honor of naming the new female. "Daenerys," I say. Because she's a badass queen (albeit fictional) and one of the last of her line.

It is said all the time but is no less true: Extinction is forever. Even a once abundant species can take only so many blows before extinction rears its head.

For Javan slow lorises and Sumatran rhinos as well as thousands of other species on Earth, that time is now. Our actions have pushed them into near extinction. I wouldn't be surprised at all if they don't make it through the century. Then again, all it takes is a few intelligent, well-meaning, dedicated people to turn things around for a single species. But it will take all of us to turn things around on our global ecological fraying.

As I board the first of three flights home, only twenty-five hours and thirteen minutes to go, I am determined *not* to repeat the journey here. No panic attacks, I tell myself. No matter how bad it gets.

So, I definitely do not see a man going in and out of bathrooms, spending way too long in them. And I *definitely* do not thoroughly check the bathrooms after him for bombs. (He was white. Steve, for all his faults, avoids racial profiling.) Even if a bomb were planted in the bathroom, I definitely am not delusional enough to think I would be able to find it.

I definitely do not do any of this.

Finally, just after 8 PM, I walk off the last plane.

I'm tempted to get down on my knees in the airport and kiss the ground. And I do not promise myself that never again, not in a million years, will I fly to Asia. I definitely don't do that because two years later I find myself in Vietnam.

But that's another story for another time.

Chapter Nine

Misadventures
in Paradise

WINTER 2012

The day began idyllically enough. What I remember most even now is not *the incident* but the sun glancing off the pristine mountain river and water as blue as a robin's egg while the canopy of cloud forest swayed above us. I remember the light that made it to the river—not refracted by stray clouds or absorbed by the foliage—casting golden iridescent pools on us as we bathed. It was this hour swimming in a jungle river—a time that seems almost dreamlike—that most typifies not only our travels in the Dominican Republic but something worth preserving.

We don't start that day at a river lost in time. Instead, Tiffany and I awake in the small, sun-drenched, parched Caribbean city of Pedernales. Like every morning in Pedernales, we wake to the sounds of unflappable roosters, cats in heat, whining dogs, men shouting in Spanish, and the *zip-zip-zip* of motorbikes. But unlike every other morning, I have a hangover from unexpected festivities the night before.

We'd planned to spend last night searching in the forests just outside Pedernales for an animal called the solenodon. But drenching, tropical rain had halted our planned activities, so instead of observing solenodons in the wild, I was given the opportunity to observe the natural behavior of Dominicans in nocturnal relaxation.

Resting on the eastern edge of the Dominican Republic, Pedernales is the country's most far-flung major town and serves as a border crossing with Haiti. With around twenty-seven thousand people, it retains a local bravado, a quality lacking in much of the overly touristed Caribbean today. Not only are visitors few and far between here, but nothing in the town feels as though it has been built specifically for foreigners—no resorts, no cheesy restaurants, no hawkers. Pedernales is what it is, unabashedly so. Viewed as a bit of a backwater by the urbane residents of Santo Domingo, it is undoubtedly alive with circling motorbikes, legal and illegal Haitians, and Dominican country music known as *bachata*.

Routed by rain, our solenodon search party spent the hours we'd planned to be in the forest chasing critters, drinking local beer—only Presidente Light here—in a bar abutting the main square. Once the torrential rain stopped, we moved outside onto the square itself, away from the head-splittingly loud music that made it next to impossible to, you know, actually talk. The smell of fresh rain mingled with beer, cigarettes, and, even more, bike exhaust as we watched half the town ride their motorbikes around and around the square in what seemed to me an impromptu parade but apparently happened pretty much every weekend.

While Tiffany wisely opted to go to bed early, I chit-chatted with Ros, a young PhD student I was shadowing because of her research on solenodons, and Juan Carlos, our driver from Santo Domingo. Both in their own ways were foreigners here, too. Ros was from the southern United Kingdom, though she'd spent practically the entire previous year in Pedernales chasing mammals no one has ever heard of, not even most Dominicans, in the undergrowth and the canopy. She stuck out with her pale skin, sharp-cut blond hair, and no-bullshit attitude, which seems a career requirement for field conservationists.

Juan Carlos, our easy-going driver, was Dominican, just not Perdernalian.

To be Perdernalian was to be a lifer, to have grown up here, be known, and accustomed to the rhythms of this little town. In this, Pedernales is like small towns everywhere.

To be frank, I had no reason to be watching the bikes go 'round and 'round at midnight, listening to the painfully loud bass, swigging beer that tasted like every other national beer on the planet, and guiltily ignoring, along with everyone else, the Haitian children begging for coins. None whatsoever.

I had no reason . . . *except* for that elusive solenodon, who, while we partied and communicated in that tipsy, awkward way of bare acquaintances socializing in a foreign country, poked amid the wet leaf litter with its long maneuverable nose for grubs, worms, and other edible goodies just a few kilometers away. Close enough, in fact, that it could not help but hear the *thump-thump-thump* of human music and the cacophony of human motorbikes diffusing all the way to its little forest, a place it had scampered about for tens of millions of years.

In the deep recesses of its wonderfully ancient brain, the solenodon was probably thinking one word: *usurpers.*

I have a theory that OCD isn't all anxiety attacks, rogue thoughts, and inane and irrational actions on repeat. Beneath all the boring terrors of the disease, there may be a special skill, even a kind of superpower, like the potential connection between mental illness and creativity. There is no medical evidence for my theory, as the research on OCD focuses solely, and understandably, on the negatives of the disorder—and indeed, the disease is defined by its shittiness and nothing else. But I think it's possible that having something like OCD may correlate to other more positive traits, including obsessing over subject matters that others may glaze over at the mere mention of.

You see, I can become obsessed, or hyperfocused, on subjects other than cancer, car accidents, and coprophobia. I can become single-mindedly interested, reading everything I can, obsessively learning and expanding my knowledge. In middle school, I was obsessed with the Middle Ages and cryptozoology. For a time in high school, it was film noir and T. E. Lawrence; then came Shakespeare and Dostoevsky; and, shortly after, the 1916 Easter Rising (hence studying abroad in Ireland). More recently the Peloponnesian War, the Sumatran rhino, and the little dodo.

And, of course, the solenodon.

In 2005 the Zoological Society of London started a new program called EDGE, which stands for Evolutionary Distinct and Globally Endangered. The program launched with a list of the hundred most EDGE mammals: mammals that are not only facing the endless night of extinction but also evolutionary distinct. These particular species have few living relatives. Some are members of a small tribe; others are the last remnants of a distant antediluvian foundation. You might call them strange, unique, bizarre, or simply lonely. Think Sumatran rhinos (of course), echidnas, hoatzin, the purple frog, and the maleo. If lost, we lose not only a distinct species but a whole swath of evolutionary wildness, a genetic branch cut off forever.

At number four on the list of mammals stood the world's only two soleno-dons: the Hispaniolan and the Cuban. As a wild-thing enthusiast, I'm ashamed to say this was the first time I'd ever heard of them.

The obsession started slowly, as many do. I became increasingly beguiled by the solenodon's many distinct attributes: its venom, its grooved teeth (solenodon in ancient Greek means "grooved teeth") built to shoot out the liquid toxin, its clickity-clacking and squeaking, which may be a kind of echolocation, its ridic-ulously long claws, its funny drunk waddle, its weird teats, which sit near the ass of the female. While it may outwardly resemble a rodent, it is in no way related.

The two species of solenodon make up an entire taxonomic family, sitting in the order of Eulipotyphla along with hedgehogs, moles, desmans, shrews, and moonrats. What joy so much strangeness lives among us!

The solenodon showed me how little we know, how little we even care, about all the other life on this planet. It's as if we live in a neighborhood of a billion and never go out, never knock on doors, never pay a call, but just stay inside with our doors barred and our windows shut. The gates of humanity closed.

It was like finding an alien life under my nose all along...and such a nose. Did I mention that the Hispaniolan solenodon is the only species in the world with a ball-and-socket nose?

The clincher for me, however, was when I learned that the solenodon is the ultimate survivor. It has been around for 76 million years. Let me just repeat that so it sinks in: This mammal has been on our planet for *76 million years*.

That means while the Tyrannosaurus Rex, Triceratops, and the Dakotaraptor (a big bad raptor) roamed North America, so did the solenodon. Remember *Jurassic Park*? Well, this baby *lived it*.

I was hooked. I read everything I could find about the two species of solenodon, which wasn't much. I closely tracked the progress of the Last Survivors Project in the Dominican Republic, which was attempting to get some baseline information on the Hispaniolan solenodon.[1]

I even considered writing a book about the solenodon. But Tiffany suggested I pick a different topic, her nice way of saying, "Jeremy, no one would buy or read a book about this rat-like thing they've never heard of." But I couldn't believe there wasn't a secret market out there for solenodon lovers. (Apparently, my delusional thinking isn't just about diseases but also the public appetite for solenodons.)

So, when 2012 came around and Rhett asked, "Where are you thinking of going this year?" I chose to head to the Dominican Republic and shadow the final stages of the Last Survivor Project.

To try to see a solenodon.

Like I said, the next day begins idyllically enough for us and likely for the now-slumbering solenodon, too, deep and secure in its warm, earthy burrow. Freed for the moment from the unending, penetrating noise of that youthful two-legged species that thinks itself so special.

My slight hangover from too much beer fades shortly after breakfast and, more important, caffeine. As our station wagon, driven by the indomitable Juan Carlos, makes its way out of little Pedernales and into the foothills of the Baoruco Mountain Range, I begin to feel light and hopeful for the day's prospects. It's probably the overdose of sunshine.

Years of writing about rainforests allow me to see the foothills of the Baorucos through an ecologist's eyes. We are driving through what scientists would call a mosaic landscape, small forest patches surrounded by pasture and agricultural plots. One might call it pastoral if pastoral can apply to the tropics. But in ecological and human terms, it is a mix of poverty-induced deforestation, livestock pasture, splashes of fields, and a few surviving forests, especially in the highlands and valleys where felling proves trickier.

We pass small, run-down Haitian homesteads where naked children run about in the yards with chickens and goats. We pass coffee fields, sometimes shaded by tall trees, and agricultural plots meant to sustain a family. We make our way past horses and cattle grazing on mountainsides, neither animal native to this hemisphere, and forest patches still standing tall in the Caribbean light. We have to climb nearly two thousand feet to reach our destination, the small village of Mencia.

I imagine that somewhere in this landscape my night-loving solenodon slumbers away, but we are putting that search on hold today. Instead, the plan is to reach the mountain village and search for the country's only *other* surviving native land mammal: the hutia.

While the solenodon drew me to visit the Dominican Republic, catching sight of a hutia would be a sweet bonus. Imagine a giant hamster scampering in tree branches in the moonlight and you have a pretty good idea of the hutia. They are big arboreal (tree-climbing) rodents with a prehensile tail, which they use to grasp branches. It acts as a fifth limb, much like the tail of a spider monkey or opossum. Despite their oddity and general cuteness, hutias are pretty much unheard of outside, and even inside, the Caribbean.

Needless to say, I was burning to get a good look.[2]

During the long and bumpy drive into the highlands, I amuse Ros, Juan Carlos, and my wife by attempting to speak Spanish. I've found time and again that nothing endears a traveler to a foreign land like butchering the local language. (The only place this doesn't work is in France.) My inability to speak foreign tongues has successfully passed the time during many travels, broken the ice with strangers, and subdued the inevitable tension that often comes with traveling with people you didn't know a week earlier.

Juan Carlos says, "Okay, try this. Jeremy. Say, 'Hola mi hermano.'"

I say, "Hola mi hermano." And everyone bursts into laughter, including me after a moment.

"Okay. Now say, 'Me gusta bailar.'"

And I repeat it exactly. "Me gusta bailar."

But it sends the whole car into fits of giggles again.

Apparently, I sound nothing like Juan Carlos—or anyone else in the Hispanophone. The words come out "too white," "robotic," and "the opposite of subtlety," says my truth-telling wife. I'm tone-deaf (you should hear me sing, I've been told it's amazing), and I think my inability to match pitch and my capacity for murdering spoken language may be related.

After I sufficiently murder every single simple Spanish phrase Juan Carlos can think of, with helpful input from Ros and my wife, we arrive in Mencia. This mountain or hillside village has been Ros's base for weeks while researching the Hispaniolan hutia. It is also the home village to her number one local assistant, Misael, a Pedernalian and father of four in his thirties.

Misael's eldest daughter, about twelve, opens the door a little to reveal a domestic scene of her younger sister fighting with their screaming half-brother while the youngest, a daughter of about two, stares naked and wide-eyed at us.

Español sparks back and forth between the eldest and Ros, and we're quickly escorted back outside to the front steps. Ros translates there for me. Misael and his wife are still passed out from the night before; they, too, had been at the Pedernales's festivities. It turns out a local politician showed up at the square after we left and bought drinks for everyone. According to Ros, this is a pretty standard way of practicing democracy in the area. It sounds better than American democracy to me. I'd rather have politicians buy me a beer than have billionaires buy politicians. At least the corruption results in free alcohol.

The door opens again and the little boy, maybe three, and the youngest come out to gawk at the newcomers in their village. Misael had the eldest two girls with his first partner and the other two with his current partner, Carmen.

"Pretty standard for the men, here," Ros says in English so the kids don't pick up on it. "Most of them have lots of exes or juggle multiple partners. The women on the other hand..."

"Yup," affirms my wife.

Juan Carlos and I wisely keep our mouths shut. Ros asks, "Who wants coffee?"

The youngest crawls unbidden into Tiff's lap. She's around the same age as our daughter back home and has similar huge brown eyes. I feel suddenly quite homesick, or perhaps I should say kidsick. It's the first time Tiffany and I have left our daughter since she was born. We practiced several times before with a few night visits to grandma and grandpa's, but this is eleven nights without our Aurelia.

Tiff wasn't supposed to be on this trip. The plan had been for me to tackle the Dominican Republic solo because we have a freaking two-year-old to, you know, nurture and parent and stuff. But the closer the trip came, the higher my anxiety rose, like a tide that doesn't stop as it should but just continues inexorably. Finally, Tiff declared she was going to keep me from madness.

Ros returns with mugs of steaming coffee made from beans growing on arabica trees we can see just down the hill.

Tiffany, Juan Carlos, and I sit in the front yard watching Mencia go by—or not, as it were—while poor Ros attempts to get the day together. As a PhD student, Ros is not a travel guide, but since I came to see her work, she's pretty much turned into one. She spends a good six days taking us from place to place, forest to forest, beach to beach and attempting to impart on us an incredible amount of knowledge about the wildlife and the people.

Rural Dominican Republic doesn't move on time. In the United States, time always moves *on time*, and when it doesn't, everyone starts hyperventilating. But in many parts of the world, wasting time is not a sin but a standard. On-timers may grumble as their on-time panic rises, but this slower pace can be a way of appreciating the present. So we sip our coffee, watch the kids and the palmchats in the palms across the street, and try not to think about whether or not we're on schedule. Or what the schedule is, for that matter.

When the coffee gets the best of me, I head into the house to find Ros in the midst of her current goal: waking up the home's parents.

"Uh, Ros, can I use the bathroom?"

"There's one down the hall, but it doesn't work. There's an outhouse." She steps through the house and points outside. "Just between the two houses. There."

"Oh, okay," I say. I hand my cup to Tiffany and cross Mencia's single street.

The mountain village is home to about a hundred or so people. A few decades ago, the government came in and built houses for everyone, three-room homes that are now beginning to crumble and mold in the tropical climate but were probably a great improvement on what came before. Because of this, every house looks generally the same—only painted different colors—giving the community a sense of village conformity. Each house also got a modern toilet, but a decade later most no longer work.

As I walk down the road, I see roosters of various sizes, colors, and ages housed in mesh boxes in every yard, waiting for their moment of glory, or gory, in the ring. Dominicans are mad for cockfighting—you know, that blood sport where two jacked-up, testosterone-fueled roosters are put into a pit together, and peck and slash each other until one is dead. Locked in their pens, these born-and-bred angry birds today egg each other on with crowing and cackling. They stop as I near and leer arrogantly at me, almost as if daring me to open their cages.

Little juveniles, currently free, run about with patchy feathers and impertinent stares, velociraptors in miniature. One can imagine their prehistoric ancestors tackling prey several times their size with cheeky finesse. Now in a bizarre fit of evolution, I'm big enough to step on them, and around the world they are raised for dinner. Sometimes we even eat them with our fingers out of paper buckets. Take that, dinosaurs.

After navigating the bloodthirsty birds, I close in on the outhouse, only to be met by a caramel-colored shaggy dog on a loop of metal chain.

Oh, come on. Really!? Can I not have just one rabies-free trip?

I slow down to about a ten-hour mile. I lick my lips. What do I do? Do I say something? Something nice like, "Who's a good boy?" or just "Hello, doggie?"

I open my mouth.

And the dog bends low and growls. I freeze. I now have a decision before me: try to make it to the outhouse or hold it as long as possible.

I take the measure of caramel-the-dog's chain and decide higher powers are at work here, over which I have little control. In a swift motion, I arc around the dog and dash for the outhouse. I make it to the shed and slam the door, not even looking at the dog who may or may not have made a snap at me.

I rush through my duties, adrenaline pumping, and then it's time to do it again. I open the door a crack, sunlight poking through, and when I see no dog, I slide my way out. He's there, of course. He strains against the chain, barks fiercely, but can't reach me. I try to move slowly, but find the harder I try, the faster I go until I'm back, full sprint, sweat soaked and cortisol snorted, at the front porch.

Tiff and Juan Carlos look at me as if nothing's happened, like it's just another morning in Mencia.

Then Ros emerges from the house and says off-handedly, "Oh I forgot to warn you—"

"Yeah?"

"The dog by the outhouse. He'll attack if you get too close," she says it with that British stoicism that borders on flippancy, a key to their ability to have once conquered a fifth of the world's population.

"You okay?" Tiff asks, suddenly in on the dog-killer loop. But my eyes are following an imaginary line to the outhouse, to that dog, which is like evil Clifford to my mind: big, crimson, and mean as shit.

On our first day in the country, we visited Parque Colon in Santo Domingo to watch feral pigeons, invasive species to this hemisphere, shit on Columbus's statue.

The original name for this paradisiacal island was Ayiti, or "land of tall mountains," a name bestowed by the indigenous Taino people. It was here on Ayiti (from which Haiti gets its name), that the first major collision between the Old World and the so-called New World occurred in that date every schoolchild knows: 1492.

Ayiti was Columbus's last stop on his first voyage but the only place he put down roots. When he arrived, at least hundreds of thousands of Taino were living here. One contemporary says over 3 million.

Within fifty years, the Taino were essentially extinct as a culture and a people. In addition to unwittingly bringing novel diseases, Columbus and his men inflicted every horror on the Taino. Slavery, mass execution, senseless slaughter, and rape were routine. Taino men were forced to work in mines and fields (men who failed to deliver tribute had their hands cut off), and Taino wives and their daughters were passed around as sex slaves. Young girls fetched an especially high price, wrote an ambivalent Columbus.

Whenever the Taino resisted, they were wiped out by steel, horses, canons, and attack dogs. It was a mass extermination, both intentional and unintentional, of remarkable brutality and efficiency.[3] With the Taino extinct, Europe turned to Africa for slaves, trading one infamy for another.

A couple of hours later and we are on our way—a whole party—thanks entirely to Ros's powerhouse organizational skills. Juan Carlos, Tiffany, Ros, an indeterminate number of children, and I all ride in Juan Carlos's car while ahead of us, Misael and Carmen, one of those Dominican beauties with a poise and grace that makes one feel shrunken and misshapen, ride on a motorbike, their two-year-old perched in front like a hood ornament. A few random villagers follow us on motorbikes as well, with one sporting a live chicken tethered to his seat.

Through the sun-sprinkled hills and down a rough road, we arrive at our destination: a small green ravine with a twisting river running through it and the canopy of a cloud forest above us, not so dense that sunlight doesn't, in patches, make its way through.

We foreigners—guests, I should say—change into swimsuits as the local adults prepare lunch. Meanwhile, the children have already rushed into the river, clothes and all.

As the river rolls through the mountains, it falls into wide shallow pools, perfect for swimming or, more accurately, bathing. Unlike the children who dance across the streams, we cross the wet rocks carefully and help ourselves luxuriously to the pools. In soaked clothes, the children play riotously about us, splashing and laughing.

Many Americans might consider these children generally poor because they live in small houses with lots of people. They aren't drowning in stuffed animals and art projects, there are no video games or computers. But at this moment, these kids appear richer than any American kid—or adult—I can name.

Poverty is a complex thing, but the more one travels and the more variations on poverty one sees, the more complexity attaches itself to the term, including the assumption that an American's version of poverty translates directly to misery. This is not to say that when anyone lacks food, health care, housing, clean water, or education they are uninjured. Of course, they are injured deeply. Yet, many US and European children are impoverished in another, less recognized way. They are impoverished by a lack of nature, a lack of real freedom and adventure, a lack of perfect afternoons like this. Swimming in a mountain river, chasing each other over wet rocks, catching little aquatic creatures, splashing one another under the branches of a forest. What wouldn't we give for our children to experience even a single day like this, a day that will stick with them for the rest of their lives?

Just on the outskirts of this paradise, a tiny drama occurs. One of the village men unstraps the squawking chicken from his motorbike. He takes a small hatchet and the struggling animal behind a boulder, where we can't see, as if not to offend the guests with the sight of blood. There is a quick motion. A flutter of feathers. He doesn't come out from behind the boulder for a while because he's plucking and cleaning the now dead bird in privacy, a creature sacrificed for our appetites.

An hour after the chicken's head has been cut off, we eat it in a spicy, delicious stew. We eat with the relish of the cool river water dripping off our skins. We chat and laugh. With lunch finished, all the adults rush into the water once again, like the children they've grown out of.

Later, I lounge on a flat rock in the sun like a lizard, letting the beads of water burn off naturally, and read a few chapters from Stendahl's *The Red and the Black*.

It's with bitter sweetness when we leave this little Eden, where appetites and souls are sated. But we have some tree-climbing guinea pigs to find.

At best thirteen different species of hutia reside on the planet today—though three of these are possibly extinct—all strewn across the Caribbean. There used to be a lot more of these tree-loving rodents. Seven other species (that we know of) have certainly gone extinct in the last thousand years. In our specific case, the Hispaniola hutia, the last survivor of its genus *Plagiodontia*, is listed as endangered

The Caribbean was once a truly wild place of wacky, diverse, and even giant mammals. Giant hutias once roamed several Caribbean islands, with one on Hispaniola the size of a friggin' black bear, amusingly called the twisted-toothed mouse. Imagine how different children's books would be had that beauty survived.

The Caribbean also used to house distinct monkeys, ground sloths and *giant* ground sloths, other solenodons (including a giant species), and a bizarre mammal family called Nesophontes, of which none have survived. Zero. All of the Caribbean's monkeys and sloths are also gone. Probably eaten to extinction.

In the last five hundred years, most recorded extinctions occurred on the world's islands. With nowhere to run, island animals are especially vulnerable to changes such as hunting, habitat destruction, or invasive species. But that pattern is starting to change as we turn the world's forests and ecosystems, and even the oceans, into increasingly smaller patches of suitable habitat, surrounded by degradation. In a sense, all the world is beginning to look like islands.

Today, Hispaniola has only two surviving *native* land mammals: the solenodon and the hutia. And how these two survived the first settlers, then the Taino people, the Spaniards, the arrival of rats, the stray dogs and cats, the mongooses, the fires, axes, and guns of the last few centuries is not only a miracle but a mystery.

I have a pretty heady obsession with endangered species no one's ever heard of. I think it's both their extreme vulnerability (I like underdogs) and the extreme ignorance with which the world treats them that makes them so fascinating. Psychologists would probably attribute some of this to my childhood experiences, but I prefer to think of it as just a natural sympathy for the strange, the outcast, and the gravely imperiled. Most of the world's species are not elephants, tigers, and pandas. They are hutias and solenodons, suicide palms and venda cycads, Dakota skippers and Bathurst coppers, Cowan's mantellas and *Sagalla caecilians*, narrowsnout sawfish and Pompeii worms,

Bridgeoporus nobilissimus and sea sparkles, and, you know, some four hundred thousand beetles.

But how many times does WWF talk about the red-crested tree rat? How many nature documentaries focus on the Frigate Island giant tenebrionid beetle? Scientists haven't even given the vast majority of the world's species a proper name. And only a select few—usually big and charismatic—get any conservation love.

My family had started as an encyclopedia family, but over the years became a DSM family.

My parents bought a set of the *World Book Encyclopedia* shortly after I was born from a traveling salesman. We kept them in the den, just ten or so feet from our kitchen table. It was necessary for the volumes to be close because invariably during every family meal, one of us would make the trek to look up something related to the conversation. Which state has the highest mountain? Is Kathmandu the capital of Nepal? What's the biggest cat?

You have to remember this was the 1980s and early '90s, pre-smartphones and even pre-internet. The encyclopedia was our Google of the time. Sure, it didn't have answers to everything, but at twenty-two volumes, it was impressively valuable. One of my favorite memories is eating spaghetti or chow mein and watching the encyclopedias pile up on the table as the conversation ranged into places far away and people long dead.

But as we got older, another book increasingly took the place of the encyclopedia: the DSM III (*Diagnostic and Statistical Manual of Mental Illness*). The discovery that we were all mentally ill created a laser-like focus on our various ailments, especially from my father, a social worker, who loved to diagnose us around the table.

I wasn't the most rebellious kid, aside from skipping school and all, but I *hated* whenever mental illness was brought up. Which, given how many times one of us ended up in the hospital or started some new medicine or therapist, was all the time. I desperately craved escape. I wanted to be in a world where there was no mental illness, where we could just pull out the encyclopedia again and talk about something that mattered, not this nightly therapy session.

In the intervening years, several of our encyclopedia's volumes went missing, so that the alphabet was slowly vanishing from our eyes, and every time one of us was sent hither, the likelihood of coming back and saying, "Nope, can't find the D," increased, almost like a metaphor for my vanishing childhood.

During the spring of my homeschooling, I realized it wasn't all it was cracked up to be. Don't get me wrong, I enjoyed the months of recovery. But it was also lonely. Meanwhile, my parents and I were told over and over that I'd never make it back to Buffalo Senior High School ("once a school avoider, always a school avoider").

But I did, and perhaps it was the DSM that drove me to it.

On the first day of tenth grade, I showered and ate breakfast. My mother drove me to school. I took a deep breath and walked in. For months I'd been telling myself I could do it. I'd chosen my classes carefully and had friends in my lunch period. My parents had gotten the school to generously agree to let me skip the first period so I could get enough sleep.

I'd been diagnosed with a sleep disorder for years. I'm not sure of the details today, but my sense of it is less a disorder and more that my sleep clock didn't fit modern society.

I did it. I did the first day. Then the next. And the next.

That fall I got cast as Roat in the play *Wait Until Dark*, playing a sociopathic murderer. The director said I was the only boy who auditioned who could convincingly play crazy.

I made new friends that year. They helped me get through the ups and downs of being sixteen, let alone the days and weeks when mental illness reared. It, of course, still did.

My junior year proved rougher, and once again I had to drop out of a play a few weeks in because of depression and stress. But I stuck with school, day by day, week by freaking week, until my senior year when the end of high school loomed on the horizon.

Once the sun begins to decline, we make the quick trip from the river back to the village to prep for our hutia hunt. To do so we stop in first at Ros's headquarters. Having done months of fieldwork in the village, she'd rented one of the houses.

But Ros has been away for a few weeks. And when you're away from Mencia, things happen. Strange things. A live rooster tied up in the kitchen. A machete on the counter. Two creepy photos on the wall (turns out those had always been there). And Ros's stuff has been flung about her room. Like Goldilocks, someone has been sleeping in Ros's bed while she was away.

Furious, she strides out to find out who has taken up in her house, leaving Tiffany and me to make up our beds in the second bedroom, i.e., sleeping bags on the concrete floor.

At the moment of rolling out our packs and unpacking a few necessities, it is hard to put our finger on it, but there is a sense of malaise that seems to rise in this house like a fog.

Perhaps it is just that some strange man could show up at any moment for his bird and his big knife. Or maybe it's Ros's warning that sometimes cockroaches and spiders run across your face as you sleep. Probably it's nothing—too many horror movies—but maybe, just maybe, Tiff and I catch a whiff of some unspeakable sin that happened in this house, like an Edgar Allan Poe tale: a beating heart beneath the floorboards or a wine-loving Italian entombed alive.

Whatever it is, both I *and* my much more reasonable and laidback wife feel unsettled by this house.

Ros saves us from our dark pondering when she returns. We assume she's delivered the message about the unwelcome lodger to the correct people. It's time to search out hutias.

While Ros and her team catch the solenodons by hand, hutias are a different story. Ros has resorted to putting traps in front of their burrows. Then the team returns to put radio collars on the captured hutias for tracking. So we are heading out to check some of the traps.

The late afternoon is still bright and beautiful, a few white as puffball clouds lolling in the sky, as Ros, Misael, Tiffany, and I leave Mencia behind.

Just beyond the village, we turn off the main road into an expansive field where cows and horses graze.

I hate cows. And horses are the most accident-prone mammals in the world.

Whoever heard of an animal that has to be put down every time it breaks a leg? Also, every horse person I know has been seriously injured at least once, sometimes multiple times, by these understandably annoyed quadrupeds. If you think about it, it's not a little insane for two-legged hominids to climb on top of a thousand-pound ungulate and then ride it around at thirty-plus miles per hour. It's amazing, of course. But also fully bizarre.

My uncle kept cows on our forty-acre farmstead, which meant whenever I'd venture into the pasture, as it was known, there'd be a chance of being charged by a pissed-off cow. The cows were also ecologically destructive by keeping any trees from growing across our otherwise unused acreage. I wanted a forest. But my father, who'd grown up with cows he'd loved like children, saw the land differently. To him, a forest growing on it felt feral, unused. To me, cows trammeling through the land felt sacrilegious.

(So, I don't really *hate* cows and horses. I mean, that would be extreme, right? And a little...crazy? I love all animals and I admit horses are awesome and beautiful—blah, blah, blah—*I* just don't want to ride them or be behind them when they kick. Cows are...I'm trying to think of something nice to say...Give me a minute...Something'll come...)[4]

Walking through the Dominican field, the domestic quadrupeds cause my palms to sweat, my breath to quicken. I want to voice my fears but don't. The image of being run over by a cow plays on repeat in my head. I stay close to the group. I work hard not to meet the eyes of the horses or cows that are docilely munching the grass, wholly unconcerned by the presence of four humans blundering by, probably a common occurrence here.

Not far in front of us, rising above the fields, looms the cloud forest, our destination. It's only when we enter the sudden coolness of the tree-giving shade and moisture that Tiffany and I discover there is no trail.

Hiking through a tropical forest when there is no trail, at least for the uninitiated, is kind of like going to Walmart to get milk at 5 AM on Black Friday. Of course, Ros and Misael slip through the forest with the ease of two fit people who have done this innumerable times. They are, it seems, in an adventure movie. We, however, are in a comedy.

For a good hour, Tiff and I struggle through the forest, stuttering over boulders, tripping on roots, and ungainly attempting to keep the backs of Ros and Misael in view. Eventually, we have to climb across a ridge, clinging to tree roots and trunks and cutting ourselves on defensive plants. Finally, hot, sweaty, bleeding, and cursing under our breaths, we catch up to Ros and Misael, already busily working at the trap site. Here would be our reward: living, breathing, bizarre Caribbean mammals.

But trap after trap is empty. Hope holds until the last one proves as barren as the rest. Then the storm arrives.

When we left, the afternoon sky had been clear with only a few cloud tufts floating leisurely like giant cottonwood seeds, but now the forest grows dark, and the noises of the birds and insects vanish. The silence is broken as thunder booms in the distance and then a wall of rain steers into our view on the horizon through the cracks in the canopy.

Ros and Misael scramble to finish their work, loathe to leave before all the traps are replaced, hoping to catch hutias another day. But within minutes, the atmosphere becomes the enemy and the rain falls on us in sheets.

"It's time to go!" Ros shouts above the thunder, saying the words Tiff and I have longed to hear the last twenty minutes.

Half running, we slip on wet roots, splash in the mud, and fight to stay together. With glasses on, Tiff and I can barely make out anything more than streams of water as we flounder on. If the way here was onerous, the way back has become perilous. Carelessly, all of us forgot to pack flashlights, assuming the daylight would last until our return.

Crossing the ravine, my feet go out from under me. Slipping in the mud, I fall maybe five feet before—*oomph*—I hit a tree in my abdomen and hang there stupidly.

"You okay?" Tiff yells from somewhere.

"Yup. Fine." I crawl my way back to the ledge, using branches and roots to pull my body through the mud.

You'd think Steve would've been using a bullhorn through all this. But I find myself actually enjoying it, enjoying the thrill. Here is adventure, immediacy, real, not imagined, peril. It's a fucking relief. I felt more terror walking by the stupid cows than I did almost plunging into a ravine, with no medical assistance anywhere in the vicinity. Somehow, for some reason, I have faith we will all get through this.

And we do.

Wet, exhausted, cursing, we emerge from the cloud forest and back onto the pasture, rain still lashing us like spit from a god. Now free from any real danger, my adrenaline dies away and Steve reappears, saying the one word that could overwhelm all the sense of adventure I for once enjoyed: *cows*.

As we skirt through the wet dark, I keep envisioning the shape of a dull-eyed cow emerging suddenly from the murk in full charge, horns aimed like spear points in a phalanx. So I stay close to the rest, barely breathing, almost paralyzed by visions of imminent attack when in fact we are far safer now than struggling through the forest.

My breathing slows only when we crawl over the fence, separating us from the potential of molestation by storm-crazed cows. Or horses. Horses could kill us, too. Really.

Opening the door to Misael's house reveals a scene very different from the muddy, soaked, thundering one outside, full of sound and fury. The family all sit in the main room, one of the older girls conducts homework in her worn-to-the-bone Justin Bieber notebook, while the other attempts to patiently erect a structure out of playing cards. The younger boy and girl rush to meet us. It's night and you know it, for the only light is glowing lazily from an oil lamp.

This is still the norm for a not-small minority of families around the world: no TV, no computer, no screens of distraction, but a life more in tune with the thousands of generations before, less out of sync with our biological and genetic rhythms.

"Are you hungry?" Ros asks as we sit down around the table.

The answer is a round of affirmatives, and Carmen heads to the kitchen to cook us up a simple but heartening dish of eggs and rice.

The toddler with the big brown eyes crawls up onto Tiff's lap. Conversation pings back and forth but almost all in Spanish, allowing Tiffany and I the freedom of our private English thoughts.

When the food arrives, we eat with abandon.

"We could still see some hutias, Jeremy," Ros says fifteen minutes later as she scrapes her plate.

"Really?"

"We have a few radio-collared near here. Just a drive and a bit of a walk."

I catch Tiff's glance. We just learned what a "bit of a walk" means to field biologists.

"Um..." I hesitate.

"Is there a trail?" Tiff asks.

"Yes," Ros said. "Short and easy."

Tiff and I exchange looks again. She's not enthused. I'm not exactly jumping up and down for joy either, but it's hard to say no to someone you just met a few days ago in a country thousands of miles from home. More important, we'd come all this way to try to see these little bastards. Well, I had. Tiff hadn't flown several thousand miles to get a look at some exotic rodents; she'd come to make sure I didn't go batshit bonkers.

"Yeah," I say. "I'm in." I look again at Tiff. "You can skip out if you want, hon."

"No, I'll come," she says.

I get it: better to be hunting for hutias in the woods at night than left alone in the house across the street with just a rooster, a machete, and two dimming photos of dead people for company.

The rain has abated, and the twilight is beginning to fill again with the sounds of insects belting their territorial needs, their lovelorn-ness, or maybe just their happiness at being alive. Can you imagine if humans got together and sang like that every night?

We drive a couple of miles to the forest and park the cars at a dark dead end. The team, including Juan Carlos now, follows a path along a forest river, forehead flashlight beams leading the way. The river is clear and uninhabited until a freshwater shrimp emerges paddling in the dark like some ghost of an older lost era. The dark and the singing of insects, the umbra of the forest and the nearly translucent shrimp—it feels for a moment as if this could be the island before Columbus's fate-soaked voyage. Before disease and death and destruction—and then truly this new world we've scrabbled together. Not discovered but built over the ashes and bones of the old.

Soon, the radio transmitter tells us to leave the river and head up a small cliffside. The path narrows until it vanishes and the soil beneath us, soaked just a few hours ago by the brief but torrential rains, has turned into mud.

Juan Carlos, not used to bumming around with naturalists, is wearing white tennis shoes. They do not fare well. As we climb, clinging to branches to pull us ever higher, I think over the string of expletives going through my wife's head at the moment. Eventually, we reach the top of the rise and stand beneath a canopy of trees filling up most of the sky, beyond which the stars glisten like the glint of sunlight on snow.

Using the transmitter, Ros quickly locates one of her collared hutias way up in the tree. This is the easy bit. Seeing it is not.

Misael takes the lead, continually grabbing me and pulling me to where I might have a good view.

"There, there, see it now?" Misael asks me so many times in Spanish that I begin to know what he means! Look at me: I'm friggin' fluent.

But all I catch is the sliver of a tail or a blob of a shape or mostly just a lot of leaves bathed by flashlight. Indeed, it seems impossible to see this rabbit-sized rodent. It moves with surprising alacrity and is easily hidden amid the thick-packed leaves of the canopy. My neck muscles strain.

Finally, I catch the glimpse I want. There it is: a giant rodent munching leaves at the very top of a tropical forest canopy. But even while one could mistake it for a rat, it certainly isn't. While its tail is short, almost stubby, it's also like that of an opossum, maneuverable, coilable, and super-strong. Its face is rounder than a rat's, more like a fat mouse or a beaver. And it is startlingly big. Indeed, while still a rodent, the hutia is firmly in the cavy family; this is the parvorder, small order, of South American rodents that includes the guinea pigs, chinchillas, agoutis, and that big ol' record-breaking rodent, my sweet love, a capybara.

I've finally gotten my view after much difficulty and several times saying, "No, no, it's okay. We can go. It's just not meant to be this time."

Tiff, though, never really gets a good look at the Hispaniolan hutia. Well, that's not exactly true. On the last full day of our trip as we are driving across the island, a different guide, Manny Jimenes with Explora Ecotour, pulls over.

On the side of the road is a Hispaniolan hutia, at 9 AM, in the bright daylight, on a busy highway. Only problem: It's dead. Struck down by some vehicle the night before. Its insides crushed instantaneously, but for all that, looking like it's just slumbering, except, of course, for the red goo and organs plunged out of one side.

I wonder as we drive off that morning—the dead hutia stuffed into a small box to be sent to scientists as a specimen—how the hutia avoided extinction when so many other mammals on this island did not. What about this particular species allowed it to survive so many onslaughts? And considering it's endangered today, and with basically zero conservation work targeting it, how much longer might it last? How much roadkill will it take? How many predations by stray dogs? How long before the Hispaniolan hutia follows its relatives into the long night of extinction?

Will there still be a Hispaniloan hutia when my daughter is seventy? How about when her daughter turns seventy? Or hers, or even *hers*—my great-great-granddaughter as a septuagenarian, which will probably be post-2150?

It's difficult for most of us to think like this, to wrap our heads around timescales beyond our own lives, but conservationists have to do it all the time. They have to think in terms of generations, in terms of threats, such as climate change, that will very well spoil even the best-laid plans. And then they have to have faith that someone—anyone, please, pretty please, seriously!—will pick up their work after they've gone. And it's not all for naught. Conservation is always an act of faith.

But days before that unfortunate roadkill, having glimpsed our elusive hutia, we cross up the hillside and through a maize field to reach our vehicle. It is high time for bed.

The three of us don't say much as we clamor into our sleeping bags in the evil, dark little house. I must have slept—some. But when I awake a few hours later, or half-awake as sleep still clings to me at the edges, increasing—as it does—my morbidity and irrationality, I find myself panting with fear. I think of cockroaches and spiders crawling over my face. I think of some hatchet-wielding Dominican maniac standing over me. I think of death and horror and extinction and madness.

And then I hear someone, some*thing*, come into the house, and all I can do is lie there. Petrified with terror, I can't move. Rigor mortis, but alive. I want to say something but don't know how to open my mouth, to speak the words. Nothing moves despite the screaming fear in my brain.

I don't know if I'm asleep or awake. But I know I can't move. I can't speak. Can't wake Tiffany. Can't even scream. Is this real? What's happening?

And then, I don't know how long after, sensation finally returns, and I feel sick. I feel hot, but not normal hot. I feel that kind of sweating, unnatural heat that portends illness. Nausea sweeps over me. I don't hear any noises anymore, and I can't tell if any of that awful spell had been real or not.

But my brain says, *Okay, okay, I'm just sick. I must have food poisoning. Or maybe not.* Steve whispers, "Maybe this is cholera or typhoid or malaria or some parasite settled in your gut. Your luck's run out, Jeremy. Boom. Chagas. Remember the Chagas."

And then my imaginary friend drops his imaginary mic.

I find I can speak now. "Tiffany. Tiffany," I say, "I think I'm going to be sick."

Bless her, she wakes quickly and takes charge. She keeps saying, "Okay, it's going to be okay."

I feel like I'm going to vomit; my stomach is tied in knots. But as we stumble around the room not wanting to wake Ros, we remember this toilet doesn't work either. Okay: outside.

Just opening the door helps—the cool air, the stars, the freedom from the stifling little house and the metaphoric demons within.

"Okay," says Tiff, "let's get to the outhouse. This way."

"Outhouse! But the dog."

"The dog?"

"The dog. On the chain. It could bite—attack. Remember? What Ros said? It's an asshole. Tiff, rabies." I say and repeat nonsensically. "Rabies."

"*Jeremy . . .*" She uses the tone that has become a mainstay of our marriage.

"I can't," I urge. "That dog is *terrifying*."

"Okay. Okay. Then we'll have to find somewhere else."

She leads me to a far side of the little lawn in front of the evil house. There's no shelter from the road, but then again since we're in a rural hill village on the border of the Dominican Republic and Haiti, no one is out. The stars are burning brilliantly above, no city lights to dampen their luminance. I try to vomit. There is trash around me, a few beer bottles, some plastic containers, a discarded old shoe. I stand there retching, but nothing comes up.

"Are you sure?" Tiff asks.

Oh, I'm pretty damned determined to vomit at this point. Still, it's all empty heaves, pointless. And then I feel it, the sick sensation has moved from my stomach to my intestines. The panic migrated.

"Shit," I say. "I have to shit."

"Shit? Christ. Okay, outhouse then."

"No, I can't."

"*Jeremy…*" Again.

But I'm already bending down. "Look away, please. Go away."

I admit, in our fourteen years together at this point, this is not our most romantic nocturnal interlude under the stars. She takes a few steps back and turns around, facing away from her husband as he poops in the yard of someone's house.

I bear down and shit—a lot. Under the stars. The undiminished stars.

When it's all done, Tiffany does what any life partner would: She covers my pile of feces with the abandoned shoe on the ground.

"There," she says. "Let's hope no one notices."

Yeah, I think, *let's hope no one notices I pooped on a village lawn last night. Let's hope.*

But, really, I can't help smiling. I feel much better now, so much better. I don't have to vomit, the flushing heat is gone, and my brain settles. I can see things for what they are now: the terrors, the exaggerations, the sleeping panic slip away. It's almost funny.

We head back inside the dark house. Ros is still sleeping. I slather my hands with sanitizer, a constant companion while traveling, and fall back asleep easily. After our 3 AM adventure, I sleep like the innocent, the unafraid. We both slumber until morning comes and the thousand-odd cocks begin crowing, including the one in the kitchen.

Thankfully, there is no evidence that Ros heard us last night. There is no evidence that any mass murderer came in and stood over us while we slept. No one notices my shit, either, underneath the unpaired, sad shoe.

We got away with it! Scot-free. Haha! A few rain showers, some tropical heat, a good number of feces-devouring beetles—not asking much here—and they'll be nothing left of our clandestine adventure.

The motley team has coffee and some sweet rolls while sitting outside Misael's house again. We soak up the morning light before we head back to Pedernales to continue our search for solenodons.

But before we leave, I head back into the Haunted House to grab my bag. Returning to Misael's, I step in something. I look down: poop on my boot. It's not mine, I've avoided that spot all morning. I look around because maybe the dog that left it will still be standing there staring at me, and then I notice my wife's face. She can barely contain her laughter. I follow her eyes. Misael's two-year-old stands pantsless, diaperless, in the yard, her shirt just barely covering her privates.

Yup, I just stepped in two-year-old human feces.

Karma is a bitch...with rabies.

Chapter Ten

The Dinosaur Mammal

WINTER 2012, CONTINUED

Francis pours out the top-shelf tequila he'd been given as a gift: one, two, three, four, five, and then, *"Salud!"* It burns—but it burns good.

We share laughter and chatter with people we just met. And then Francis asks, "Another?" I'm pretty sure Francis doesn't do this for all his guests. We all nod.

We're in Punta Rucia, on the northern coast of the Dominican Republic, nearly a straight line north of the Pedernales Peninsula. This morning we started a four-day tour with an eco-tourism group known as Explora Ecotour, run by the husband and wife team Manny Jimenez Gomez and Olyenka Sang Luciano. Over the next few days, they will take us to some of the Dominican Republic's most splendid natural sites. But tonight, we're doing shots.

Francis, a forty-year-old friend of Manny and Oly's, owns a little eco-guesthouse in Punta Rucia and had just served us one of the best meals of my life: pastelón de papa, cooked to perfection. Of course, no meal can be truly great without the best companions, and Tiff and I have taken to Manny and Oly like ducks to water.

They'd picked us up that morning from our hotel in Santo Domingo, and over the five-hour drive, we bonded. Just in their twenties and newly married, Oly and Manny had started their company the year before because they loved the natural landscapes of the Dominican Republic and wanted to see them protected. Both had grown up in the United States but had moved here, their ancestral home, to embark on this adventure.

According to Manny and Oly, part of eco-tourism is to involve local people at every stage because that spreads the financial love around and supports those who are also working toward a greener Dominican Republic. Francis was one of their connections.

A few hours before tequila, Tiff and I sprawled out on colorful hammocks on a balcony, watching the sun descend into the sea as Francis's adopted Haitian daughter played with a puppy beneath us.

As we watched, I again felt that sense of paradise surrounding me on this beguiling island. And I thought once more of the Taino people, of how many generations had lived here, of their lives, their loves, and their delights. The countless sunsets they, too, enjoyed. The world is populated by ghosts, and for some reason, they always seem more present when traveling.

There's a knock on the door. The dying light of day catches the girl below, now spreading a red blanket over waves of bright green grass as the puppy tugs on one corner.

"Coming," I say.

It's Manny.

"Dinner in a half hour. That okay?"

"Yes, of course."

He turns and then swings back around. "Oh, Jeremy—"

"Yeah?"

"Sorry the snorkeling didn't go a little better this afternoon."

"Oh, no problem. It was my first time doing it here, after all."

He nods, smiles, and then like any good guide, repeats: "Half-hour."

It turns out snorkeling is pretty much playing dead.

You lie facedown in the water and float. Yes, of course, you breathe through a plastic tube and watch in awe, I hope, as the colorful denizens of what seems another world flit, float, and scatter beneath you. But aside from engulfing oneself in wonder, it's also good practice, I think, for the grave. You know, keep still. Go with the flow. Have a coin for Charon.

When Tiffany declared at the last minute that she would go on the trip to the Dominican Republic with me, her one stipulation was, "I want to go snorkeling."

So that's how I find myself, earlier that same afternoon, in the blue dreamy Caribbean Sea trying hard to play dead. The only problem is that the ocean isn't playing along. It's rolling over us like vast round hay bales.

This is our first stop with Manny and Oly, but according to the rules, once we reach our destination, they hand us off to a local guide. He's young, maybe eighteen, smiley and intimidatingly fit in his swimsuit.

"Hola—Nice…meet you. Me llamo Diego. Boat…over here," he says, struggling with his English.

The boat ride is short. We're headed just off the coast to a little spot called Cayo Arena, a sand island known colloquially as Paradise Island, which is ever shrinking and expanding. Think: an ivory sand hump rising out of the sea, with nothing but a few thatched buildings on top, surrounded by turquoise water.

Tiff and I had gone scuba diving years before in Tobago, but this is her first time snorkeling and my second. Diego gives us a talk, but his accent is thick and English wayward, so I pick up only bits and pieces that are summed up in my brain: Let the waves play with you, toss you, treat you like some flotsam and jetsam. Just float. I translate: pretend, you know, you're really dead.

And we're off, treading water blue as blue can be, flashing with mercury splotches from the undiminished sun.

We all know that the ocean covers over 70 percent of our very blue planet. But I think most of us don't know it in a way that matters. We still view the land, the global minority, as somehow paramount and treat the sea like both an inexhaustible resource—even as we've exhausted it—and a trash bin. Now the ocean is heating up, acidifying, and losing its oxygen. Yup. Coral reefs are dying en masse. Fish are being overfished, i.e., slaughtered to the point of extinction. And millions of tons of plastic enter the ocean annually while trillions of micro-plastics already reside in the sediments. All this in just a few decades of misrule.

We have solutions to all of these problems. We know what needs to be done. We've known for decades. We just choose. The word *grief* doesn't even begin to capture the loss. If we don't get our collective act together, we'll have to start inventing new words.

I feel the motion of the sea all around me as if I'm engulfed in some water titan's breath. A few fish swim haphazardly above the sand, but we're headed toward the breakers over the ridge where the coral reef rises. I lie still, try to breathe, and just look. Of course, lacking glasses I can't see a damn thing; the sea denizens gaining definition only if they come within a foot of my face, which few seem to want to do.

But it turns out that I have bigger problems. The Titan Oceanus's breath grows deeper and deeper, the rolling swells breaking over me. I start to stop playing dead and come alive.

I can't breathe! Salt water floods my goggles and my mouth. I put my head out of the sea like an ugly seal, and a frothy fountain of seawater bursts from my lips.

Okay, I'm flailing now as the sea tugs at me like I'm caught on a monster marine yo-yo. Clumsily, I put my goggles back on, as if that will magically give me control. I try to swim, but my dog paddle seems no match, and the sea inexorably pulls in me toward the coral reef and away from Tiffany and Diego. Suddenly, I'm over the top of the coral reef, scrambling.

Will the current reach me? Will I be swept out to sea?

Then I feel strong arms underneath me and a voice from above says, "¿Estás bien?" Diego has me. His muscular arms, his dexterous strokes pull me from the coral. "¿Estás bien?"

I try to speak but spit seawater into my snorkel instead. Then I manage a seaworthy, "Glurb, glurb, yep."

Diego helps me refit the goggles with the snorkel and gives me some sage advice. "We...no swim...en el coral. You understand?"

"Si, si," I respond breathlessly, seawater still dribbling from my mouth. Then he lets me go.

Minutes later, I'm in the same position, at the sea's mercy, struggling and panicking. This time I'm pulled directly over the coral, and as I kick my legs frantically, I can feel my flesh and bone connecting. Flashes of pain as the coral cuts through my skin like sea razors.

I can't see but feel like I'm colliding hard, breaking off coral with my aimless, stupid flailing. Coral built rigorously generation by generation over years, if not decades, ruined by one sloppy-swimming environmental journalist. Once again, just as I think I might certainly be lost at sea, Diego's arms grip my torso, and he swims me easily back to safety.

It's the third time—with the sea pulling me out again, with the water in my eyes and mouth again, with the *clunk-clunk-clunk* against the coral and thrashing against death, with savior Diego swooping in like a Marvel hero to my rescue—when Diego finally says, "You swim only Cayo Arena."

I'm regulated to swim around the little island's edge in three feet of water like a kid who thought he was ready to ski the black diamond slope but is sent back to the bunny hill. Only in this case, I'm the only thirty-three-year-old on the bunny hill, like a creeper.

There aren't many fish to see here, and when I do see one, indistinctly due to my lack of glasses, we look at each other morosely but sympathetically, as if the fish is also an exile from the great wide sea.

I stand, my feet against the sand, my torso immediately popping out of the water, as if I'm standing in a kiddie pool. Across the waves in the big ocean, I can see on the swell for a moment two floaters who look like they're playing dead quite well: Diego and my wife exploring the ocean like adults.

It's true, I've never been a strong or skilled swimmer, mostly relying on swinging arms and thrashing legs to get me from one end of a watery locale to another. It's also true I'm about as athletic as a retired data manager.

I've come to terms with the fact that I'll never be a blue reporter. Not that I don't love writing about the oceans, but you know you can drown in there, right? Ships can sink. Scuba gear can fail. Even snorkeling, apparently, has its hazards. The ocean is deeply uncomfortable, almost as if we didn't evolve in it.

I love being near the ocean. I do. I love the sight of it, the sound, the smell. I'm obsessed with seabirds and sperm whales. But mostly, I love it all from the shore.

Like the reason I'm here at all, the solenodon, I prefer to have a little earth under my feet.

On our last day in Pedernales, we awake to the same orchestra: crowing roosters, barking dogs, a cat really wanting a fuck, and puttering motorcycles. Opening the shades, lying in the sun, I think, *This is our last chance to find a solenodon.*

And then Tiffany, who's already up checking her email, starts to cry.

"What's wrong?" I ask.

Unable to speak, she hands me the computer. I look at the screen and stare, almost disbelieving. By *almost*, I mean that it is believable in America, given our long tradition of gun massacres. Twenty *children*, six- and seven-year-olds, six teachers and administrators also dead, slaughtered by a madman with a semiautomatic weapon at Sandy Hook Elementary in Connecticut.

Children.

I hold Tiffany and start to sob myself. In a moment when I think every parent in America wants to hold their children, ours is three thousand miles away, and I wonder, not for the first time, if this whole trip was a mistake. Shouldn't we have stayed home with our two-year-old Aurelia? Shouldn't we be home with our child?

What difference can I really make here? How does one with a pen and paper stop the onslaught of extinction, halt deforestation, stop stray dogs, black rats, and mongooses?

It's a question I ask myself on every trip: *Really*? Is this going to matter? How many articles have I written about climate change, mass extinction, and global ecological collapse? Honestly, how many have mattered at all? Out of over three thousand, maybe, a handful? At best.

Pre-FaceTime, we're not able to connect with our daughter and will have to wait until the grandparents email the next update.

Eventually, cried out, hunger and the need for caffeine get the best of us, so we head downstairs to the hotel's breakfast. But our brains remain thousands of miles away, caught on the chain of a tragedy that's as gut-wrenching as it is senseless.

After the much-needed meal, we meet up with Ros and Juan Carlos. They've both heard of the tragedy, but for them, it doesn't pierce quite so deeply. Instead, it offers another indication of the bizarre nature of the United States, a nation that's increasingly seen by the wider world as not only inexplicable but unrecognizable.

Today, or tonight, rather, is our final solenodon search, but there are many hours between now and when we can start. The solenodons are slumbering just as we are waking.

Ros has lots of plans, and I must say I'm thankful to be kept busy this morning. First thing's first, we head to visit one of the matriarchs of Pedernales for coffee. The wizened old lady, a relative of one of Ros's assistants, lives in the middle of the town in a small, by American standards, tidy home. Outside her house sits a couple of large bags of freshly picked coffee beans.

She is a fierce little lady with a twinkle in her eye and a sometimes-sharp tongue. One gets the sense that this is how the women here survive such constant displays of dramatic, in-your-face masculinity. They persist; they harden like clay in the kiln.

Unlike the sparsely furnished homes of Mencia, her house is filled with furniture, albeit slightly stiff, as well as small trinkets and even doilies. There are a few Christmas decorations out, including a small elegant crèche. It is a picture of intentional domesticity in what seems to be middle-class Pedernales. The coffee is, of course, ridiculously good. And we listen patiently as Ros and the dowager chat in Spanish.

After coffee, we head to visit the Haitian market, a biweekly Pedernalian tradition, where vendors come over the border to sell everything under the sun. The market sits adjacent to the border crossing between the Dominican Republic and Haiti, which consists of a gate, a fence, and some Dominican police. We ramble the market and find pans of loose medication, old TVs, a slew of fresh produce, Christmas decorations ('tis the season!), fresh eels, whole fish, fried fish, black cauldrons stewing up Caribbean delights, very used stuffed animals, boxes of clothes, toys, shoes—so many pairs of shoes. Much of this, we are informed, came from earthquake donations. Haitians don't have a use for Christmas sweaters, but we see many a jumper.

The market is another visible way in which the Dominican Republic and Haiti do this highly volatile dance between sometimes despising each other and often relying on each other.

The Dominican Republic and Haiti have a relatively porous border: Many Haitian women work as maids, while Haitian men work in construction and other manual labor in the Dominican Republic. In a myriad of ways, the Dominican Republic rests on Haitian labor, just as the United States depends on the labor of immigrants from Mexico and beyond.

Haitians have been immigrating to the Dominican Republic for over a century. While many Dominicans have a less than favorable, in some cases flat-out racist, view of their neighbors, that doesn't stop the immigration.[1]

Haiti is today the poorest nation in the Western Hemisphere, but it wasn't always so. The first nation to see a successful revolt of slaves against the whip and the chain, Haiti was once the wealthy pride of the Caribbean until it was decimated by decades-long dictatorships of the Duvaliers. The 7.0 earthquake in 2010 only worsened conditions.

Aside from this market, the closest we physically get to Haiti is a glimpse of it from the highlands.

It is a stunning sight: on one side, the rich pine forests of the Dominican Republic in the Sierra de Bahoruco, and then just across an invisible line, the forests vanish for denuded, eroding hills, as if they had been napalmed out of existence. That invisible line, that border between forest and unnatural desert, is a stark reminder of why conservation matters.

It's not like the Haitian people set out to destroy their forests, but poverty and instability meant turning to the forests for charcoal, for slash-and-burn agriculture, for survival. Now there is little left, and Haitians are increasingly crossing the border to cut down trees in the Dominican Republic in an illegal business that can turn deadly.

Haiti does have one spectacular surviving forest. The Massif de la Hotte on the southern peninsula is home to over a hundred species found nowhere else in the world, including a greater diversity of frogs than anywhere else of similar size. Also, the wonderfully named Massif is home to the Haitian solenodon, either a subspecies of the Hispaniolan or a full species unto itself. But we don't even know if it still survives.

After visiting the market and buying food for our picnic, we head to the beach, a somewhat incongruous switch in the day from the news of Sandy Hook to the Haitian market to the sun, sand, and waves of Bahia de las Águilas, "Eagle's Bay."

Despite being overrun with resorts and unplanned mass tourism, Hispaniola is *still* a magical island. Tiff and I crisscrossed much of the western half of the island over our twelve days, from the Pedernales peninsula to Los Haitises National Park in the northeast (which, despite days of practice, I never learn to pronounce correctly). We visited a forest blanketed in clouds with mini-ferns and carnivorous plants found nowhere else in the world, tunnel-like mangroves hiding manatees, dark coastal forests that seemed out of a Hollywood adventure movie, caves where the Taino people painted their world, waters as blue as Easter candy, and islands of sand.

Still, no beach could rival Bahia de las Águilas in Jaragua National Park, about an hour east of Pedernales. Sand so soft and pale you could almost mistake it for cocaine spread for unbroken miles across a turquoise sea that shades into lapis lazuli farther out.

Not a single dwelling sits on this gem. No resorts, hotels, or restaurants mar this ecosystem because it's in a protected area. Had it not been so, over-tourism and development would've turned this beach into a shit stain within a few decades.

This late morning, the beach is empty but for us and a few carrot-and-ruby-colored hermit crabs shyly retreating into their shells. We all swim in the ocean—me in my hat, of course—in water as warm as a bath, truly pacific (we should've snorkeled here) as the sunlight floods our senses. Then we eat our lunch on the cocaine sand.

At times throughout the day, I recall the news from Connecticut like a nightmare that sneaks up on you, and I think of my daughter thousands of miles away in the cold, dark, silent, snow-felled winter of Minnesota.

It was a much different day in Minnesota—late spring, sunshine, butterflies breaking from chrysalides, flowers bursting with hope—when I graduated from high school. In cloak and gown, I took my diploma, shook the principal's hand—whose face I can't even remember—and quickly walked off the stage.

My senior year had been my best in a long time. I'd collected a small group of friends, all of us misfits in various ways, and we turned ourselves into a little community. I'd done a ton of theater. I'd even fallen in love.

The world suddenly seemed quite different on the day I graduated than it had even a year before. It seemed full of possibilities. If I could survive high school, and even *like it* in the end, maybe I could make a real go of this living thing. After all, high school isn't life.

I didn't realize at that moment what graduation meant. It's hard for an eighteen-year-old to understand that transition from adolescence to adulthood. But it's there. It's real. It doesn't happen all at once. But it does happen. The silly madness of high school (whoever thought putting hundreds of teenagers together with minimal adult supervision was a good idea?) soon submerges like the horizon against a revolving earth.

A few weeks after I graduated, I found myself in the alleyways of London, creeping up on the Thames. It was my first time outside North America. I'd started in France with my high school French class (I couldn't speak a friggin' word but *zut alor!*) and then on my own visited a family friend in London.

Here, I got to spend my days largely alone, roaming the museums, churches, and monuments, marveling open-mouthed at this nearly millennium-old city.

I always knew the world was much bigger than the one I lived in, but here I experienced its largeness for the first time. It was in some ways a victory lap for just surviving the last eight years since my mother's breakdown to my graduation. In other ways, the kind of bridge I desperately needed at that point between my past and my future.

In London I discovered that I can do this. I can be an adult. I can be *myself* again. My future, while it may never be easy, could still be bright.

In recent years, psychologists and researchers have become increasingly interested in something called resilience: the capacity for those living with chronic mental illness to deal in healthy ways with stressors, even crises, and move forward.

I don't think I heard the word *resilience* in relation to my mental health until I was well into my late twenties, but over the last decade, it's become my go-to concept.

While no one could tell me how to toughen up, except by denying my very self, resilience offered a clearer path to managing my mental health.

Now when I ask myself how I can become more resilient, I have an answer: make sure I'm getting plenty of sleep, exercise, meditation, and yoga, as well as swimming regularly and dosing myself with nature as often as I can. Don't forget my meds. Spend lots of time reading. Watch movies. Have time alone.

Of course, none of this would be possible without the love and support of both Tiff and Aurelia. Resilience is also — maybe mostly? — about surrounding yourself with good human beings, people who not only won't condemn you for your mental illness but will be supportive and patient with your daily challenges. Not easy to find.

This is not what some had in mind when they told me to toughen up, but it turns out that lots of sleep, good meditation, and finding a kickass partner makes me stronger.

And then, of course, practice. Practice. More practice. Sure, it won't ever make perfect, but it will make possible. The only reason I have been able to travel with mental illness as far and as frequently (around once a year) is because I have practiced building up skills and experience over decades.

Resilience, to me at least, isn't a destination I've somehow reached but a constant journey. It implies work and restructuring, not an end goal. It implies both self-care and keeping up on therapy and meds.

But maybe, most important for those who suffer from mental illness, resilience denotes the existence of limits. Push someone with mental illness enough—or anyone for that matter—and they *will* break. People break every freaking day. And some of them never recover. Developing resilience is not about becoming superhuman but acknowledging and accepting the limits of being human, of being you.

Should I work nine to five in an office? Nope. Should I go grocery shopping at Trader Joe's on the weekend? Definitely not. Should I drive myself cross-country in a moving van? Over my very dead body.

Resilience is not a fantasy such as pull your bootstraps up, nor mental torture like toughen up. It's a strategy that has worked for me so far on how to live an imperfect but good life (and even to travel) with chronic mental illness.

I'll never be a great traveler. Indeed, I'll probably never be a very good one. I'll never speak your language, summit your mountain, or traverse your nation on foot or bicycle, never explore terra incognita or spend a year living with an indigenous tribe. I'll never do that trip around the world that I used to dream of in my twenties—are you friggin' kidding me?

But can I do a ten-day trip to report on jerboas in Mongolia? Yes...I think, so long as I take extra care of myself before and after, so long as all my meds and podcasts are packed, so long as I use all the tricks from my cognitive therapy basket, so long as I have my animal totem and say my prayers. In discovering your limits, you discover your potential.

What I have become is a practiced traveler. I know what can go wrong and how to plan well so things are more likely to go right. I've learned one panic attack doesn't mean a trip is a failure and one bad day doesn't mean the next can't be better.

And most important, I know why I keep doing it. One of the reasons is selfish: I'm addicted to novelty. I love encounters with new places, new people, new foods, and, of course, the nonhuman denizens that are the foundation of our world.

The other is less selfish: I have a job to do, really the only one I can do and the only one I'm good at, and that is to tell stories for species and places that can't tell their own.

All I feel I can give back to this planet, which I love so maddeningly, are stories. But if that means having to skirt street dogs, ride motorcycle death machines, get tested for Chagas, and get on yet another fucking plane, so be it.

(Also, the test for Chagas was negative.)

Returning to Pedernales, we have only enough time to shower the sand away and grab a quick bite before it's back into the car. We're heading toward the forests a few miles out of town, toward our last chance to find a solenodon.

Juan Carlos's trusty wagon carries us north into the sparsely wooded hills that surround Pedernales. Behind us ride several of Ros's assistants: Misael, Nicolas, and the latter's son Adalberto on their motorbikes.

The sun has nearly set as we park on a dirt road cutting through the forest, the motorbikes sliding to a stop behind us.

Tiff and I take in our surroundings as Ros and her team get things together, their discourse in Spanish. On both sides of the road is a squat dry forest, the trees only a few feet taller than we are. The shine of our light catches hundreds of little glimmers, like drops of dew. But as we get closer, we realize these glimmers are actually the eyeshine of innumerable small spiders on the roadside. With a little more searching, Tiffany and I find amid the trees a broad-billed tody, fluorescent green with a blood-red throat. The little bird, found only on Hispaniola, is trying to sleep as Tiff takes its nighttime portrait.

"Okay, Jeremy," Ros says when everything is ready. "You're going to go with Nicolas. Just follow him, and hopefully, he'll catch one."

"You're not coming?" I ask Ros. I know Tiff doesn't *want* to come after the hutia fiasco.

"You'll have a better shot with fewer people."

"Okay."

"You wanted to be there if he catches one, yeah?"

"Of course!" I'd come thousands of miles for this.

Nicolas Corona Peralta, in his forties, with long curly black hair and a scruffy beard, motions to me as he pulls out his machete and heads into the dark forest. He wears a green shirt, a machete sheath strapped around his chest using a belt, and a green Che Guevera hat (with his good looks, Nicolas could almost pass for Che). Having grown up here, Nicolas knows this forest like we know our neighborhoods. He hunts wild pig here regularly and is the go-to guy for catching solenodon *by hand.*

A sallow, overgrown path winds through the forest, but we don't use it. Instead, Nicolas plunges in, moving ghost-like around branches, vines, and spines; up and down rock faces; into and out of dry ravines. I crash, stumble, and scrape my way through the forest, my shirt tearing on branches, thorns poking my flesh.

"Iguana," he says, stopping suddenly and turning his headlamp onto the
ground. "Today." And as he runs his hand over the vegetation, he makes a
swooshing sound. I can't see much difference, but Nicolas can tell an iguana
passed this way not long ago.

"Big one," he adds.

While Nicolas leaps across shallow ravines or simply dances across a fallen
tree, I fall into the ravine and have to crawl my way out. Where he finds a way
through clumps of brambles, I get stuck. So stuck, that every step forward, I
catch on another vine that just won't budge. I have to backpedal and go around,
for a moment losing Nicolas altogether. Thankfully, when I rediscover him,
he's stopped to light a cigarette.

The orange glow emblazes his countenance momentarily and his puckish,
shining eyes. At this moment, I have the bizarre sense that I'm in some Vietnam movie, just the burst of flaming nicotine outlining a dark tropical forest.

"Wait for me here. I go. I come back for you," Nicolas says.

Before I have a chance to respond, he's off. Within moments, I can no longer
see the bounding light of his headlamp.

I'm not worried. Maybe it's the adrenaline or my confidence that Nicolas
won't lose me. I try to find a way to settle down, but there's only undergrowth,
and for some reason I don't want to sit on it, worried I'll damage it. I turn off
my flashlight, squat, and wait in the dark. I'm not bored. I listen to the forest,
look at the stars, and hear the low *boom-boom* of music from Pedernales, only
a few miles away.

The dry forest is unexpectedly enchanting. A green plant, not grass but
almost clover-like, known as water herb, blankets the ground this time of the
year. Short, winding trees curl around me. Large boulders jut out of the soil,
and at times an aggregation creates a mini-mountain range. Everywhere,
snails in beautifully colored conch-like shells hang from tree branches, like
nature's Christmas ornaments. From time to time I hear a whirring as a nearby
roosting bird takes off. The forest is almost hobbity, as if built for small things.
One could imagine old-school fairies and elves, mischievous creatures, living here, which is why it seems such a suitable place for the strange, cryptic,
elfin-faced solenodon.

A bird lands in the canopy not far from me. Its shape is that of a dove or pigeon. It perches there, too obscured for me to guess the species, but something about it sticks with me: the beautiful bird in the dark, not asleep but vibrantly awake. My body covered in sweat, my heart pounding, my shirt torn, but here I am: alive in a forest, just me and this bird in the dark.

Suddenly, the bird takes off. Nicolas has returned.

He motions. "Come."

We start moving together again. A few minutes later, Nicolas stops and aims his light just in front of him. He points.

"These, a week old," he tells me, showing me small divots in the ground. They are solenodon nose pokes, where the animals dig in the dirt and then stick in their long noses, hoping for a tasty treat. The fact that Nicolas can look at *this*—just a bit of a hole in the water herb—and know when it was made is bonkers.

Finding solenodons is not easy. Nocturnal, rabbit-sized, and easily hidden in the undergrowth, the search seems almost fruitless. But Ros had told me how Nicolas can actually hear solenodons moving through the dry leaf litter and scraggly brush if he gets close enough. If it's wet, searches are called off since solenodon feet fall silent on damp ground.

Another time, Nicolas points and says breathlessly, "Tonight."

And then he stops, listens, moves a bit, stops again, and listens. Suddenly, Nicolas becomes a burst of action. He plunges into the thicket, hands scrabbling, feet kicking him forward. He attempts to catch something, but in the dark, in thick undergrowth, and with bare hands. I never see the beastie and am not surprised when Nicolas comes up empty-handed.

"Two," he says. Then after cursing in Spanish, "Got away."

After this, Nicolas leads me back to the road where the team is parked. We emerge from the forest like a pair of wanderers, long lost in fairyland.

Tiff hands me a bottle of water, which stupidly I forgot to bring with me. While Nicolas updates the team, she picks as many thorns as she can manage out of my T-shirt—I'm bleeding in a couple of places—but her effort is fairly futile since after a few minutes, the hunter waves me on and we're heading back toward the forest.

Round two.

Through some kind of miracle, the solenodon survived the asteroid or comet (scientists are still debating) that caused an extinction-level event, including killing off 75 percent of species, 99 percent of living things, and all the non-avian dinos.

No one knows where exactly the solenodon populations were when the six-mile-wide asteroid hit on that fateful day, but it's almost certain they were pretty damn close to Chicxulub. Whether they lived on the North American landmass or were already on the islands that would one day become what we know as the Caribbean, the solenodon somehow survived what was essentially a direct hit.

How? Only the heavens know.

Perhaps, though, the solenodons' intimate connection to the earth allowed it to survive. The solenodon spends most of its time in dens beneath the ground. Some of them on that autumn day perhaps had been slumbering a few feet below the surface in their dug-out dens. The earth must have shaken terribly at the initial impact, the dirt probably filling in much of the critters' holes. Perhaps the solenodon was busy digging its burrow clean as the asteroid's debris—falling, sun-hot—turned the entire planet into a tinderbox, engulfing everything on the surface like some mad god gone ballistic.

During the next few months, most of the solenodons that survived that first day would've starved or frozen to death, but a few, lucky and particularly skillful, held on. With the whole planet shrouded in dust-choked darkness, these die-hard few may have eked out a frayed life by keeping to their underground dens and living off grubs and insects. The air beneath would've been warmer than that on the surface where, without the sun, an unnatural winter had fallen.

Until, eventually, one day, after months of planetary death, the sun peeked through the apocalyptic haze. The solenodon emerged from its life-preserving hole and found itself truly in a new reality, a world where all the giants had vanished. Only the charred, frozen skeletons of the big animals that had ruled the earth for 175 million years stood as any reminder, while this little, venomous mammal poked around the dead forest.

Maybe on that day, the solenodon bumped into another iconic survivor, a small bird-like dinosaur, crow-sized, full of feathers, and scavenging on whatever it could. Both would be malnourished, near-death, psychologically pushed to the edge but still *there*. Perhaps they eyed each other askance before going on their way just as acid rain, once again, began to fall.

Neither of them would've known that they were inheriting a new earth.

I've noted a lot of reasons why I love the solenodon. I think, though, there is another, almost subconscious, reason for my obsession: It's the poster child of survival.

Survived T-Rex. Check. Survived the 10-billion-Hiroshimas asteroid. Check. Survived the Ice Age. Check. Survived the arrival of the first humans. Check. Survived the Taino people. Check. Survived Columbus and the Spanish Conquistadors. Double Check. Survived the rats, pigs, cats, mongoose, and all the novel diseases they brought. Check, check, check, check, and check. Survived the industrial age. Check.

Do you know what the solenodon says to human hubris? Grow up. Talk to me when you've been here for 50 million years.

I like that fierceness, that tenaciousness, that resilience of the long-ignored and often underestimated.

And it's not just the solenodon. Tenacity is arguably *the* overriding characteristic of all life on our planet. While the solenodon is an extreme example, all long-adapted species are remarkably resilient. Ecosystems—that collection of all living things in a given area—are even more resilient, built as a collective to last hurricanes, fires, earthquakes, and sometimes even humans with our clever technical know-how.

You can see the resilience of nature by just letting your lawn grow or walking through a vacant lot. It can be seen in the spiders in your basement, the rats of New York City, or the ants everywhere. Or why not the forests and animals that have taken over the Korean DMZ or the Chernobyl Exclusion Zone? Or, you know, the American bison in Yellowstone, the mountain gorillas of Rwanda, the tigers of India, the bald eagles of North America, and the humpback whales that are nearly back to pre-whaling numbers.

Leave nature alone and it will flourish. Help it along a little, and it will come back all the faster and richer. Life is tenacious. Life will find a way, but we first have to leave it a path.

Still, like psychological resilience, nature—and species—have obvious limits. Kill too many individuals and a species will vanish in extinction. Attack our ecosystems for too long and they will fail. Put too much CO2 in the atmosphere and it will respond to basic physics and overheat the whole planet.

Nature is resilient both for its ability to bounce back and in the reality of its limitations.

And the solenodon is the same. It survived a real apocalypse, far worse than any that our species has ever seen, but it may not survive us.

Today, the solenodon in Haiti might already be extinct. The Cuban solenodon, a distinct species, or singular genus, is hopefully still around, but no one has recorded it in years. Meanwhile, the Hispaniolan solenodon continues to decline. Ros's research has found that stray dogs likely pose the greatest threat to the solenodons' ongoing survival. The earth's longest-living mammal potentially killed off by man's best friend.

And the tragedy of it all: About zero dollars are going into solenodon conservation at this moment. The Last Survivors project ended in 2012. And today there are no programs devoted to either the Hispaniolan or the Cuban species. The Hispaniolan hutia, as well, has been given next to nothing. And while all these species inhabit protected areas, that doesn't protect them from the rats, dogs, mongooses, and cats that imperil them. Or even human hunters.

Ironically, the animal that survived the dino killing needs *our* help. But there it is. Welcome to the Anthropocene.

I follow Nicolas back along the road to a different part of the woods. He shines his flashlight on about a dozen different tarantulas just hanging out on the road, either to show me just how many there are—an insane number—or so we don't step on them. (Why here? Are they bathing in the moonlight? Sleeping? Is it the heat still left in the concrete?) And then it's back into the shelter of the trees, where tarantulas are not so easily sighted.

We begin again rushing, scrabbling, breaking through the woods, trying to find our Cretaceous prize.

It's only now that I realize I'm completely superfluous to this hunt. There's nothing I can do to help Nicolas track, find, and lay his hands on a solenodon. In fact, I'm pretty sure I'm a hindrance. My breathing and running are so much louder than his. While this should've been obvious from the get-go, it takes a while to come to me. I wanted to believe that I could provide some help, some service.

However, this realization also allows me to let down, to speed through the forest after Nicolas without worrying whether or not we find the mythic solenodon that I traveled so far to see. It's quite simply out of my hands.

I become almost unthinking, just scraping, plunging, pushing, ducking as the time goes by unheeded. How long have we been doing this? Twenty minutes? Three hours? How much longer? Should we just call it a night?

We stop. He points his flashlight to a pair of nose pokes that have become quite familiar, almost prosaic, in the last few hours.

"Last night," he says. Then he pauses. "No, no, no. Tonight. *Tonight.*"

And with that, the long, sweaty, hypnotic hunt takes on a sudden intensity. Nicolas moves forward just a few steps, motioning me to wait behind, flashing his light here and there, listening, it seems, with ears that can pick up sounds I've never heard. Suddenly he's crashing into brambly bushes, and yelling, "Aqui. Aqui. *Aqui!*"

I can't tell if he wants me to do anything. What can I do anyway? But he yells so insistently that I find myself crashing dumbly into the brambles, hoping maybe, on some off chance, my floundering scares a solenodon into his hands (and not the more likely outcome that I scare it away).

Then all of a sudden Nicolas rings out with joyous sounds, in Spanish or English or some bizarre combination of the two. He pops up from the brambles, where he was lying face first at the end, with something in his hand. I scramble closer, flashlight trained on him. And then I see it. A ginger-colored, large beastie with coal-black eyes, and the world's most magnificent nose.

In two words: a Hispaniolan solenodon, or *Solenodon paradoxus.*

"Here," Nicolas says holding the creature—this antediluvian survivor, the mammal under the feet of the dinosaurs—out to me.

"No, no, no," I say. "It's okay. I don't need to hold it."

"Yes, by tail," he says. His face flush with his success, his hands grasping the tail as it hangs upside down.

Researchers always hold solenodons by their tails to avoid a nasty bite and also because the animal seems much less stressed in this position. It flings and flails a little, but it's noiseless and relatively docile, more bewildered than anything else. The upside-down solenodon doesn't seem to be in pain or fear.

"I need to put aqui—here," Nicolas says. With his solenodon-free hand, he holds up the canvas bag.

I probably still look bewildered, but he coaxes me. "It's fine. It's fine. By the tail, and it's fine."

I do something I never expected: I hold a solenodon. As I grasp her scaly tail, I almost drop her—she's heavier than I'd expected. But I hang on as she wriggles, holding her by the tail as far away from my body as possible.

It's one thing to want to see an animal in the wild, another altogether to handle it. I'm not the type of person who usually likes to touch wild animals. I know better.

Nicolas scrambles the bag open, and after a few movements, he's able to slip the bag carefully from under to over her. I let go, and in a flash, he has the bag tied. We're ready to head back to the group, who has probably heard our victorious whooping, when Nicolas pats the belt around his chest.

"Your machete?" I say.

"Si. Si."

It's gone. He must have lost it in the brambles somewhere.

"I go look," he says and hands me the solenodon in a bag. As he disappears into the dark forest, only his flashlight denoting occasionally that he has not been swallowed up, I stand there dumbly.

I'm holding a solenodon in a bag. I'm holding a solenodon in a bag. I'm holding a solenodon in a bag. Years of obsession, months of planning, and thousands of miles over land and sea have led to this ludicrous moment in a shadowy forest in Hispaniola.

She wiggles a few times. I can hear and see the outline of her sickle claws as they attempt to burrow through the canvas bag, just as they would, more successfully, pluck through the earth. I'm still standing in a stupor—though I've wondered a couple of times if Nicolas should give up the machete hunt, how much does a machete cost? Maybe it has personal value?—when he returns, machete in hand (I'd find out later that he's had that same machete for years and never leaves it behind).

By now he's yelling to the team on the road, who have been wondering what happened, given the silence after the joyful whoops. "Si, si, we have a solenodon. Si, si, we are on our way. Just had to get my machete." I imagine his words go something like this as machete in one hand and bagged solenodon in the other, he clears the quickest path for us to get to the road.

When we emerge, everyone looks much relieved and even celebratory. But Ros is in full science mode. She's already opened her kit and is rifling through the equipment. As we wait for her to get set up, Nicolas tells the story of the catch in español.

The solenodon is kept in the bag until all is ready. Then Nicolas, his son, and his cousin gingerly pull off the bag. Nicolas is holding her by the tail as she scrabbles at the road.

"Female," Ros says. "You can see the teats there, low on the body."

She's as beautiful as anything that's ever lived. Deep black pinprick eyes, dark brown fur progressing to sunset orange around her face and forelegs, a blond patch on the right side of her head. Tiny ears, ridiculously long sickle claws, and a squiggly nose rolling on its ball and socket complete this lovely little gremlin. She is also covered in the same tiny green seeds that cover me.

Even my partiality aside, solenodons are ridiculously adorable, made up of parts that seem incongruent but only make them more beguiling. Like a living Muppet, tens of millions of years before Jim Henson invented them.

The whole group is in a state of delight, making jokes and fawning over her as Ros finalizes her preparations. Now, it's time.

Adalberto and Misael grab her gently but firmly around the head and body so she can't get away and also can't reach anyone to bite and inject the venom through her teeth as a cobra would. Tiff is busy taking photos, and I'm standing by just soaking it all in.

"Now there might be a bit of shrieking," Ros warns.

And there is. The minute she's secured, the animal lets out an incredibly loud, high-pitched banshee squeal as Ros and her assistants work incredibly quickly to fit the radio collar around her neck. Her piercing cry of alarm and anger makes me realize just how much she didn't mind being carried about by the tail. In a wiggling frenzy to escape, she spits out venom onto the ground and shits. She's feisty and furious. Is this one of the reasons her line of decedents survived more cataclysm than pretty much any other mammal on Earth? Because they are badasses?

It's nice to see, honestly. It shows that the animal has learned a healthy fear of humans, as it bloody well should. I've watched videos of solenodons on leashes (seriously) and solenodons attempting to escape researchers, and they are never docile. They scramble away and do the first thing they can to escape: dive underground.

And then it's over. Maybe thirty seconds have passed. The collar is on her neck, and it's secure and working. They hold her up by the tail again and she quickly calms.

We follow Nicolas as he carries the now collared female back into the forest. He sets her down on the ground gently, forelegs first, scraping against the beloved earth. And then Nicolas lets her go. She waddles quickly through the undergrowth—with that characteristic drunk-style solenodon walk—up and over a few rocks and then deeper into the forest. She's gone.

But now her movements will tell Ros something about this individual: How far does she roam? How many different dens does she use? How much forest is she utilizing for foraging? Although seemingly innocuous questions, these are hugely important if we are to have a chance to save the solenodon. The problem? Such research rarely gets put to good use. We often have the knowledge and the data, but lack the resources or the will to act.

I stand there even after she's long gone.

This night has proven one of the best of my life, spending ten minutes with a gorgeous female solenodon was pretty much the highlight of my career. I realize that makes me weird and unusual. But, hey, I'm used to that and, honestly, wouldn't have it any other way.

The dark drive back to Pedernales is full of laughter and chatter. By the time I reach the bed, I'm so exhausted I think I'll slip into delicious sleep instantly.

I don't.

Instead, I can't stop thinking of *her*. That collared solenodon, now scurrying around the undergrowth of the dwarven forest looking for something to eat. Her orange fur. Her rotating snout. Her comedic waddle. Her black eyes, as dark as the universe, will remain, immovable, in my memory till the moment it's my time to flee this life.

Epilogue

JULY 2019

And once again, ladies and gentlemen, thank you for your patience. We're now ready to board…"

I stop listening, but I take a deep breath as I stand up and head to the end of the line. Another agonizingly long journey to Southeast Asia—some ridiculous twenty-four hours of various flights—for a longshot chance to see a recently rediscovered small mammal in the bush.

I'm pretty sure I'm going to die. Yup, this'll be the trip that does it. Kills me. Kills me real good.

"Don't get on that plane, Jeremy," Steve says. "If you do, you'll die. I'm not fucking around this time."

I put on my headphones. I turn on a podcast. I hand the flight attendant my ticket—one of the most vulnerable moments in any journey, as there is a sense of "Well, I can't back out now"—and they scan it. They don't say, "No sir, you're mistaken. This ticket is for another day," like I hope to hear.

"Are you listening, Jeremy?"

Step by step, I get on that plane.

"Are you listening, you sad sack of fear?!"

I have a trip to complete. People to meet, things to do, endangered species to pursue. And stories, oh so many stories, to write.

Vietnam, here I come.

About the Author

Jeremy Hance is a writer and freelance environmental journalist. Hance cut his teeth at *Mongabay* as a lead writer and editor for six years. For over three years he wrote the blog "Radical Conservation" on *The Guardian*. Today, he is a columnist for *Mongabay,* writing articles under the banner "Saving Life on Earth: Words on the Wild."

His journalism has also appeared in *HuffPost, Ensia, Yale E360, Sydney Morning Herald,* among others. A story on the history of the Sumatran rhino in *Mongabay* was chosen for the 2019 edition of "The Best American Science and Nature Writing."

In pursuit of stories, Hance has traveled to over thirty countries on five continents. He considers himself ridiculously lucky to have spent time with singing rhinos, dinosaur mammals, and angry clown fish.

Hance is a 2002 graduate of Macalester College with a major in English and minor in history. He is also a 2009 graduate of St. John's College's Great Books Master's Degree program.

He lives in St. Paul, Minnesota, with his wife, daughter, and pooch. When not writing, he enjoys time with friends, cups of tea, long hikes, longer naps, even longer novels, and playing Dungeons and Dragons.

Notes

PART ONE: BROKEN DOWN

CHAPTER ONE

1. Peru built a vast and surprising economic empire on bird poo in the nineteenth century. Farmers worldwide used the guano as a fertilizer to feed an agricultural system that was becoming increasingly industrialized, commercialized, and globalized. The guano market collapsed after the invention of synthetic fertilizer in 1910, a discovery that helped usher in the past hundred years of unparalleled human population growth. Today, the Islas Ballestas are once again the domain of seabirds and mammals, though artifacts of the past linger in the form of poo-covered docks.

2. Old World diseases likely wiped out tens of millions of people in the Americas. Whole civilizations collapsed and those that survived limped on in a kind of staggered condition. It was probably the biggest loss of life globally since the Black Death of the fourteenth century.

   This might explain why on November 16, 1532, Francisco Pizarro, in one of the strangest twists of human history, was able to overthrow the entire Incan Empire with less than 200 men. The Incan Empire was already in rapid decline due to decades of repeated epidemics.

3. On this square, the Spanish removed Tupac Amaru's head from his body. Amaru was one of the last members of the Incan royal family. Two hundred years later, two infamous indigenous rebels, both who took the name Tupac, were also torn limb from limb by Spanish horses.

4. A mountain peaking at 14,593 feet, Pillku Urqu is also one of Cuzco's dozen apukuna (singular: apu). Apu are spiritual guardians of mountains and other stony places for the Quechua people. Many Peruvians leave offerings to these mountain gods to this day.

CHAPTER TWO

1. The book is Time Life's *The Amazon,* 1973. The photo is on pages 114–15, though it is nothing like I remember.

2. It wasn't always that way. For millennia, the Mashco-Piro, and numerous other tribes in the region, had trading contacts with peoples on the Peruvian coast just over the Andes. But things eventually soured.

   In the fifteenth century, the Incan Empire tried, and partially succeeded, in conquering Amazonian tribes in the region.

   Then came hemisphere-shattering Columbus.

Juan Alvarez Maldonado was the first European to make it to the Manu River in 1567, probably trailing disease in his wake like a train spewing smoke. Who knows how many peoples, languages, cultures were lost in the ensuing conflagration brought by conquistadors and explorers like Maldonado?

The inhabitants of Manu were largely left alone for the next three centuries until the rubber boom.

In 1896 rubber baron, Carlos Fermin Fitzcarrald, showed up in the area. Fitzcarrald had already enslaved the Campa and Piro tribes, forcing them to deconstruct, carry, and rebuild a steam ship across an indigenous land path to the Manu River.

As Fitzcarrald sailed down the Manu, in what must have looked like a beast from hell to native peoples, he used his enslaved army of indigenous people to attack the Mashco tribe, slaughtering hundreds. (Werner Herzog's film, *Fitzcarraldo,* may be an incredible piece of art, but it ignores the bloody brutality at the heart of the rubber trade, turning Fitzcarrald into a whimsical dreamer who just wants to have an opera in the jungle).

All the Mashco-Piro people today are direct descendants of those who survived Fitzcarrald's War. While 1894 may seem a long time ago, let's not forget the power of collective memory—what happened to the Mashco-Piro undeniably lives on more vividly through oral stories than anything found on Netflix. It's not that uncontacted indigenous tribes have never had contact; they've had enough contact to know that it only brings disease and death.

3. In a single day two birders once recorded 331 bird species in Manu—or nearly a new bird every two minutes. For a comparison, Canada houses 468 bird species, when you subtract sightings of vagrants.

4. If we start to *really* identify the world's tropical insects and fungi, I believe it would change our understanding of tropical diversity forever, shattering current records and projections.

A study in 2008 found twelve hundred species of mushroom in an area covering just six hundred square meters in Guyana. That's one-tenth the size of a soccer pitch. Scientists believe that *half* of the mushrooms in that survey (six hundred in total) are new to science. Now, think about all those unsurveyed places around the tropics. Damn, someone get me some mycologists, stat!

5. An oxbow lake is created when a river meanders due to erosion, making a loop like a bunny ear in tied shoelaces. Then there is a flood, and suddenly the neck of the meander is pierced by water and the river creates a new, straighter course, cutting off the loop. The leftover river, now a lake proper, is called an oxbow due to its extreme crescent or U-shape, resembling the U-shaped pole that would go under the neck of an ox pulling a wagon, cart, or plow.

PART TWO: MEETING NATURE
CHAPTER THREE

1. Nairobi doesn't have the long history of European cities. It was founded as a railway depot in the last year of the nineteenth century by the British, so in that way it's more like American cities—an architecture largely of the post-war eras and a kind of "sprung up feel" of both newness and the disjointedness that comes without the anchor of history. I have no memory of seeing the river it's named after.

2. Some scholars have cast doubt on Herodotus's Egyptian vacation, but I tend to trust Herodotus. I find the scholarly mistrust of everything written by ancient authors—as if they sat around deliberately writing lies in order to confuse the future—self-defeating.

Ilium (or Troy), of course, is the most famous example. Many scholars for centuries thought it was a legend, brewed in Homer's heady brain. That is, until Heinrich Schliemann found the lost city on the coast of Turkey, proving that a real place, and no doubt actual events, underpinned Homer's *Iliad*.

3. British Lieutenant Colonel John Henry Patterson, who made that claim, eventually shot dead both the lions. He then wrote a book about his escapades. You can see the stuffed skins of the man-eating pair—poorly preserved because Patterson used them as rugs for a quarter century—at the Chicago Field Museum of Natural History. The stuffed lions are significantly smaller than they were in life. Their skulls are at the museum as well.

4. It's not completely insane that a lion would sleep on a tent with someone inside it. Kick-butt lion researcher, Amy Dickman, once had this very thing happen to her in the bush. You can watch her tell this story on National Geographic's *Sleeping with Lions*.

CHAPTER FOUR

1. The military dictatorship under Dési Bouterse was battling a coalition known as the Surinamese Liberation Army (SLA) headed by Ronnie Brunswijk. The SLA was fighting for greater recognition of Suriname's maroon population, those survivors of the Middle Passage and the death plantations run by the Dutch.

   On November 29, 1986, Bouterse's army headed on this highway to Brunswijk's home village of Moiwana, where they slaughtered thirty-nine people, mostly children and women, and burned the village to the ground. Hundreds of survivors fled over the border to seek refuge in French Guiana.

   Today, Bouterse is the democratically elected president of Suriname—seriously. Ronnie Brunswijk is a representative of the General Liberation and Development Party and owner of a football club. Politics are strange the world over.

2. The Dutch first showed up in what is now Suriname in the 1600s and decided, as Europeans did everywhere, that this strange land was theirs, because.

   Viewing the verdant, tropical land as nothing more than a profit-maker, Dutch companies brought African slaves to live and die—mostly die—in sugar cane plantations. The region was known for some of the most savage and cruel slave masters in the world, and that's saying something.

   During the Age of Enlightenment and the Dutch Golden Age, slaves were quartered and dumped in the river, broken on the rack, burned alive, hung by iron hooks in their ribs, beheaded, and de-limbed for minor offenses. The banks of the Suriname River in Paramaribo were decorated with the heads of escaped slaves, including young girls. Dutch Suriname makes Westeros look like a day camp.

   Aside from death, Suriname's slaves had only one mode of deliverance: escaping into the seemingly impenetrable interior of the rainforest, building villages and cultures outside the white man's lash and boot.

   These "maroons" became known for enacting brazen raids on the plantations to survive, leading to guerilla warfare between them and the Dutch army. Eventually, the maroons would secure agreements—the first during the 1760s—making their freedom official.

   Still, the Netherlands was the very last country in Europe to abolish slavery: it lasted until 1873 there—eight years after the end of the American Civil War.

3. The first humans arrived in South America some 11,000 years ago and may have crossed this very region. But, to date, archeological evidence shows human habitation in Suriname beginning around five thousand years ago—about the time that the Sumerians and Egyptians invented writing.

   Today, Suriname has a population of just over half a million people (the United States' *least* populous state, Wyoming, has more people than that).

Nearly half of the Surinamese are of African descent, maroon and creole. So, who are the rest? Not Dutch. Over a third are of Indian descendent, and fifteen percent Indonesian. After the abolition of slavery, plantation owners still wanted cheap and expendable labor, so they turned to China, India, and Indonesia. These people weren't slaves, but the soil is made up with their blood as well.

The various Amerindian people (the term used for indigenous people in the Guianas) make up about 3 to 4 percent of the half-million people in Suriname. These include the tribal groups of the Caribs (including the Kalina) and the Arawaks on the coast, as well as the Trio and Wayana in the interior forests.

Suriname's incredible diversity is marked by dinners. You can choose from Javanese cuisine, Chinese, Indian, Amerindian, or distinct flavors of Latin America, including dishes found nowhere else in the world.

The widely diverse cultures, most of them brought here against their will or as expendable labor, has created a country that struggles with its various identities.

4. Apparently, all that Sunday school teaching successfully sank into my subconscious: The Book of Malachi is the last book in the Old Testament and the final book in the Nevi'im. In it the prophet Malachi, which literally translates into "my messengers," harangues the Israelites and priests for their misbehavior.

CHAPTER FIVE

1. It's believed the word Guiana or Guyana came from an indigenous language meaning, "land of many waters"—an apt description for a land that runs with rivers, drips with rain, and produces its own clouds.

The Spanish were the first to write about this region, to them terra incognito. Just seven years after Columbus's first voyage, a Spaniard named Alonso de Ojeda is believed to have reached the mouth of Essequibo River, the largest river in Guyana (and the one to which we are heading).

But the first European to actually write about the *interior* of Guyana was the tobacco-loving, poesy-penning, adventure-addicted, lady-in-waiting seducing, war criminal (by today's standard), all-round Renaissance dude, Sir Walter Raleigh. In 1595, Raleigh somehow succeeded in sailing 400 miles up the Orinoco River in the area then known as the "Guianas" (present day Venezuela, near the western border of Guyana). Raleigh wasn't after knowledge or cross-cultural understanding; this wasn't *Star Trek* utopianism. He was following a gossipy trail of gold.

He'd heard from a friend who'd heard it from a Spanish governor that a certain Spaniard, one Juan Martinez de Albujar, had escaped a death sentence by securing a canoe and heading out alone in the Guianan interior. Albujar showed up eighteen years later claiming he'd been to El Dorado, the famed city of gold (the story of El Dorado had been drifting around Europe for years, despite any real evidence).

Out of favor with Queen Elizabeth I, Raleigh decided on a course to make the queen adore him again: discover El Dorado. Although he had adventures aplenty, he never found it. There's a lesson here: Don't trust a tale that depends on a game of telephone.

Raleigh's narrative of the voyage, *The Discoverie of the Large, Rich, and Bewtiful Empyre of Guiana*, is full of what today may be called humble bragging (or not so humble). While many scholars believe Raleigh massively hyped up his visit to the Guianas, I think the tour is more interesting, and the book's strangest passages more revealing, as a reflection of cultural and ecological disconnect. Raleigh is struggling to write about cultures and people who lived wholly different from his own ragged tribe back home. He's writing about a place that couldn't be more different from the island of England; he simply can't fully understand many of the things he sees with his own eyes—or the tales he is told. Not to mention the potential for accuracy to be "lost in translation."

Europeans and Americans, at this point, had been separated by some 10,000 years of cultural evolution. Like two species left adrift, they had created different cultural and civilizational species, their minds and ways wholly unlike one another.

2. If we truly take the word at its definition, then some things can never be sustainable. Fossil fuels are not sustainable in any way, shape, or form (solar, wind, geothermal, tidal are sustainable—after mining is done).

Mining by its very nature is wholly unsustainable. I'm not saying it's not necessary to society, but let's not pretend it's "green." It's wholesale destruction—and we should at least be clear-eyed about that, even as we find ways to mitigate and repair the damage.

3. Scientists are not sure why, though I'd hazard overstimulus of the mind as one option. I couldn't survive New York City because of my mental illness. And there are days when even St. Paul, Minnesota, feels way too much.

Adding green spaces to a city can help. You don't have to go white water rafting or mountain climbing or backpacking to benefit from nature—you can get many of these same boons from a simple walk in the woods or a park. Even sitting on a bench outside helps. Exercise in nature is great, but the benefits appear to come largely from simply engaging your senses in nature. Just looking out a window at a tree is good for you, which is probably why cubicles and gray cities are so dispiriting. But, of course, longer "doses" of nature seem to provide more and longer-lasting benefits.

4. Scientists don't yet know why nature is so good for so many. Is it that seeing the fractals in nature calms our minds? Is it the aerosols released by trees? Is it the increased exposure to microbacteria? Is it the mitigation nature provides from air pollution, noise pollution, and concentration pollution (i.e., lack of tech)? Scientists like to find one single reason behind a phenomenon—and sometimes physical reality rewards them: The apple falls because of gravity—but I suspect there's no *one* reason why nature heals us and makes us happy. I suspect it's a multitude of complex reasons, all interacting.

Also, much of this science is new—only in the last couple of decades—and should come with a caveat that while we are starting to put the puzzle together, many pieces are still missing. And many still need to be fully corroborated. In fifty years, we'll know so much more.

5. Like many indigenous tribes, the Macushi did fight back against enslavement and destruction. In 1790, the Macushi rebelled against Portuguese colonizers who had forced the tribe into Christian missions. At this time, such missions were often a way of pacifying and dividing tribes while exploiting their resources. Information on the Macushi rebellion is sparse, but many of them were able to escape into the forest and undercut Portuguese control until the rubber boom arrived, and with it, re-enslavement and death.

6. Caused by a parasite transmitted through various species of mosquito, malaria is still one of the world's biggest killers. In 2017, the World Health Organization estimated that malaria killed 435,000 people that year—most of them children under five. During the same year, malaria struck around 219 *million* people—nearly 3 percent of the entire global population. And climate change is now helping to spread malaria upslope and potentially into new regions.

Hope springs eternal, though. A vaccine, the first ever, has just been trialed in four African countries.

PART THREE: NATURE DISTURBED

CHAPTER SIX

1. Though living in the shadows for much of ancient history, northern Borneo certainly traded with powerful neighbors like China, India, and Sumatra. The region also bounced between various empires and kingdoms, including the Majapahit Empire, the Bruneian Sultanate, and the Sultanate of Sulu.

   It was in the nineteenth century that Europe entered the equation, as it so often did as the meddler of the world. By some labyrinthine history, a rando British dude named Arthur Dent came to *own* Sabah. He founded the British North Borneo Chartered Company, which ran the country for over sixty years. And by that, I mean exploited the bejesus out of it. Northern Borneo didn't free itself from being a corporation until after World War II.

   In 1963, Sabah united with Sarawak, Singapore, and Peninsular Malaysia—known then as Malaya—to become the newly independent nation: Malaysia (Singapore, however, would be expelled from the agreement after two years).

2. Palm oil began to really take off in Malaysia around the 1960s. By the 1980s the country had planted a million hectares (2.5 million acres) of the lucrative oil crop. That number has now more than quintupled, around half of it in Sabah and Sarawak, and often at the expense of Bornean forest and local people.

3. The bustling Sandakan is a miracle city. In 1941 Japan invaded Borneo, largely for its oil. This led to a brutal three-year occupation in which one estimate says 16 percent of northern Borneans died.

   At the end Sandakan city was pretty much an ash pile. Today, it's the second largest city in Sabah and feels like a noisy, turbulent teenager to the more laidback Kota Kinabalu.

CHAPTER SEVEN

1. One researcher recorded nearly fifty different species being sold commercially here, over twelve tons of bushmeat annually.

2. The name Orellanna rises over everything here. In fact, the city of Coca's real name is Puerto Francisco de Orellana, but you'll forgive locals for calling it El Coca over this mouthful.

   Francisco de Orellana was a conquistador, and like most, he lived hard and died young. He is famous (or infamous) for being the first European to ever sail down the entirety of the Amazon River —and he started here on the banks of the Napo.

   Orellana's fame begins, as so many of these disastrous tales do, with an attempt to find El Dorado. The expedition, headed by his cousin Gonzalo Pizarro, went terribly from the start. As Pizarro's men dropped like flies to disease and exhaustion, clever Orellana took some of the men downriver to find supplies.

   Orellana's journey became much more than a supply run: It turned into what is arguably the craziest boat trip in the history of the world.

   When Orellana did find supplies six hundred miles downriver, he decided not to return to his cousin, possibly assuming Pizarro was lying dead in a swamp somewhere. Instead, Orellana carried on downriver, hoping to reach the ocean, which he had no idea was around four thousand miles away.

   Fortunately for us, Orellana brought with him a literate monk, Carvajal, who recorded the journey. The monk described a heavily populated land of riverside villages and even, according to sixteenth century standards, vast cities. At this point, the Amazon, at least along major rivers, was heavily populated.

Natives of the region grew understandably hostile to these strange men who did not speak their language; who looked pallid, ghastly, starving, and ill; and who imperiously demanded food and supplies. The Spaniards found themselves fighting—but mostly fleeing—downriver.

At one point, according to Carvajal, the Spaniards were set on by a hoard of female warriors, an encounter that would give the river, the region, and the world's great ecosystem its name: Amazon. The moniker stems from the ancient Greek tales of the mythical Amazons, a group of female fighters allegedly from Asia Minor.

The biggest outcome, historically speaking, of Orellana's ride down the Amazon was not his eventual success on navigating the river and reaching the Atlantic, but the viruses his men spread. No Westerner would ever see the Amazon River quite like this again. It is only now that archeologists and ecologists are beginning to find evidence of these long-lost rainforest civilizations that had been wiped out by novel diseases.

Some scholars even argue that the indigenous people living here in some ways *created* the Amazon rainforest—a claim that remains contentious and debatable. Enhanced and shaped the forest in select places, through large-scale planting of preferred trees, is probably a more likely reality. But whether these lost civilizations planted or enhanced the Amazon—or simply learned to live within the ecosystem without destroying it—we now have physical proof of their reality.

Orellana's end came when he attempted a second voyage on the Amazon, resulting in the deaths of himself and over two hundred of his crew.

3. Scientists have found more tree species in a *single hectare* of upland rainforest of Yasuni—655 species—than in all of North America.

PART FOUR: SURVIVORS

CHAPTER EIGHT

1. Scientists keep discovering new species in Indonesia—a far more difficult task than in the United States. For one thing, the United States has been far better studied, but also because it's simply *much less diverse*. Much of Indonesia lies in the Coral Triangle, the most biodiverse marine area on the planet.

2. Krakatoa actually cooled the entire Earth for a few years. All that ash swept into the stratosphere—up to fifty miles high—reflected the sun's rays and caused average global temperature to plunge more than two degrees Fahrenheit the next year. Temperatures didn't come back to normal for about five years.

One of the most promising geo-engineering ideas to mask climate change is to simulate something like Krakatoa by deploying reflective aerosols in the atmosphere. Recent research has found that this sci-fi idea would probably successfully cool the Earth but would need to be done repeatedly and would be incredibly expensive.

Still, I'm pretty confident future generations will turn to climate engineering of some kind or another. People always say: but what about the negative impacts of geo-engineering? Yes, there will be impacts, and they probably won't be minor. But global warming will likely be so catastrophic—and our children and grandchildren so goddamn desperate—that any potential geo-engineering impacts will look like no biggie compared to the climate Cthulhu that is battering them every year.

3. A study in 2017 by the World Health Organization found that air and water pollution are the world's biggest killers—more than malaria or HIV or warfare, or really anything. According to the report,

air pollution kills over 7 million people a year, and water pollution kills near 2 million. That's equivalent to the entire population of Hungary or New Jersey. And, according to the report, it's probably an underestimate.

4. As I write, California is on fire. Australia, too. Indonesia has had one of its worst burning seasons on record. The Pantanal, the world's largest wetland, is ablaze. And ranchers have just felled vast areas of the Brazilian Amazon and then ignited it, leading to a crisis that, for once, broke into the mainstream news. But vanished just as quickly as the smoke.

CHAPTER NINE

1. If you've ever watched *Unbreakable Kimmy Schmidt,* you've actually seen a photo of a Hispaniolan solenodon. Only in the show the characters call it the Haitian toilet rat. The "toilet rat" plotline is funny—and the picture they chose is one of my favorite solenodon pics. But alas, the species may now be more famous as a Haitian toilet rat than as my dear dinosaur mammal.

2. Hutias even have a footnote in global human history. Columbus, who called them rats, brought back a few to Isabelle and Ferdinand after his first voyage. This makes the hutia one of the first animals to make the trip from the so-called New World to the Old.

3. Five hundred twenty years after Columbus, indigenous people the world over remain some of the most trampled, vulnerable, and under siege human beings around the world. However, that's not the end of it.

   Little told, the last fifty years have seen a spectacular rise in indigenous activism. Tribal peoples are throwing off the, at times, defeating label of victims and actively raising their voices and unfurling their power. From the Amazon to Australia to the frigid north, tribal groups are now asserting themselves in new ways: employing protests, media, and new organizations to attempt to survive ongoing colonialism, neoliberalism, and politic ambivalence.

   They are not disappearing without a fight.

4. While I clearly have issues when it comes to domestic cattle, I'm weirdly fascinated by wild ones. I love banteng and guar. African buffalo are badass. I went all the way to Poland just to find European buffalo, and I'd cross the planet again to have a chance to see some tamaraw or anoa. Oh, how I wish aurochs and kouprey were still with us. When I first read the line "I am thinking of aurochs and angels" in Nabokov's *Lolita,* I nearly wept.

CHAPTER TEN

1. The million or so Haitians who live permanently in the Dominican Republic do so in an opaque stateless condition, given the inability for either government to come to terms with this long-going migration. Meanwhile, the Dominican Republic recently ended birthright citizenship—meaning Haitian children born in the Dominican Republic are now stateless as well.

When I was three, my parents built me what we affectionately called "the jungle," a cut-up four-by-four of different ecosystems for my plastic animal toys.

Photo ©Erva Hance

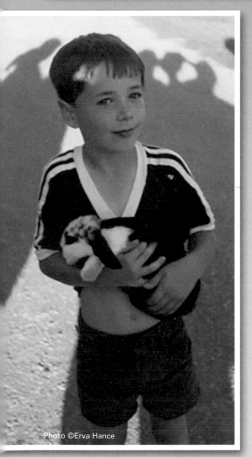

Photo ©Erva Hance

There was no question that I loved animals as a child, including this adorable bunny.

Me as a super chill eighteen-year-old.

Peruvian bills mixed in with "falso" money.

A sea lion colony on the Islas Ballestas, Peru.

A few sea lions at Islas Ballestas, near Paracas, Peru.

The fairytale-like desert oasis of Huacachina, Peru.

The cute killer kitty in Huacachina, Peru. Look at her eyes. She definitely has rabies.

Running away from Huacachina's rabid cats and dogs. Metaphorically, that is.

The Andean condor, the world's heaviest flying bird, soars above Colca Canyon, Peru.

Taking in the sunrise view of the famed Machu Picchu, Peru. The famed Incan ruins are on a spectacularly steep jungle mountain top.

Tiffany eats lunch at the top of the Andes, overlooking the Amazonian cloud forest.

Our guide through Manú National Park & Biosphere Reserve shows off his impressive climbing skills. I do not attempt to follow.

We found this bad boy in our bunk in the Peruvian Amazon. Even our guide was impressed.

The Nauta mushroom-tongue salamander, found on a night hike in Manú. Check out how this beauty can turn itself into a spiral.

Reading Charles Dickens' Bleak House in the Peruvian Amazon.

Po tries to make me feel better at the Lima Zoo, but he only makes Tiffany laugh at me. Hard.

A mother cheetah scans the horizon for a meal for her cubs in Kenya.

Tiffany examines the bloated, decapitated corpse of a large anaconda on our boat ride to Galibi, Suriname.

A baby green sea turtle, before being released back into the sea in Suriname.

A very rare sighting of a mother leatherback laying eggs during the day. She disguised her nest by flinging sand in every direction with her impressive flippers.

Tiffany stands directly in the sun without even a hat. There are very few pictures of me outside the protective shade of a tree. And I always wear a hat.

I watch the magic of a leatherback laying her clutch in Suriname.

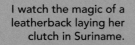

A church in remote Guyana built out of logs from the surrounding rainforest.

The Iwokrama River Lodge dining room in Guyana.

Sankar, the giant black caiman of the Iwokrama River Lodge, chomps his chicken snack.

Tiffany and I on top of Turtle Mountain, Guyana, with a spectacular view of unbroken rainforest.

The beautiful smile of a piranha caught in the Essequibo River, Guyana. The piranha went back into the water alive and well.

Beauty reflected in the calm waters of the Essequibo River.

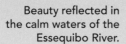

I catch some much needed sleep in Johannesburg airport.

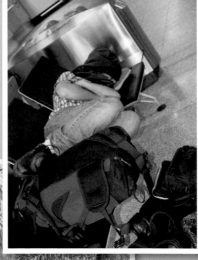

The ubiquitous and measured green of an oil palm plantation in Borneo.

Tam, the last known male Bornean rhino, enjoying his brunch.

Tam heads out into his jungle enclosure to enjoy a spa day in his mud wallow.

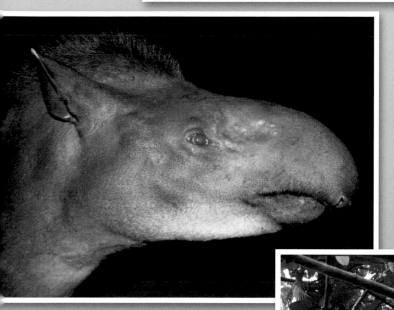

This lowland tapir was taken in by the Huaorani tribe after they hunted her mother. She was hand-raised, but then released back into the wild.

A monk saki monkey in Yasuní Biosphere Reserve.

My guide at the Yasuní Research Station decides to take the tree down rather than the ladder. I take the ladder.

A gorgeous collared puffbird in the Ecuadorean Amazon.

Hoatzins chill on an oxbow lake in Ecuador.

My first view of the unforgettable Napo Wildlife Center Ecolodge.

A many-banded Aracari takes off.

A golden-mantled tamarin raids the garden at the Napo Wildlife Center Ecolodge.

Photo ©Rhett A. Butler / Mongabay

An adult capybara hangs out with a bunch of youngsters in Colombia. They tend to be quite communal, hanging out in large groups.

Harapan, a male Sumatran rhinoceros, enjoys a morning repast.
The sanctuary is working hard to breed these nearly-extinct animals.

I plant a tree in Bukit Barisan Selatan National
Park in Sumatra, Indonesia.

Scientists with the Little Fireface
Project check the radio collar of
a Javan slow loris. The research
will help conservationists better
protect and rerelease this species.

A Javan slow loris is measured by scientists.

The beautiful, venomous mammal of my dreams. This solenodon is sporting some cute grass seeds on her face.

A sleeping broad-billed tody in the scrub forests of the Dominican Republic. This bird is found nowhere else in the world.

A Dominican forest river where we spend a magical afternoon bathing.

Prized roosters are kept in cages for cockfighting in the village of Mencía.

Juan Carlos and I enjoy the crystal blue waters of Bahia de las Aguilas, Dominican Republic.